This anthology is dedicated to our late beloved colleagues Tsering Dhundup Gonkatsang and Christina Lee Monson.

Gen Tsering was an accomplished teacher and translator who dedicated his life to imparting the wonders and wisdom of the Tibetan language to others.

A close disciple of Chatral Sangyé Dorjé, Christina spent her life practicing the dharma and translating Tibetan teachings—exemplifying heartfelt devotion.

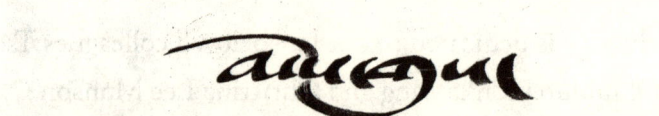

LONGING TO AWAKEN

Traditions and Transformations
in Tibetan Buddhism

David Germano and
Michael Sheehy, Editors

Longing to Awaken

Buddhist Devotion in Tibetan Poetry and Song

Edited by Holly Gayley and
Dominique Townsend

University of Virginia Press
CHARLOTTESVILLE AND LONDON

University of Virginia Press
Printed in the United States of America on acid-free paper

First published 2024

1 3 5 7 9 8 6 4 2

Library of Congress Cataloging-in-Publication Data
Names: Gayley, Holly, editor. | Townsend, Dominique, editor.
Title: Longing to awaken : Buddhist devotion in Tibetan poetry and song / edited
by Holly Gayley and Dominique Townsend.
Description: Charlottesville : University of Virginia Press, 2024. | Includes
bibliographical references and index. | Poems translated from Tibetan.
Identifiers: LCCN 2023052268 (print) | LCCN 2023052269 (ebook) |
ISBN 9780813950686 (hardcover) | ISBN 9780813950693 (paperback) |
ISBN 9780813950709 (ebook)
Subjects: LCSH: Buddhist poetry, Tibetan—Translations into English. |
Buddhist poetry, Tibetan—History and criticism. | Didactic poetry, Tibetan—
Translations into English. | Didactic poetry, Tibetan—History and criticism. |
BISAC: RELIGION / Philosophy
Classification: LCC PL3735 .L66 2024 (print) | LCC PL3735 (ebook) |
DDC 294.3/432—dc23/eng/20240108
LC record available at https://lccn.loc.gov/2023052268
LC ebook record available at https://lccn.loc.gov/2023052269

Epigraph translation by Anam Thubten. Reprinted with permission of the author.
Material in chapter 7 first appeared in Sarah Harding, *Shangpa Kagyu:
The Tradition of Khyungpo Naljor, Part Two*, pp. 587–90. © 2023 by Tsadra
Foundation. Reprinted with permission of Shambhala Publications.
Material in chapter 9 first appeared in Dominque Townsend, *A Buddhist
Sensibility: Aesthetic Education at Tibet's Mindröling Monastery*, pp. 110–12. © 2021.
Reprinted with permission of Columbia University Press.
Material in chapter 10 first appeared in Alison Melnick Dyer, *The Tibetan Nun
Mingyur Peldrön: A Woman of Power and Privilege*, pp. 114–15. © 2022. Reprinted
with permission of the University of Washington Press.

Cover art: "Morning Mist in a Himalayan Valley" (detail), Matthieu Ricard, 2006.
(© Matthieu Ricard)

Calligraphy on page v.: "Mögü" (devotion) by Pema Bhum,
used with permission.

རང་སེམས་སངས་རྒྱས་མ་མཐོང་བར། །
བླ་མ་སངས་རྒྱས་ཟེར་ན་ཡང་། །
བཙོན་མ་གཞན་གྱི་ལྀད་མོ་ཚམ། །
དད་པ་དེས་ཀྱང་ཀྱེན་མི་ཐུབ། །

Without seeing one's own mind as Buddha,
even if you say "my guru is a buddha,"
such devotion will not withstand difficulties.
It's just a contrived imitation of others.

    —Third Karmapa Rangjung Dorjé

CONTENTS

NOTE ON TRANSLATION
AND TRANSLITERATION

This anthology invites readers of English into the literary world of Tibetan poetry and song. To highlight the distinctive qualities of Tibetan forms of versification and the varied dimensions of devotion, we asked our contributors to pay special attention to literary style in addition to semantic meaning in their translations. For general accessibility, we provide phoneticized versions of Tibetan terms and names. Where phoneticized Tibetan is given in order to maintain the original flavor of a translated passage, an explanation is provided in the notes. Wylie transliteration is used in parentheses, notes, and bibliographic entries as necessary. An exception is the introductory essay by Lama Jabb, "An Act of *Bardo:* Translating Tibetan Poetry," where the Tibetan script is provided for the rich poetic examples in the original Tibetan followed by English translation. Diacritics are used for Tibetan and Sanskrit terms.

Editorial Introduction

AT A TIME when so many are thinking critically about the promise and pitfalls of devotion in Buddhist contexts, this anthology of Tibetan poetry and song invites readers to experience a range of devotional expressions. Far from being a uniform or static tradition across time, Tibetan devotional literature invokes a variety of emotions and perspectives—from grief and longing to skepticism and humor—meant to inspire, educate, and transform its readers. This variety is revealed in the poetic imagination and the translator's rendering just as vividly as it is lived in the dynamic nature of guru-disciple relationships. The poems and songs selected for this anthology are gutsy, adoring, sensual, mournful, rhythmic, balladic, introspective, skeptical, and uproarious. By playing with experimental approaches to translation and foregrounding the literary qualities of the poems and songs, these translations demonstrate the ways that poetry can generate human experience as readily as it reflects and expresses it. At the same time, the source materials elucidate the complexities of devotion, providing examples of how animated its affective dimensions can be and revealing how a student's relationship with their guru can be fraught and filled with twists and turns.

WHAT IS DEVOTION IN BUDDHISM?

Devotion is more than the first flush of inspiration. Having goosebumps upon encountering a charismatic teacher is a trope in Tibetan literature. Yet devotion is so much more. It takes time, discernment, cultivation, and a curious blend of humility and confidence. It can be directed at various objects yet ultimately transcends the need for an external reference point altogether. In Tibetan literature, we find numerous expressions of the bond between teacher and student, such as when the eighth-century yoginī Yeshé Tsogyal exclaims after a vision of Padmasambhava, "Just by the sight of you, I am perfectly liberated" (chapter 6), or when the seventeenth-century adept Tsang Khenchen states when grieving his teacher, "There will never be another master like you" (chapter 8). Yet devotion can also be directed at sacred sites, lineage founders, buddhas and bodhisattvas, the nature of mind, and more. For example, the visionary Jigmé Lingpa (1729/30–1798) exhibits devotion to a physical location, in particular the Yarlung Valley of Central Tibet, which is saturated with the blessings of Nyingma progenitors, who used sites like Samyé Chimphu as a retreat hermitage. In chapter 11, Willa Baker draws an analogy between Jigmé Lingpa's longed-for "wild and sparsely inhabited landscape" in which to engage in solitary retreat and the uncontrived "ground" of one's being discovered there.

Through these poems and many more, this anthology offers readers an expansive vista from which to reflect on devotion in Tibetan Buddhism at a time when recent allegations and revelations of abuse have raised urgent and often painful questions about the guru model. We, the editors, are firm in our support of survivors of sexual abuse within Buddhist saṅghas and other religious communities. Questioning the nature and parameters of devotion, and by extension the guru model as it has been translated into new contexts, is crucial and timely, and we return to this issue below. With this in mind, we hope these translations can contribute a useful perspective by offering wide-ranging literary examples of devotion that include but also go beyond reliance on the external guru on the path toward recognizing one's own nature.

The translations included here showcase poetry and songs composed by Tibetan religious figures affiliated with a range of traditions and from a range of time periods, including classical and contemporary sources. These examples are specific to Buddhist tantra, also known as the Vajrayāna, or "adamantine vehicle," with its emphasis on the guru as a conduit for wisdom and blessings handed down over time. Yet, as we note, the guru is not the only object of devotion, and inspiration is not the only type of affect involved. Through the songs of Shabkar (1781–1851) in chapter 13, for example, Rachel Pang shows how natural wonders, such as a rainbow over Mount Tsari, can provoke realization and reflect Shabkar's "profound feeling of reverence and awe toward the awakened state itself." In some cases, the issue of human fallibility is taken up in critiques of false piety and misguided devotion. For example, misrecognition provokes humor when the twelfth-century Kagyu adept Rechungpa is shunned unfairly by a group of Kadam monks and thrown out of their monastery, only to get his foot stuck in the gate. Each verse of his song (chapter 3) calls out their hypocrisy, followed by the refrain "Ow! Ow! Ow! You rash little monks, don't crush this leg! / Let this leg go!" There is also plenty of room for skepticism, as suggested by this verse from the Jonang master Kunga Drolchok (1507–1566): "They say the root of spiritual powers is the guru. / They say the guru is the actual Buddha. / They say one must regard the guru's acts as good. / They say beautiful things, but it's just noise." In chapter 7, Sarah Harding explores the implications of this provocative statement.

From its early foundations in India, there have been evocations of faith in Buddhist literature. For example, in the jātaka tales recounting the Buddha's past lives, acts of heroism and sacrifice epitomize the virtues to be cultivated along the Buddhist path and instill admiration for the Buddha. One famous story features the Buddha-to-be as a hare who sacrificed its body to feed a wandering mendicant.[1] Such tales of extreme generosity are meant to inspire "faith" or "esteem" (Skt: śraddhā, Tib: dad pa) rather than emulation and thereby encourage more conventional acts of merit-making through ritualized offerings.[2] The "ethics of esteem," as Maria Heim has called it, is expressed through generosity to Buddhist adepts and the monastic community, orienting the giver toward a set of values epitomized by the historical Buddha.[3] This is a classical sense of faith relevant to all Buddhist traditions, though its expression has taken different forms across Asia. Three types of faith are operative in Tibetan Buddhism—inspiration (dang ba), confidence or conviction (yid ches), and irreversibility (phyir mi ldog pa)—and these overlap with the term usually translated as "devotion" (mos gus).

But is devotion the right word? Etymologically, the Tibetan compound mögü entails "conviction or inclination" (mos pa) and "respect or reverence" (gus pa).[4] Its closest correlate in Sanskrit is adhimukti, with a semantic range that includes inclination or adherence towards an object and faith or conviction based on study, reflection, and meditation.[5] There is only partial overlap with the English term devotion and its associations with piety, worship, and religious zeal or, in secular terms, loyalty and enthusiasm for a person or cause.[6] Moreover, mögü in its standard translation as "devotion" can be easily confused with bhakti, also translated as "devotion." Bhakti is a Sanskrit term employed in Vaiṣṇava and other Hindu traditions in which love for the divine is central. In such contexts, different rasas, or "flavors," of love are vehicles for liberation (Skt: mokṣa), as attested in the celebrated songs of Mirabai or Andal addressing Kṛṣṇa through the eroticism of śṛṅgārarasa.[7] These distinct conceptions can be conflated mistakenly through the single English term that renders them all, *devotion*. That said, within Tibetan literature, in the specific context of consort relationships,[8] love can blend with devotion, as can be seen in chapters 17 and 18, featuring songs by the female visionary Sera Khandro (1892–1940).

Another vexing issue in translating Buddhist terms related to this theme is that the religious lexicon in English is saturated with Christian meanings and their theistic associations. When a term that indicates nobility (*rje*) is translated "Lord," the effect, even if unintended by the translator, is to divinize and gender its referent. Likewise, when *mögü* is rendered "devotion," the connotations of Christian piety and worship are invoked, however inadvertently. These are some of the questions we have grappled with as translators and editors.

The Spectrum of Devotion

We are fortunate that Jetsün Khandro Rinpoché, of the Mindrolling lineage, agreed to do an interview with us for inclusion in this anthology. The interview in full, titled "Devotion and Discernment," follows immediately after this introduction. In the interview, Khandro Rinpoché emphasized to us that *devotion* fails to capture the spectrum of what *mögü* means in Tibetan. Not only is it multifaceted but, importantly, *mögü* matures along the Buddhist path. In her words, it begins as the "longing for liberation, longing for buddhahood, or longing for the qualities of one's own primordial nature." This is inspiration, the first type of faith, or *depa* (*dad pa*), and then it develops into a more mature type, *yiché* (*yid ches*), which is confidence, trust, and conviction in the teachings, practices, and one's own potential to realize them. In its fruition, according to the three types of faith mentioned above, that conviction becomes unshakeable; one no longer relies on an external support, such as a human guru, but actualizes the qualities of enlightenment that have always been within oneself.

In its most basic sense, then, devotion is a "longing to awaken" and proceeds from there, with the teacher-student relationship as just one of its possible expressions. Felicitously, we heard this phrase "longing to awaken" from Anam Thubten a few months after choosing it as the title for this anthology. Elucidating the phrase, Anam Thubten said, "Why do we have a teacher? To find out who we are and go back to the heart of the matter, returning to the buddha-nature within. Thinking it's all 'out there' leads to disappointment and all kinds of pitfalls."[9] Put another way, the point of the teacher-student relationship is to empower the student to discover and manifest their own buddha-nature rather than to create a perpetual dependency on or a chauvinistic loyalty to a single teacher or tradition. In mature form, devotion—as conviction in the teachings—expresses itself as an aspiration to follow in the footsteps of past masters and the commitment to practice wholeheartedly to be able to attain awakening oneself.

Such conviction comes about through meditation practices that include tantric liturgies in which one visualizes oneself in the form of an enlightened deity in order to invoke its qualities within oneself. In chapter 1, the first poem is a praise to Sarasvatī, or Yangchenma in Tibetan, the goddess of arts and literature—a fitting opening to this anthology. In it, the Geluk polymath Tsongkhapa (1357–1419) praises Yangchenma in lavish terms and sets her form vividly in mind in order to evoke the very qualities of literary prowess he demonstrates in the poem itself. It is common for teachers to praise deities or lineage masters while remaining humble about their own human failings. Even the most revered lamas are forthright about any shortcomings, and we should not take this as empty rhetoric. A lineage prayer by Longchenpa (1308–1364) in chapter 4 and a song by Jamyang Khyentsé Wangpo (1820–1892) in chapter 14 are illustrations of this. So *mögü* may begin with an inspiration or inclination, but it does not end there. Like writing poetry, devotion of this kind is cultivated, practiced, and mastered, even as it appears to manifest spontaneously.

If devotion is focused excessively on an external teacher, it can foster what Amanda Lucia has called "proxemic desire." This is the desire to be close to a charismatic guru, which tends to structure a religious or spiritual community and its institutions around the guru in ways that are susceptible to abuse.[10] As Tibetan Buddhism has become popular in Europe and the Americas, this has led to systemic issues whereby some gurus are siloed and protected from feedback and accountability by an inner circle, allowing harmful behaviors to occur and go unchecked. This is only compounded when gurus are viewed as beyond conventional ethical standards, or when secrecy prevails around their conduct. These and other pitfalls can enable abuse and leave individuals and communities devastated and shattered, as attested by reports of sexual abuse in several of the larger international Vajrayāna communities, including Rigpa, Shambhala, and the Foundation for the Preservation of the Mahayana Tradition (FPMT).

While recent events may suggest that this is a modern crisis, abuse is an age-old problem across cultural, social, and religious contexts. Needless to say, Tibetans are and have long been well aware of the potential for teacher misconduct. Numerous folktales, satirical accounts, and contemporary short stories recount how monastics and lamas might take advantage of their position and harm vulnerable followers.[11] In addition, Buddhist writings on the teacher-student relationship emphasize the importance of discernment in finding a qualified teacher, which is a tacit recognition of the risks involved.[12]

Given the traumatic disruption to survivors' lives and fragmentation within multiple Buddhist communities in recent years, now is a crucial time to reexamine the systems in which these relationships are forged and to affirm that the responsibility for harm lies squarely with those who abuse their power. To address the problem holistically, it is urgent to call attention to and uproot the Orientalist legacy and tendency in public discourse to idealize and romanticize Buddhism. This tendency, often evident in English-language publications, might seem innocuous or even positive—after all, it helps attract people to the dharma—but in reality it contributes to the problem and helps support systemic dysfunction by flattening the complexity of human relationships and their diverse expressions. For this reason, we as editors have chosen to showcase a spectrum of devotional expression in Tibetan poetry and song that can serve as a resource for exploring anew the nature and dynamics of the teacher-student relationship.

What is devotion, then, beyond the initial longing to awaken and the subsequent development of conviction in the teachings? In "Devotion and Discernment," Khandro Rinpoché discusses *mögü* as the further maturation of faith. In her terms, it involves "humble respect" and "gratitude" for all that has supported one on the spiritual path, even the breath in meditation practice. This includes gratitude for any teachers who hold a genuine lineage, have practiced and studied extensively, embody the teachings to the best of their ability, teach them appropriately, and exhibit ethical behavior. These are the very qualities of a vajra master, authorized to bestow tantric initiations, according to the Tibetan polymath Jamgön Kongtrul (1813–1899).[13]

Yet Buddhist masters in Tibet, past and present, recognize that living gurus are human and can make mistakes. Thrangu Rinpoché cautions against "blind faith" (*rmongs dad*), saying:

Faith in one's guru does not mean blind faith. It does not mean believing "My guru is perfect," even though your guru is not perfect. It is not pretending that your guru's defects are qualities. It is not rationalizing every foible of the guru into a superhuman virtue. After all, most gurus will have defects. You need to recognize them for what they are. You don't have to pretend that your guru's defects are qualities, because the object of your devotion is not the foibles, quirks, or defects of your guru, but the Dharma that your guru teaches you. You are not practicing the guru's foibles. As long as the Dharma you receive is authentic and pure, then that guru is a fit object for your devotion. The result that you get, you get from the Dharma that you practice.[14]

Khandro Rinpoché echoes this statement when she discusses the problematic tendency to overlay "pure perception," or daknang (dag snang), in an attempt to minimize teacher misconduct. Unequivocally she states, "If you think, oh, I have to close my eyes and pretend it's not happening and then think purely of whoever is doing something that is inappropriate, that is not daknang. That is really ignorance." This pernicious misunderstanding of "pure perception" may inform constituencies within Buddhist saṅghas that dismiss or minimize the impacts of teacher misconduct and Buddhist organizations that fail to adequately address abuse and create accountability processes.

In line with this, Ringu Tulku has made the point that Western practitioners are too focused on the teacher, whereas the Buddha said: "I show you the way. Understand that liberation is up to you."[15] The teacher serves as the conduit for the teachings, rather than the focal point, and the rest is up to the student. Perhaps this is why prostrations are done before a lineage tree, whereby humility and respect are distributed toward a host of enlightened figures—buddhas, bodhisattvas, lineage masters, tantric deities, and protectors. One prostrates to what these figures embody (enlightenment and its qualities) and practices what they teach (the dharma according to their lineage) instead of simply admiring them as individuals. As a case in point, in chapter 15 an homage by the ecumenically inclined Sakya master Jamyang Khyentsé Wangpo to Avalokiteśvara contains a praise of compassion embodied by this bodhisattva as well as a critique of narrow-mindedness and the pretense of religious observance. When the enlightened qualities are embodied, a "non-dual form of devotion" arises in which the guru is no longer external, as evoked in a "non-song" of realization by the contemporary Dzogchen master Khangsar Tenpé Wangchuk (1938–2014) in chapter 20.

In contemporary Tibetan poetry and songs with a devotional tenor, Buddhist teachers stand for so many other things: faith in Buddhism as a whole, loyalty to Tibet as an ancestral homeland (or the Nubri Valley of Nepal, as in chapter 25), and a commitment to its language, culture, and lifeways. A common theme in the final chapters of this anthology is nostalgia, which includes a sense of loss and longing for connection to historical places, figures, and traditions. Conditions of cultural rupture and rapid social change in Tibetan and Himalayan contexts, as well as among Tibetan exiles across South Asia, heighten that sense of separation that is already paradigmatic in common devotional song forms, such as "calling the lama from afar" (bla ma rgyang 'bod). Chapters 21 and 22 contain songs by and about Khenpo Jigmé Phuntsok (1933–2004), founder of Larung Gar, the largest Buddhist institution on the Tibetan plateau, and a key figure in revitalizing Buddhism in the aftermath of the Maoist period and the Cultural Revolution. These songs lament the loss of tradition and contain rousing calls for Tibetans to unite in a path forward in line with Buddhist values.

The threat of loss also figures in the poetry of Wo Jik Jil, who portrays faith embodied in pilgrims in her depiction of Tibetan mothers circumambulating the Jokhang Temple in Lhasa. In "Mothers in the Barkhor Circuit" (chapter 24), the steadfastness of their maintenance of tradition is more palpable and enduring than the fleeting goosebumps of inspiration. Therein devotion is directed at Tibetan culture and those who uphold it: the tenacious mothers who pass on the Tibetan language and culture across the generations in cyclic fashion akin to circumambulation.

POETRY AND SONG IN TIBETAN LITERATURE

This anthology includes twenty-five chapters with translations of Buddhist devotional poetry by celebrated Tibetan authors from different Buddhist traditions and historical periods, both classical and contemporary. The forms are diverse, spanning the ornate, cultured, and crafted as well as the spontaneous and colloquial. The chapters begin with exceptional illustrations of two main forms of versification in Tibetan literature: ornate poetry (snyan ngag) and more colloquial songs (mgur), sometimes referred to in religious contexts as "songs of experience" (nyams mgur). The first shows the refinement of ornate poetry and honors Sarasvatī, the goddess of arts and literature, while the second celebrates Milarepa, the tantric adept who popularized singing profound spiritual instructions in vernacular song styles. While these forms of versification have overlapping features—and *poem* and *song* are sometimes used interchangeably by our contributors—there are notable stylistic differences.

The ornate poetic form *nyen-ngak* literally means "melodious speech," reminiscent of Coleridge's famous statement that poetry is "the best words in their best order," as Lama Jabb reminds us in his opening essay to this volume. It derives from Sanskrit poetics, or *kāvya*, and the enduring influence of Daṇḍin's *Kāvyādarśa* in Tibet. Translated into Tibetan during the thirteenth century,[16] the *Kāvyādarśa* details the stylistic features of ornamentation involving simile and metaphor, sonic repetition and wordplay, and the use of kennings (figurative compounds in the place of single terms). The praises to Sarasvatī by Tsongkhapa in chapter 1 are eloquent examples of this ornate poetic form. Gedun Rabsal and Nicole Willock carefully unpack Tsongkhapa's use of poetic embellishments from the *Kāvyādarśa* to aid the reader in appreciating the work. All of that said, Roger Jackson explains that no single Tibetan term covers the full range of the English word *poetry*: "From among the vast number of versified works found in their language, Tibetans have separated out certain pieces because of their greater concentration of rhythm, image and meaning, their heightened 'imagery' (*gzugs*), 'vitality' (*srog*) and 'ornamentation' (*rgyan*).... These works are designated in Tibetan by at least three separate terms: *glu* (songs), *mgur* (poetical songs) and *snyan ngag* (ornate poetry)."[17] Notice that there is no mention of content in this definition since what makes a versified work poetic has to do much more with *how it is said* than with *what is said*.

Like ornate poetry, Tibetan songs also utilize imagery, vitality, and ornamentation, which overlap with the poetic devices systematized in the *Kāvyādarśa*, although Tibetan song forms historically preceded them.[18] Oral accounts and written documents make it abundantly clear that poetic verse and song are pervasive and even constitutive aspects of Tibetan cultural production and have been a mainstay of Tibetan societies and identities since before the advent of Tibetan writing. In its origins a "performative tradition," *gur* contains melodic meters meant to be sung.[19] For this reason, *gur* retains the language and cadence of orality and sometimes also the pretense of being uttered spontaneously, only later to be recorded as a literary artifact for posterity. The eleventh-century adept Milarepa is a paradigmatic figure in this regard, having synthesized the tradition of spontaneous insight from the *dohās* and *caryāgīti* of Indian tantric masters with colloquial Tibetan song styles.[20] Chapter 2 is dedicated to an edifying exchange of songs between Milarepa and an irascible hunter, his rapacious wife, their fierce dog, and a frightened deer. It is a charming account of their conversion, one by one, after arriving at the great adept's retreat hermitage in the midst of the hunt, only to realize the futility of saṃsāra after listening to Milarepa's songs.

Thus, we begin the anthology with prominent examples of *nyen-ngak* and *gur* by Tsongkhapa and Milarepa, respectively, to set the stage for the variety of forms of versification found in subsequent chapters. From there, the anthology proceeds roughly chronologically, from a satirical song by Rechungpa—successor to Milarepa—forward in time according to the dates of the author. Because we have arranged the entries according to the Tibetan authors' dates, revelatory literature from the terma (*gter ma*) tradition appears according to the approximate period of its revelation, not according to the time the teachings are understood to have been concealed. That means that figures like Padmasambhava and Yeshé Tsogyal, renowned for their activities in promoting Buddhism in Tibet during the eighth century, are positioned in this anthology after the Nyingma master Loncghenpa, because the narratives in which they appear in chapters 5 and 6 were recorded by later figures: Orgyen Lingpa (b. 1323) and Dorjé Lingpa (1346–1405), respectively.

In Buddhist literature in Tibet, *gur* are often embedded within larger narratives that provide the context and rationale for a specific song, whether to offer spiritual advice, to express longing or realization, to call out for guidance and blessings, to encourage oneself while on retreat, or to engage in pedagogical dialogue. The introductory essays by our contributors provide the historical and narrative contexts for their translations, and the narrative frame is sometimes included in the translation as well. Thus, a song about the "mighty guru" is prompted by a "masculine showdown" between the Tibetan emperor Tri Songdetsen and the Indian master Padmasambhava in a foundational myth of the advent of Buddhism in Tibet, as translated by Joshua Brallier (formerly Shelton) in chapter 5. The destruction of Mindrolling Monastery by Dzungar Mongols in 1717 provides the poignant backdrop for Mingyur Peldrön's lament in chapter 10, as she flees her homeland and calls out to her deceased father, Terdak Lingpa (1646–1714), in despair. When songs appear in letters (*'phrin yig*) or collections of songs (*mgur 'bum*) without a narrative frame, the context may have to be discerned from the song itself.

This is the case with a letter written by Terdak Lingpa to his younger sister, Sonam Palzöm, to advise her after the tragic death of a child (chapter 9), reminiscent of Khandro Rinpoché's reference to Tibetan songs as a "balm that soothes the mind." Solitary retreat is the context for Jigmé Lingpa's expansive tributes to the natural environment at Samyé Chimphu (chapter 11) and for the renowned hermit Shabkar's simple and profound songs of experience and advice to himself (chapter 13). Closer to the present, in chapters 19 and 20, Khenpo Gangshar Wangpo (b. 1925) and Khangsar Tenpé Wangchuk offer riveting testaments to the violence of modern Tibetan history and songs of advice for practicing in the worst of times.

The works translated here are largely *gur*, with some important exceptions. Also featured are several examples of *nyen-ngak*, which has received less attention to date from scholars and translators.[21] After the first chapter, chapters 8 and 12 return to ornate poetry and deal with historically significant events during the perils of war. Chapter 8 features poems from Tsang Khenchen's autobiography, written as he fled the Mongol armies that rampaged through Tibet in the mid-seventeenth century. And chapter 12 brings the reader into the cosmopolitan milieu of Central Tibet in the eighteenth century through Doring Tenzin Peljor's account of the Gorkha War (1788–92) in an acrostic poem that is part of a mixed prose-verse narrative. In his introductory remarks, Riga Shakya addresses the potential for reading history through literature and interpreting literature as historical documentation, rather than the more typical treatment of these as distinctive spheres. In chapter 23 a praise to Jetsünma Mumtso (b. 1966), niece and successor to Khenpo Jigmé Phuntsok, likewise employs the formal features of *nyen-ngak*. Composed by Khenmo Norzin and translated by Padma 'tsho, it unabashedly calls attention to the female master Jetsünma Mumtso's exalted stature among the leadership of Larung Gar. Beyond that, chapter 16 showcases the distinctive genre of Tibetan epic, bridging the oral and the literary. It contains a prophetic song from the Gesar epic by the maiden Nechung, who casts a shadow over the celebrations following Gesar's victory over demonic forces and return from hell by foretelling the doom of his kingdom of Ling. Natasha Mikles highlights the epic nature of the ballad in her translation to exquisite effect.

Some works embody the characteristics of poetry and song in exciting combinations. For example, in chapter 20 the "Non-Song" by Dzogchen master Khangsar Tenpé Wangchuk synthesizes the spontaneity of songs of experience with ornamentation more typical of *nyen-ngak*, even though the author received little by way of formal instruction during the turbulent era of his youth and wrote the song while in prison. In chapter 24, Miranda Smith refers to Wo Jik Jil's poem "Mothers in the Barkhor Circuit" as an example of "*gur*-influenced free verse," given its metrical variety and loose structure. Free-verse poetry is popular in contemporary Tibetan literature, alongside a revival of *nyen-ngak*, in Tibetan literary journals and blogs. In line with this, Mindrolling Monastery in Dehradun, India, holds the equivalent of a poetry slam every year, and monks prepare eagerly by composing devotional poetry and practicing reciting it.[22] The event is a contest showcasing the virtuosity, pleasure, and sometimes bravado associated with Tibetan poetry even today. As another syncretic impulse, chapters 22 and 25 feature devotional songs performed in contemporary musical styles in Tibetan pop music videos. In those chapters, selections include *gur* and folk song (*glu*) styles, which are composed by Buddhist lamas and cleric-scholars and performed by popular singers as either *dunglen* (Tibetan vocals accompanied by the mandolin) or pop music (vocals accompanied by MIDI, musical instrument digital interface).

REFLECTIONS ON TRANSLATION

Lama Jabb begins his essay in this anthology, "An Act of *Bardo*: Translating Tibetan Poetry," by stating that "poetry is in the Tibetan DNA. Therefore, translation of Tibetan poetry is vital for a more nuanced and fuller understanding of and more meaningful communication with Tibet." For too long, translation of Buddhist literature from Tibet has been focused on semantic meaning, without adequate attention to literary style. This is, in part, the consequence of the doctrinal and philosophical focus of Buddhist Studies in early scholarship and the liturgical and instructional needs of multilingual Vajrayāna communities burgeoning beyond Tibetan and Himalayan areas. In the past decade or so, scholars and translators of Tibetan texts have at long last turned their attention to literary considerations in conferences and publications, including the first Lotsawa Translation Workshop, in 2018, during which most of the translations included in this anthology were first presented. Indexing this turn toward the literary, as this manuscript was in progress, two online journals for translations and studies of Tibetan literature were founded, *Yeshe: A Journal of Tibetan Literature, Arts and Humanities* (yeshe.org), and *Journal of Tibetan Literature: Research, Translation, Criticism* (journaloftibetanliterature.org). Given the context, it is fitting that this anthology of Tibetan poetry and songs instigated among its contributors a focus on the formal, literary considerations in translation.

Lama Jabb characterizes translation as a "liminal *bardo*-like zone between two languages—a communicative act between two separate worlds." The *bardo* (*bar do*) is a Tibetan rubric for articulating existence as a series of transitory, in-between experiences, particularly the transition between death and rebirth.[23] For Lama Jabb, translation enacts a rebirth of a literary work in a new language. He uses this framework to theorize translation as another expression of the nature of reality as always contingent, attending to the debate over whether it is even possible to translate poetry and addressing the not uncommon doubt of the value of translated verse, in whatever language. Part of the problem is what gets lost in translation, which is as much an ethical question as it is a semantic and literary one.[24] Along similar lines to Lawrence Venuti,[25] Lama Jabb calls attention to the potential for "destructive violence" in translation, the "tendency to erase the original in the memory of the target language reader." This tendency, found in the typical English-language mode of domesticating translations, threatens cultural erasure in a context in which the survival of Tibetan language and cultural production is already at risk. One of the several ways that Lama Jabb works against this hazard is through the selective preservation of Tibetan terms or in some cases, Tibetan sounds and wordplay, in the English translation. Some translators in this volume follow suit. In translating songs by the female visionary Sera Khandro, note how in chapter 17 Christina Monson leaves the calling sounds *ki ki* and *kyé hud* untranslated and in chapter 18 Sarah Jacoby calls attention to the lexical variety of terms referring to *ḍākinīs* (tantric female deities) in Tibetan. Lama Jabb emphasizes that foreignizing moments "help the English reader be conscious of the source language and appreciate its cultural matrix," thereby resisting the erasure of the Tibetanness of this literature.

A middle way between domesticating and foreignizing impulses in translation is Paul Ricœur's notion of "linguistic hospitality." Articulated in his work *On Translation*, this is a method by which the translator considers the needs of both the author of the source text and the reader of the target language. Acknowledging that there is no perfect translation, due to phonetic, lexical, and syntactical differences between languages, he suggests that some experience of loss is unavoidable in translation, even as something is salvaged in the process. Like a good host who considers the needs of diverse guests in one's home, the contributors to this anthology make an effort to be hospitable to their Tibetan authors and their English-language readers, as equally welcome guests. As Ricouer puts it, "the pleasure of dwelling in the other's language is balanced by the pleasure of receiving the foreign word at home."[26] For this reason, our call for translations submitted for the Lotsawa Translation Workshop and revised for this anthology was to pay more attention to formal, literary features than has been typical in the translation of Tibetan texts. Even if it is not possible to recreate the meter or precisely reproduce Tibetan poetic forms of alliteration and word play, as Lama Jabb puts it, "our challenge is to find a way of translating these poetic turns of phrase that does justice—even a modicum—to their expressiveness, rhythmic beauty, and visual intensity."

With full recognition of the challenges, the contributors to this anthology agreed to foreground formal aspects of their translations of verse and to experiment with the possibility that this would lead to a more lively and poetic result in the English. Meter might well be the most challenging aspect of Tibetan poetry to approximate through translation. Although line-length is not by any means an equivalent to meter, playing with the number of syllables in the Tibetan line when rendering it in English, as Dominique Townsend does in chapter 9 and Oriane Lavolé does in chapter 14, can have a compelling effect. In her translation of Jamyang Khyentsé Wangpo's song, Lavolé subtly refers to the consistency of the eleven-meter Tibetan verse by translating it in fourteen-syllable lines in English, using repetition and refrain to highlight the rhythmic flavor. In addition, allusion and sonic wordplay can seem impossible to carry over into the target language, but when the "trappings" of poetry are ignored, the results can be impoverishing to the translated text. In chapter 20 Lowell Cook takes seriously the classical poetic form known as "matching initial letters" (*thog ma'i sgra mtshung*) and attempts to approximate it in English by translating the Tibetan syllable *ma* with English prefixes such as *un-*, *in-*, *im-*, or *non-* or negating initial terms such as "without." The effect is arresting, calling attention to the form and highlighting in the process Khangsar Tenpé Wangchuk's use of negation to point to the freedom beyond contrivance discovered in Buddhist meditation.

Tibetan literature demonstrates an almost dizzying display of virtuosic wordplay, which can be daunting to readers and translators alike. In chapter 1, Gedun Rabsal and Nicole Willock demonstrate the significance of capturing phonemic repetition, in the technique known as *yamaka* in Sanskrit (Tib: *zung ldan*). In one instance this is the duplication of syllables and in another it is the repetition of initial words of subsequent lines. They also pay special attention to the translations of kennings (*mngon brjod*), which are notoriously difficult to translate, by maintaining the combination of terms such as "rain-holder" (*chu 'dzin*) instead of using their referent, "cloud." In chapter 11, Willa Baker calls attention to the structure of a pair of songs, one embedded within the other, like nestled *matryoksha* dolls through using indentation and taking appreciative note of what she describes as "Jigmé Lingpa's ability to envelop a didactic religious instruction . . . in the spontaneous sensuality of the natural world." In other cases, translators call upon non-Tibetan poetic forms to render the work anew in English. For instance, in chapter 16, Natasha Mikles employs the style from English epic ballad and folk literature with its "iambic tetrameter rhythm, as well as the playful inversion of subject, object, and verb" to evoke a resonant tone to the Gesar epic in English and conjure both horror and melancholy at the fall of Ling. The result of her experiment is stunning.

Since we encouraged experimental approaches, some contributors work in innovative ways with familiar terms. As an example, Renée Ford chooses to use the term "love" rather than the more literal and conventionally translated "look on me with compassion" (*thugs rjes gzigs*) in chapter 4 to emphasize affect in Longchenpa's lineage prayer. Acknowledging that there is no perfect equivalence in translation, our contributors, each in their own way, aimed to bring some of the liveliness and ingenuity of the original into the English, and we embrace the riskiness of that commitment. The particular poetics of Tibetan is not the only challenge in the process of translation, of course. Much of the content here is highly specialized and even esoteric, having to do with advanced meditation instructions and experiences. These are hard to understand, let alone translate without expert interpretation, often in the form of consulting a Tibetan lama or cleric-scholar. In the spirit of facing apparent paradoxes and other challenges head-on, Sarah Harding's translated verses are an inspiration. Note the elegance of this description of meditation: "Fixation on equipoise and subsequent attainment faded, / I forgot the distinction of meditation sessions and breaks, / let go of judgment whether 'this is it' or 'this isn't it,' / and lost the bias of self and other, close and distant." Her translation in chapter 7 is an example of what Ricoeur calls "the inseparable combination of sense and sonority" in poetry.[27]

Elsewhere, in "Toward a Hermeneutic of the Idea of Revelation,"

Ricoeur offers this apt reflection on poetry and poetics, remarkably resonant with the Buddhist themes of the volume: "Poetic language alone restores to us that participation-in or belonging-to an order of things, which precedes our capacity to oppose ourselves to things taken as objects opposed to a subject."[28] We hope the translations collected here might elicit such a sense in readers.

ABOUT THE ANTHOLOGY

Longing to Awaken emerges out of a groundswell of interest in the translation of Buddhist literature from Tibet. Since 2008 there have been numerous conferences regarding the translation of Buddhist sources from Tibetan into English, culminating in the large Tsadra "Translation and Transmission" Conferences held in Colorado in 2014 and 2017. Parallel to that, there has been an increasing interest in the literary features of Tibetan religious texts, as exemplified in the five-year American Academy of Religion Seminar on "Religion and the Literary in Tibet" (2010–14) with concurrent and subsequent events at various institutions. The first Lotsawa Translation Workshop, held at the University of Colorado Boulder in October 2018, was a successor to these endeavors. We chose the theme of devotion, broadly conceived, in order to explore poetic expressions of affect within a Buddhist framework. This anthology contains a number of the translations that were originally presented at the workshop with a few additions.

We would like to express our appreciation to the Tsadra Foundation for their generous support of the Lotsawa Translation Workshop. Thanks also to the Tibet Himalaya Initiative at the University of Colorado as host, the Chancellor's Office for additional funding, and Joshua Brallier for his time and efforts spent on logistics. One of the driving intentions of us as organizers was to encourage more experimental and literary approaches to the translation of Buddhist poetry and song in Tibetan sources. We also sought to forge a community of practice around translation through bringing together scholars and translators at various stages of their careers for dialogue and feedback around translations-in-process. Too often translation, like reading and writing in today's world, happens in solitude. We found it enriching to read the Tibetan source texts and workshop translations-in-progress together in small groups, and this volume is the result of that effort.

We would also like to express our appreciation to Jetsün Khandro Rinpoché and Lama Jabb for contributing to the opening reflections for this anthology. Lama Jabb delivered the keynote address at the Lotsawa Translation Workshop and has kindly allowed us to print his lecture in full. Our interview with Khandro Rinpoché on the complexities of devotion provides the volume with a Buddhist master's perspective. Thanks also to Anam Thubten for offering the verse and translation by the Third Karmapa Rangjung Dorjé for use as the epigraph, Pema Bhum for his calligraphy of *Mögü* (devotion) on the opposite page, and Matthieu Ricard for permission to use his photograph, "Morning Mist in a Himalayan Valley," on the cover of this book. Finally, we would like to thank the editorial team at the University of Virginia Press for their sustained interest and care in bringing this anthology forward.

We dedicate this anthology to the accomplished teacher and translator Tsering Dhundup Gonkatsang (1951–2018), Tibetan language instructor at Oxford University, who had planned to attend the first Lotsawa Translation Workshop but died tragically in a car accident earlier that year, and to Christina Lee Monson (1969–2023), a dedicated practitioner and talented translator who contributed a chapter to this anthology and passed away after a long battle with cancer as the book was being finalized. The dedications in the first pages of this anthology were composed by Lama Jabb and Sarah Jacoby, longtime friends and colleagues.

Notes

1. See Khoroche, *Once the Buddha Was a Monkey*, 32–38.
2. Reiko Ohnuma refers to jātaka tales depicting the "gift of the body" (*dehadāna*) as super-jātakas." *Head, Eyes, Flesh, and Blood*, 46. These portray an "inimitable act," not recommended for the ordinary person, who is instead encouraged to perform ritual gestures in order to gain merit.
3. See Hibbets (now Heim), "Ethics of Esteem."
4. The *Bod rgya tshigs mdzod chen mo* glosses *mos pa* as *yid ches pa'am yid 'dun pa* and *gus pa* as *yid dang bas 'dud pa*. Krang dbyi sun, *Bod rgya tshigs mdzod chen mo*, 361 and 2125, respectively.
5. On the semantic valences of *adhimukti*, see Benedetti, "Etymology and Semantic Spectrum." Its Tibetan correlate is *mos pa*. See also Buswell and Lopez, *Princeton Dictionary of Buddhism*, 16; and Edgerton, *Buddhist Hybrid Sanskrit Grammar and Dictionary*, 14.

6. For a genealogy, see *OED Online*, s.v. "devotion, n.," accessed 30 August 2022, https://www.oed.com/view/Entry/51579?redirectedFrom=devotion.

7. For a useful comparison, see Schelling, *Oxford Anthology of Bhakti Literature*.

8. On the consort relationship in Tibetan Buddhism, see Gayley, "Revisiting the Secret Consort."

9. Interview with Anam Thubten, 2 October 2 2021.

10. Although Lucia focuses on a Hindu devotional context, her observations on the desire for proximity and its structuring properties for religious communities are relevant here. See Lucia, "Guru Sex."

11. For an analysis of contemporary Tibetan short stories about sexual violation by "fake" lamas, see Gayley and Bhum, "Parody and Pathos."

12. See, for example, Jamgön Kongtrul, *Teacher-Student Relationship*.

13. See Jamgön Kongtrul Lodrö Tayé, *Buddhist Ethics*, 47–52.

14. Thrangu Rinpoche, commentary, 92.

15. ངས་རེ་ཁྱོད་ལ་ཟར་བའི་ཐབས་བསྐུན་གྱི་ །ཟར་པ་རང་ལ་རག་ལས་ཨེས་པར་ཤུས། ། Talks in Boulder and Denver, CO, October 2019, clarified with Ringu Tulku by personal communication in August 2023.

16. See van der Kuijp, "Tibetan Belles-Lettres," and chapter 1, below, for the historical details of the *Kāvyādarśa*'s translation and transmission.

17. Jackson, "'Poetry' in Tibet," 368.

18. The modern intellectual and writer Döndrup Gyal (1953–1985) emphasized this point in his history of Tibetan songs. See Don grub rgyal, *Bod kyi mgur glu byung 'phel gyi lo rgyus*.

19. See Larsson and Quintman, "*Opening the Eyes of Faith*."

20. See Kapstein, "Indian Literary Identity in Tibet."

21. See Lin, "What Language We Dare Learn and Speak."

22. Poetry is not always part of the monastic curriculum, but it is in some Nyingma monasteries such as Mindrolling, and the proliferation of literary journals published by monasteries makes clear that poetry is a highly valued aspect of monastic life and expression today. On aesthetics at Mindrolling, see Townsend, *Buddhist Sensibility*.

23. The traditional six *bardos* (*bar do*) are (1) life, (2) dreaming, (3) meditation, (4) dying, (5) dharmatā, and (6) rebirth.

24. This question was taken up in a recent panel on "Lost and Found in Translation" at the 16th Seminar of the International Association of Tibetan Studies in Prague, 3–9 July 2022.

25. See Venuti, *Translator's Invisibility*.

26. Ricouer, *On Translation*, 10.

27. Ricouer, *On Translation*, 6.

28. Ricoeur, "Toward a Hermeneutic," 24.

References

Benedetti, Giacomo. "The Etymology and Semantic Spectrum of *adhimukti* and Related Terms in Buddhist Texts." *Buddhist Studies Review* 36.1 (2019): 3–29.

Buswell, Robert, and Donald Lopez. *The Princeton Dictionary of Buddhism*. Princeton, NJ: Princeton University Press, 2014.

Don grub rgyal. *Bod kyi mgur glu byung 'phel gyi lo rgyus dang khyad chos bsdus par ston pa rig pa'i khye'u rnam par rtsen pa'i skyed tshal* [The pleasure grove of play: A history of Tibetan songs in terms of origins, dissemination, and distinctive features]. Beijing: Mi rigs dpe skrun khang, 1997.

Edgerton, Franklin. *Buddhist Hybrid Sanskrit Grammar and Dictionary*. New Haven, CT: Yale University Press, 1953.

Gayley, Holly. "Revisiting the Secret Consort (*gsang yum*) in Tibetan Buddhism." *Religions* 9.6 (June 2018). https://doi.org/10.3390/rel9060179.

Gayley, Holly, and Somtso Bhum. "Parody and Pathos: Sexual Transgression by 'Fake' Lamas in Tibetan Short Stories." *Revue d'Etudes Tibétaines* 63 (April 2022): 62–94.

Hibbets, Maria. "The Ethics of Esteem." *Journal of Buddhist Ethics* 7 (2000): 26–42.

Jackson, Roger. "'Poetry' in Tibet: Glu, mGur, sNyan ngag and 'Songs of Experience.'" In *Tibetan Literature: Studies in Genre*, edited by José Ignacio Cabezón and Roger Jackson, 368–92. Ithaca, NY: Snow Lion, 1996.

Jamgön Kongtrul. *The Teacher-Student Relationship*. Translated by Ron Garry. Ithaca, NY: Snow Lion, 1999.

Jamgön Kongtrul Lodrö Tayé. *Buddhist Ethics*. Translated by the International Translation Committee. Ithaca, NY: Snow Lion, 1998.

Kapstein, Matthew. "The Indian Literary Identity in Tibet." In *Literary Cultures in History: Reconstructions from South Asia*, edited by Sheldon Pollock, 747–802. Berkeley: University of California Press, 2003.

Khoroche, Peter (trans.). *Once the Buddha Was a Monkey: Ārya Śūra's Jātakamālā*. Chicago: University of Chicago Press, 1989.

Krang dbyi sun, ed. *Bod rgya tshig mdzod chen mo* [The great Tibetan-Chinese dictionary]. Beijing: Mi rigs dpe skrun khang, 1985.

Larsson, Stefan, and Andrew Quintman. "*Opening the Eyes of Faith*: Constructing Tradition in a Sixteenth-Century Catalogue of Tibetan Religious Poetry." *Revue d'Etudes Tibétaines* 32 (April 2015): 87–151.

Lin, Nancy G. "What Language We Dare Learn and Speak: Decolonizing the Study of Tibetan Poetry." In *Living Treasure: Tibetan and Buddhist Studies in Honor of Janet Gyatso*, edited by Holly Gayley and Andrew Quintman, 321–34. Boston: Wisdom, 2023.

Lucia, Amanda. "Guru Sex: Charisma, Proxemic Desire, and the Haptic Logics of the Guru Disciple Relationship." *Journal of the American Academy of Religion* 86.4 (December 2018): 953–88. https://doi.org/10.1093/jaarel/lfy025.

Ohnuma, Reiko. *Head, Eyes, Flesh, and Blood: Giving Away the Body in Indian Buddhist Literature*. New York: Columbia University Press, 2006.

Ricoeur, Paul. *On Translation*. Translated by Eileen Bennan. London: Routledge, 2006.

———. "Toward a Hermeneutic of the Idea of Revelation." *Harvard Theological Review* 70.1/2 (1977): 1–37.

Schelling, Andrew. *The Oxford Anthology of Bhakti Literature*. New Delhi: Oxford University Press, 2011.

Thrangu Rinpoche, Khenchen. Commentary to *Creation and Completion: Essential Points of Tantric Meditation, by Jamgon Kongtrul*, translated by Sarah Harding. Boston: Wisdom Publications, 2014.

Townsend, Dominique. *A Buddhist Sensibility: Aesthetic Education at Tibet's Mindröling Monastery*. New York: Columbia University Press, 2021.

van der Kuijp, Leonard. 1996. "Tibetan Belles-Lettres: The Influence of Daṇḍin and Kṣemendra." In *Tibetan Literature: Studies in Genre*, edited by José Ignacio Cabezón and Roger Jackson, 393–410. Ithaca, NY: Snow Lion, 1996.

Venuti, Lawrence. *The Translator's Invisibility: A History of Translation*. New York: Routledge, 2017.

Devotion and Discernment

EDITORS' INTERVIEW WITH
JETSÜN KHANDRO RINPOCHÉ

To start with a basic question: what is devotion in Tibetan Buddhism? Would you say it's primarily an emotion, or a set of commitments, or something else?

Everybody seems to be asking this question these days—what is devotion? Actually, I think it's good that people are exploring this. There are some wonderful teachings explaining what devotion is, so there's nothing different to add to that. But this is a question coming up for many Vajrayāna students, and of course for all those who are exploring dharma, due to all the unfortunate experiences that many people have encountered here and there. I don't think there is an answer that can be arrived at in a direct way. It's not like asking what's two plus two and then you get an answer of four. In the same way, there is not any one single answer.

I don't think the word *devotion* can capture the whole spectrum of what it means in Tibetan Buddhism. I always like to look at words and try to figure out what they mean. The English word *devotion* is limited. If we are to understand the terms for the Vajrayāna concepts of *depa* (*dad pa*), *yiché* (*yid ches*), and *mögü* (*mos gus*) or other such terms, I myself am not sure that the word *devotion* captures all of this. Of course we have *faith, confidence, devotion,* and other words in English that we could explore. So, when trying to understand it myself, I have often referred to these Tibetan terms for what we are calling *devotion*.

In the beginning *depa*, or faith, has the characteristics of engaging the wisdom of discernment—that's very important. Any understanding of what the Vajrayāna or Buddhist concept of devotion means has to be born out of discernment, for which knowledge is very important. If we try to get to the fruition aspect without really going through the first steps, then I think we encounter difficulties. So, discriminating wisdom is born out of knowledge and study, hearing and understanding. At that point, we can work with variations of taking refuge in the dharma and having some semblance of what devotion means, but it is not on a par with the Vajrayāna sense of indestructible confidence. So, I think people need to understand the various levels of this step by step.

In the beginning, out of that wisdom of discernment, is born *depa*. I call it *depa* although I don't think *depa, yiché,* and *mögü* are exclusive terms. Still, I like to see them as a little bit distinct from one another because of what each of these words suggests. *Depa* seems to be born out of discernment, and this discernment leads to really being inspired by enlightened qualities. So *depa* entails seeing enlightened qualities, wishing for these qualities, and understanding how wonderful it would be to have these qualities. Even simple things such as wishing to be free from suffering and learning the dharma are included. Therefore, *depa* means seeing these enlightened qualities in masters, being able to focus on and have admiration for them, and then really being encouraged to follow their example.

After you work with wishing for enlightened qualities, then I think the *yiché,* or confidence, comes. *Yiché* is a more mature state of faith that begins to become powerful. It has a power that can withstand and even cut through your own doubts and hesitations. This is a transition from the first longing for the enlightened qualities, because simply longing for liberation, longing for buddhahood, or longing for one's own primordial nature isn't sufficient. This is especially true when the deluge of one's own *kleśas,* or negative emotions, become very strong. But then there is *yiché,* when that longing has matured. At that stage, it has to become so powerful that it can actually stop the neurosis from gaining strength. If it is weak, maybe that kind of *yiché* can at least help you recognize your own neurotic mind at that moment. If it is powerful, it can transform or even transcend neurosis.

So, the power of devotion at that point is knowing the true qualities of the Buddha, dharma, saṅgha—as well as knowing the true qualities of the master and one's own primordial nature. As that grows to include more awareness, it is able to stop doubts and hesitations that come from one's own *kleśa*-ridden mind. When one continues to work with that, more and more, then I think *mögü* develops. This is interesting because *mögü,* or humble respect, is a state of equilibrium. It's a balanced state in which that awareness and trust in what you have taken refuge in, and that you have generated devotion toward, is more powerful than the normal processes of your own emotional mind. So, I think once you develop a respectful state of mind, then the humbling aspect comes. It is powerful enough that it devours self-absorption and the self-cherishing mind altogether.

After you first see the enlightened qualities in teachers and really wish to emulate and embody those qualities, and as the longing becomes stronger, it becomes more of a presence of awareness in your mind, until it finally matures into a full state of unimpeded and continuous devotion. At that point, it is so powerful that the mind no longer gets distracted. At that time you are truly grateful. It's not just saying, "I'm very grateful to my lama," but you are truly grateful. It's an unquestionable sort of gratitude for all those who have been able to give you that sense of confidence that cuts through the ego-cherishing.

This is a journey of maturation: first seeing something extrinsic and then knowing that you can embody it. In time you find that it was always within you, inseparable within you. So that is a tremendously important journey for any practitioner, but especially within the Vajrayāna. That's why the concept of devotion is emphasized. Whether or not it starts with emotion, it is as with any other topic of buddhadharma. As sentient beings in the relative world, we are so dependent upon the emotional mind to recognize something of value. We have the transcendent nature already, but we rely at first upon emotion to know what is good and what is bad, to know what to abandon and what to cultivate, although at the ultimate level everything is beyond purity and impurity. Still, we have to recognize purity and impurity as long as relativity exists, and therefore the emotional mind is engaged initially in developing the quality of devotion.

But eventually we have to understand what true faith is and go beyond that. At a certain point, one is no longer reliant upon any particular object. The true supramundane devotion is the absolute confidence of knowing that the qualities of the guru, the Buddha, and our own buddha-nature have never been separable or distinct from our own selves. At that point, we no longer are operating within the realm of emotion. But to get there while in saṃsāra, most of us will have to rely upon emotion and make it more and more pure.

To follow up on the external aspect of devotion, to what extent is devotion mainly for one's guru, or should it also be directed toward lineage and toward the teachings? In other words, is it something broader?

I think it is very important to consider the capacity of the student. One thing I have noticed is that we have very little discussion of capacity.

When we request a teaching, we usually request that the master turn the wheel of the dharma in accordance with the potential of the student. Then we promptly forget about capacity. We begin to think that all of us are exactly the same, and we're all going to experience the same thing. I think that's something to consider more deeply. Individuals have different capacities and different potential. Of course, in the modern world no one likes to be told there are different potentials. We are all supposed to be equal and perfect, but that's wishful thinking in some ways. Because there are diverse potentials and diverse capacities among students of Buddhism, the approach has to be in accordance with the student. So, you have to consider your own capacities.

In Buddhist terminology, when we talk about potentials we are not talking about a stagnant state. Potential is an ever-changing process: otherwise how could we ever talk about liberation and enlightenment? Because the nature of potential is impermanent, it is also changeable; it is also transformable. Therefore, potentials always have to go through processes, and that's the path. On the path, what you rely on is in accordance with whatever your potential is. Some people need to rely a lot more on objective phenomena and some less, depending upon how clear their mind is. So, nobody is the same in that way, although of course we can generalize about certain things. Some depend more on external conditions of the guru, lineage, and saṅgha, and so on. But some rely less on external conditions. I think it's different for different individuals.

That being said, a lot of people do get a bit optimistic and think that they can do it on their own. That also has to be considered very carefully—there has to be a certain humility. That humility helps you know how much guidance you need, which teachings you need, which transmissions you need. The more reliant you are upon something to give you that ultimate wisdom, how could one not be grateful? How could one not then consider the profound relationship to teachers, lineage, transmissions, and so forth? But the teacher, lineage, teachings, and everything are not separate entities. They're all within oneself. So, the whole concept of the lineage tree is actually your core. It's your own buddha-nature. And the whole root of that tree branches out from you. It is rooted within your own primordial nature, and then it streams forth. These manifestations are unlimited and manifest in diverse ways, and the branches are innumerable as well. Then you have the whole concept of lineage: the many lineages and many masters. There are different displays your mind makes. They're all connected to the root of your own fundamental nature, and they are indistinct from your own self. So, the inseparability has to be understood.

I think a lot of problems come about when the objective conditions are seen as something different from yourself. From that perspective it's as if you are *you*, and the teacher, the teachings, and the lineage are like Noah's Ark. You have to sort of jump into it. But that's not the Buddhist view. You don't have to jump into another ship. You have to realize that it's all indivisible from your own mind stream. But how wonderful it is that there are those conceptual, relative manifestations available for as long as they are needed, that can be a reference for you for as long as reference is needed. But ultimately, it's not separate: the Buddha is not, the teacher is not, the lineage is not, the teaching is not, the transmission is not, the deity is not, and the meaning is not. The realization is also not divisible from yourself. And the one who really points that out to you becomes the root teacher.

Recognizing that devotion is so important to the Vajrayāna, would you say it's because devotion serves as a kind of conduit for blessings? Or does it open the student's mind to be able to hear the teachings? How does devotion work?

The whole view of the Vajrayāna is about developing confidence in your own primordial nature. It's your own primordial nature, but there's always doubt and hesitancy. We're not able to really believe that. So that's what makes us reliant externally. So therefore, there's the outer guru. Rinpoché [Mindrolling Trichen, who was Khandro Rinpoché's father] used to always say that the best guru is the one who gives you a boost by letting you step on their shoulder when you need to climb up high. So, a guru is the best when they can give you a "leg up." That's the outer guru. So, the outer guru refers to all those whom we receive teachings from. This is the concept of blessing and receiving empowerment. When you are able to receive transmissions and teachings, you practice *guruyoga* and generate devotion. Then that takes you to the inner guru. The inner guru is something you have to really work with. That is when even the physical guru sort of intermixes and becomes indivisible with your own *yidam* [tutelary deity] practice. Whether it is form or formless meditation, the essence of the path allows confidence to come about. That's when you're working with the inner guru. And then that inner guru also has to be let go of at a certain point.

That inner guru has to give you the "leg up" to send you off to the secret guru. And that is where you remain more and more. That's why in the Dzokpa Chenpo [Great Perfection] tradition, for example, all the formlessness of being able to rest within the nature of mind becomes the secret guru practice. But you have to progressively go from one stage to the next. So, the first stage would be the blessings, the second would be the *siddhis* [accomplishments], and then the final stage would be the attainment. So even in the *guruyoga* practice, first you take the *abhiṣekas* [empowerments], and you get the blessings. The conclusion is always the moment when you dissolve the guru within yourself. That's more the inner aspect. And then there's the absolute, or the secret aspect of remaining indivisible. The guru and your mind become indivisible, and you just rest within that.

So, in the beginning, a lot of blessings are needed for the mind to be stabilized and purified and to accumulate merit and so forth. But ultimately, there has to be more and more a sense of confidence. And that is the *siddhis,* or accomplishments, and then gradually one is able to not even worry about the *siddhis.* At that point, one is just being and resting within the continuum of the indivisible nature. That itself is the core where everything is, including devotion. But devotion no longer becomes the word *devotion* that we have some kind of a conceptual idea about. If you look at the great teachers, you never would ask them, "Do you have devotion?" I don't think they ever ask themselves, "Do I have devotion?," "Should I have devotion?," or "Should I not have devotion?" If we were to ask our teachers, "Do you have devotion, and how can you know you have devotion?," I'm sure they would laugh. My teachers would laugh at that question. I never asked a direct question exactly like this, but once Rinpoché pointed out that he'd never accomplished anything other than what he had received in terms of the teachings. He didn't have to define that as devotion. It is. What else would it be?

Sometimes in liturgies there are statements like "I rely on you," "I place my hopes in you," or "I pledge myself to you." How do those liturgical statements square with the notion that it's really up to the practitioner in terms of the effort, perseverance, and discipline to traverse the path.

When you do śamatha practice, often people say to focus on the breath. It's a very popular thing to do. So you know, you could also write a praise of the breath: "there's nobody to rely upon but you, breath—my breath."

We may not write about it like that, but we really rely upon the breath to bring our concentration to one-pointedness. Many of these compositions [like the ones in this volume] come from the heart of somebody who appreciates the fact that there are these references that can keep our distracted minds focused. There has to be gratitude for that.

That's my own personal experience. When I do my *guruyoga*, and when I read supplications, tears come to my eyes out of gratitude that there have been those who have taken time to give teachings, and to make some sort of human being out of what I am. Without my teachers there would be no difference between me and a buffalo, for example. From all the distractions, neuroses, *kleśas* and every kind of negativity—to find some kind of awareness within that, and to make an individual like me sane, how does that happen? It could only be the enlightened activity of the great masters that could make a human out of me. How can one not appreciate that? Why not appreciate what we rely upon, that which awakens our own primordial nature to a state of enlightenment? That's marvelous. How can one not be utterly grateful for that? It's very humbling.

Rinpoché, I'm sure lots of people are asking you this. Do you have advice for students of the Vajrayāna whose teachers have engaged in abuses of power? As you mentioned, so many people are asking these questions right now.

It really saddens me. I think there's no other word. What to say? It breaks my heart to hear and learn of the experiences of some women. We can't be naïve and say, "No, no, there's a misunderstanding," or "That's something that didn't happen," and so forth. But what saddens me a great deal more is when practitioners give up on the dharma. I won't say women only, because it's everybody. Many people are going through these difficulties. When practitioners aren't able to differentiate between an individual [teacher] and the dharma, they say, "That's why I gave up practicing," or "That's why I gave up the dharma or quit the saṅgha." Some even give up their vows. That's deeply disturbing and saddens me greatly.

My first instinct always is to ask, What could be done to keep their faith and devotion to the path intact? So, I think more talk needs to happen along these lines. When we learn of lamas and teachers who have done things that are harmful and hurtful to others, how can anyone that has any amount of wisdom or understanding ever condone that kind of activity? That's very simple to say. On the other hand, there is the relationship to the dharma, which is more important. And I think we need to really work on making sure that the support is there. I know that there are several organizations and people who have come together to create that kind of a support group for people to still stay connected to the profound dharma.

It saddens me when people think that devotion means you stop thinking, analyzing, and questioning. Devotion and discernment complement each other. These are the things that need to be discussed, and this is one area where we all need to work a little bit more. We need to know that this is something that is not acceptable. And thankfully, it is still not widespread; it's rare, comparatively speaking. So, I'm happy about that, and I think talking about it is very helpful.

Educating the monastics is also very important. Just as much as the education of practitioners around the world, primarily the Western world and the lay community. I think there's a lot of training required for those who are leading saṅghas, especially those who hold the monastic vows. That's very important. One can try to see that there is something positive coming out of any difficult or adverse situation. So, I think this discussion is also very timely, and it is needed. If we don't address these issues now, it won't be healthy for the growth of dharma.

This is a time of maturation for the dharma in Europe and the Americas. It's still so new, especially Tibetan Buddhism, and there has been so much confusion. One site of confusion has been about daknang (dag snang), *"pure perception" or "sacred outlook," and what it means to see the guru as a buddha and one's environment as a buddhafield.*

Daknang will come, *daknang* will come eventually, but it will come later. In the beginning, *daknang* can seem forced. We have to keep reminding ourselves of that. How many times have I said things to my teachers that led them to laugh at me and say, "*Daknang gom, daknang gom,*" or "Meditate a little bit on pure perception." But I fail miserably, even today. *Daknang* is very good, but forced *daknang* is a work in progress. It takes time. If you think, "Oh, I have to close my eyes and pretend it's not happening and then think purely of whoever is doing something that is inappropriate," that is not *daknang*. That is really ignorance.

Daknang has to be born from the dissolution of all the trappings of your own self-cherishing mind. When you have nothing to hold on to, it just falls apart. Then *daknang* arises. *Daknang* is very subjective; it's less about the object.

Let's turn to one or two examples from the anthology. There's a translation of the story of Milarepa and the hunter in which the hunter is converted after hearing Mila's songs. With utter devotion, the hunter, his wife, their dog, and the once fearful deer sit harmoniously and listen to the teachings and gain the realization of Mahāmudrā. How should we understand these kinds of stories, which can make it sound so easy, given what you've said about devotion as a maturation process that happens over time.

It doesn't happen often. Beyond the beauty of that moment in the story, there are so many things to consider. There's the activity of a great master like Milarepa and his own realization of the Mahāmudrā mind, which transforms all the environment and external conditions into the vessel within which such realization arises. Even if one is born as a hunter, the karmic timing of just that moment, of physically being tired and frustrated, plus every other experience that he has been through, must lead him to reach a point of being completely disarmed. In that moment of encounter, he's totally disarmed. There has to be the deer being hunted, the fear and helplessness, this sense of utterly giving up. It's all of those causes and conditions coming so beautifully together.

It's like an orchestra that's building to a crescendo. At the moment of the peak, everything that you have otherwise held on to with stubbornness just falls apart. And it falls apart in the presence of somebody who is a realized master. That's called *tendrel* (*rten 'brel*, auspicious coincidence). It's the power of *tendrel* that brings all of this together, and it's so unique. When we speak about marvelous moments such as these, it's true that the activities of great realized beings are such that they can transform and purify lifetimes of negativities in beings and bring them onto the path of liberation. But on a pragmatic level, the right ripening of karma has to be there. It's like the straw that breaks the camel's back, isn't it? Something has been percolating in the mind, and then there is that one more thing that just disarms completely all the sense of holding and being stuck. When this happens at a moment with one's own karmic fruition and merit, as well as in the presence of a great master, that is a very powerful moment.

When we make aspirations and wishes for something like this to happen, it's easy to ignore the fact that there was a process leading up to that. The frustrations have to add up; the revulsion has to add up. With that, questioning has to happen: What am I doing? Is this really meaningful? You have to be brave to hold that mirror in front of yourself to really see what you're doing and admit that ultimately you cannot hide anymore. Then there's a sense of being fully naked, when you cannot hide from either yourself or others. So, in those moments, if one is able to meet with a guru, or the mind transmissions are given at those times, it's really very powerful. That's what happens in some of the accounts given.

In our anthology, there are several supplications for blessings in order to gain the strength to renounce the world and attain realization. Can the guru actually grant these things? And if not, what is the role of supplication?

Other lineages have what is called the *myurjon soldeb* (*myur byon gsol 'debs*), a supplication for teachers who have passed away to swiftly return. Mindrolling doesn't have a "swiftly return" prayer. We have what is called the *Jetsün Soldeb* (*Rje btsun gsol 'debs*). This is a supplication to follow the teacher's example. One of the best compositions is the *Jetsün Soldeb* by Terdak Lingpa [founder of Mindrolling Monastery]. I recite that every day. I cannot remember any day that I have not done this and felt it very strongly. It just binds my whole day and everything that I have to do in that one simple aspiration to follow the example of past teachers. Not to look like them. Not to speak like them. Not any of these. But if I can be even a little bit like what Terdak Lingpa and other Mindrolling masters embodied, I feel fully confident that my *guruyoga* practice for the day has been well done.

So, all of these supplications and aspirations are very powerful. It's very important. It's like when we wear monastic robes, we gather all those pleats, and we hold them up with our hands, and then we have the sash, or the belt, that you tighten. That's what keeps the whole thing up. So, these supplications are like that for our mind—it is like the sash that binds everything together to remind us why we are Buddhist. All that I am doing is so I may recall your teachings and follow your example. This is recalling the qualities, and it is very important. Then you really have the aspiration to generate those qualities and ultimately actualize them. As I said in the beginning, the enlightened qualities are inherent in you.

We supplicate as a method to be able to embody those qualities. That is the whole meaning of *guruyoga* and supplications to the guru.

Before we conclude the interview, is there anything else that you would like readers to know about this anthology's theme—devotional poetry from Tibet?

It's really very timely. I can't speak for anyone other than for practitioners, but I think it is really very timely. I think we've become too clever. Knowledge is good, being clever and smart is good. But sometimes your own cleverness makes the mind become a little bit more scattered. You become either critical of others or, much worse, you become self-critical. Songs of realized masters and supplications have a balming effect on you. It's like a balm that soothes the mind. It's almost like your mother cuddling you and telling you it's going to be alright. This is needed as the world bleeds everywhere, and especially today with the internal bleeding of the human spirit. Some people are just busy and oblivious, lost outside themselves in certain ways—as they say, ignorance is bliss. But if someone tries to be a little more observant, one cannot help but feel the pain, confusion, and suffering of everyone. A balm is definitely needed for the mind, for the soul. The wisdom that is not lost in the sophistry of cleverness but speaks to the heart of a human being is needed. People need the encouragement that everything is going to be alright, that we can all do it, and that there are those who can help us. If one day we open up to that help, we will ultimately realize that what we have opened up to was never distinct from who we are.

བོད་ཀྱི་སྙན་ངག་སྒྱུར་བའི་བར་དོའི་ལས།

An Act of *Bardo*

Translating Tibetan Poetry

LAMA JABB

One would be hard-pressed to find a single Tibetan writer worth their salt who has not dabbled in writing poetry. In fact, it would be extremely difficult to find one literate Tibetan who has not tried their hand at composing poems. Likewise, Tibetan oral culture is saturated with poetry. A Tibetan proverb tells us: བོད་མི་རེའི་ཁ་ན་གླུ་རེ།། གླུ་མི་ཤེས་ཟེར་བ་བོད་མིན།། (In every Tibetan mouth there is a song / To claim not to know a song is not Tibetan). I think it is not an exaggeration to say that poetry is in the Tibetan DNA. Therefore, translation of Tibetan poetry is vital for a more nuanced and fuller understanding of and more meaningful communication with Tibet.

Although highly rewarding, translation is no easy task. Translation operates in a liminal *bardo*-like zone between two languages; it is a communicative act between two separate worlds.[1] A scrupulous dismantling of the original text is required before its substance can be transported into the target language. This is like the complex dissolution of corporeal existence at the time of death. The target language itself also goes through a process of deconstruction before being reassembled to absorb the content and sometimes even the form of the original. Walter Benjamin concludes his "Task of the Translator" by stating, "To some degree all great texts contain their potential translation between the lines."[2] When one appreciates this enigmatic statement within the context of Benjamin's notion of translation as survival, then it is within the interstices of words and lines that we find the roaming consciousness and the potential for its rebirth.

Like a journey through the *bardo* realm, translation is full of pitfalls and enlightening opportunities. I will discuss these challenges and rewards, drawing on my own experiences as a translator. Through my English translations I will demonstrate my attempts to assist the rebirth of Tibetan poems in English. I usually recite or present the Tibetan original first so as to underscore some aspects of its sound, cadence, and mood as well as to highlight the obvious fact that the English rendition is a recasting. Although translation is enriching in various ways, it also entails destructive violence—in that sometimes it erases the original in the memory of the target language reader. Reciting or presenting the source material helps to foreground the continued life of the Tibetan original and by extension the continued life of Tibetan language. Translation takes one closer to the original poem, but it is in no way the real thing. Let me start with a typical formulaic beginning of a Tibetan wedding recital:

གཏམ་ཞིག་མི་གཏམ་ཟེར་ན། གཏམ་ཞིག་གཏམ་དགོས་ཟེར་གི་སྐྱེ་བོ་རབ་ཞིག་གིས་གཏམ་རེ་གཏམ་ན། བྱ་ཐང་དཀར་སྐོང་པོས་ ནས་འཕང་བཏང་འདྲ། འཕུར་གི་འཕུར་གི་རེ་མཐོ་ཡིན་རུང་། གཤོག་སྟེ་དགུང་ལ་མི་ཐུག་པའི་ཡིད་ཚོན་ཞིག་དགོས་གི་ སྐྱེ་བོ་ འབྲིང་ཞིག་གིས་གཏམ་རེ་གཏམ་ན། སྐྲག་རོག་པོ་ཚང་ལ་གཟོལ་འདུ། གཟོལ་གི་གཟོལ་གི་རེ་དམའ་ཡིན་རུང་། གཤོག་སྟེ་བྲག་ ལ་མི་ཐུག་པའི་ཡིད་ཚོན་ཞིག་དགོས་གི་ སྐྱེ་བོ་ངན་ང་འདྲ་བས་གཏམ་ཞིག་རེ་གཏམ་ན། བྱ་ཕུག་རོན་སྔོན་མོས་ཟ་འཚས་ འདུ། གཡས་ལ་གཟིགས་ལྟ་དགོས་གི་ གཡོན་ན་གཟིག་ཉན་དགོས་གི་ སྨུར་སྨུར་ཡས་བཟང་ནས་གཟིག་འཛུ་དགོས་གི་ སྦོང་སྦོང་ ཡས་བཟང་ལས་གཟིག་མྱིད་དགོས་གི

"I won't give a speech," I said. But I'm beseeched to give a speech. When a great man gives a speech it's like the white vulture cutting through the high heavens. As it flies and flies—it soars ever higher, yet it needs mental alertness so that its wing-tips won't touch the extremity of the skies. When a middling man gives a speech it's like the brown eagle swooping down to its nest. As it swoops down and down—it falls ever lower, yet it needs mental alertness so that its wing-tips won't touch the rock. When a lesser man like myself gives a speech it's like the blue pigeon foraging for food. It needs to look to the right, it needs to listen to the left, it needs to bend down and down to pick it up, and it needs to hunch over and over to swallow it![3]

These are some of the many Tibetan figurative expressions for the act of public speaking that describe and instruct the potential speechmaker. I think they would also serve as apt metaphors—especially the blue pigeon in my case—for translators of varying competences.

The works of the accomplished translators might appear graceful and effortless like the flight of the vulture and the eagle, but behind them lie many hours of hardship, headache, and struggles for mental alertness. Like the blue pigeon's foraging for food, the act of translation in general is an arduous process that requires heightened senses and diligence and even entails existential danger. In spite of all these factors that go into the act of translation, something of the original still remains uncommunicated. In particular, translation of poetry is deemed to be difficult if not impossible.

Arthur Schopenhauer writes that "poems cannot be translated; they can only be transposed, and that is always awkward."⁴ Percy Bysshe Shelley goes further and speaks of "the vanity of translation" and posits: "It were as wise to cast a violet into a crucible that you might discover the formal principle of its colour and odour, as seek to transfuse from one language into another the creations of a poet. The plant must spring again from its seed, or it will bear no fruit—and this is the burthen of the curse of Babel."⁵ As poetry is a specific fusion of words and musical elements, I take heed of this notion of the untranslatability of poetry. If poetry is what Samuel Taylor Coleridge claims it is—"the best words in their best order"⁶—then translation inevitably disrupts this scrupulous ordering. *Kāvya*-influenced Tibetan scholars state that poetry is རྣ་བར་སྙན་ ཞིང་འཇེབས་པའི་ཚིག་གི་སྒྲིག་པ་ཞིག (an arrangement of words that is melodious to the ear).⁷ John Dryden's definition of poetry, "the harmony of words," would not be an unfaithful translation of སྙན་ངག, the Tibetan term for poetry.⁸ Once again, this accentuated element of harmony might fade into discord when a poem is transported out of one language into another, despite the translator's best efforts to retain it.

Regardless of these seemingly insurmountable obstacles, it is also a simple fact that without the labor of translation there could not be much poetic communication across cultures divided by language—let alone any possibility of overcoming that perennial linguistic confusion captured by the Tower of Babel story. Indeed, Tibetan scholars acknowledge the illuminating role of translation in opening one's eyes to a foreign world when they reverentially address the accomplished translator in Sanskrit as Lotsawa and in Tibetan as འཇིག་རྟེན་མིག, "the eyes of the world." Tibetan translators do not seem to dwell much on the untranslatability of poetry but get on with the task at hand. The ninth-century royal decree on translation found in སྒྲ་སྦྱོར་བམ་པོ་གཉིས་པ, the Tibetan and Sanskrit glossary of Buddhist technical terms, respects the syntax of the original language

but is more concerned with the transference of the meaning.⁹ It instructs
the translator to retain the order of words or sentences both in prose and
in verse but to change it if it does not make proper sense in Tibetan.

I take this practical royal reflection on translation seriously. So, it
might be impossible to transport—to borrow Shelley's words—"a cer-
tain uniform and harmonious recurrence of sound" within a specific
poem from one specific tongue into another.¹⁰ However, it is still pos-
sible to transfer some of its subtle qualities concerning sense, tone, imag-
ery, and general meaning. It is also possible for translation to carry over
the heightened emotions and thoughts that constitute poetry. I will now
present some of my translations for appraisal to show how I both succeed
and fail in assisting the rebirth of Tibetan poems in English. We will
see if my translations are still stuck in that twilight *bardo* realm between
the Tibetan and English languages or if they can be considered worthy
reincarnations.

TIBETAN POETIC DEVICES

Let's look at an excerpt from a poem-song, or *gur* (Tib: མགུར), by the great
monk-scholar and poet ཞང་སྟོན་བསྟན་པ་རྒྱ་མཚོ, Shangton Tenpa Gyatso (1825–
1897):

མིང་ནུ་མ་ཆེན་པོའི་གྲགས་པ་ཅན།།
ཕུགས་ནི་ཐམས་གཏད་པས་བཞུགས་དུས་མེད།།
མཚོ་དྭངས་སྟོན་བསྐྱེད་པའི་བུ་གོད་དེ།།
ཁོ་སྐྱབ་སྟེ་སྐྱབ་མེ་རོ་ལ་འབོར།།

ཐས་དཀོར་ཐས་འཆོལ་བའི་གྲོང་ཆོག་པ།།
ཁ་ལག་པ་གཉིས་ཀ་དགལ་དུས་མེད།།
ས་རེ་ཕུག་དཀྱིལ་གྱི་ཟུ་ཚོག་དེ།།
མཆུ་མོ་རེ་མོ་རེ་དགལ་དུས་མེད།།

གནས་རེ་ཕྱོད་འགྲིམ་པའི་སྐྱོམ་ཆེན་པ།།
ཕྱོང་ཕྱིམ་སྐྱོ་ཞུལ་ནས་ནས་ཕྱར་འཕྱུ།།
ཉེན་ལུང་སྐྱོང་འགྲིམ་པའི་སྐྱུང་སྐྱོག་དེ།།
མཆན་ཀུག་གི་ཀུག་གི་ཏུ་མཐའ་ཞུ།།

མིང་གོས་མཚོ་འདོད་མི་ཆེན་ཚོ།།
ཕུག་ཡོང་གི་ཡོང་གི་སྒུན་དུས་མེད།།

མཚོ་རྟ་རེ་ལུལ་བའི་ན་པོ་དེ།།
ཁོ་གྲབ་བེ་གྲབ་བེ་འདུག་དུས་མེད།།

The lama known for his greatness and fame
Is never present when beseeched by the pillowed dying.
The vulture that soars high in the blue sky
Circles over the corpse with its wings — flap, flap.

The ritualist who forages for food offerings
Never ceases to move his mouth and hands.
Pikas and mice on the ground and amidst the crags
Never cease to move their muzzle — nibble, nibble.

The great yogin who roams through wild mountains
Wanders at villagers' doors collecting fistfuls of barley.
The hungry wolf that roams the empty valleys by day,
By night prowls the encampment's edge — sneak, sneak.

Powerful men who crave after fame and status
Never tire though hardships accumulate on the way.
The stag that wanders through high rock mountains
Never for a moment stays still — stumble, stumble.[11]

This is an excerpt from the epilogue to Shangton Tenpa Gyatso's བསྐྱབ་
བྱ་ནོར་བུའི་ཕྲེང་བ, *Jeweled Rosary of Advice*, a famous tract of elegant sayings consisting of fine verses of advice. Here our poet attacks the hypocrisy, irresponsibility, avarice, and dishonesty of high lamas, monk ritualists, ascetic yogins, and powerful Tibetan men, who are likened to restless, hunger-driven vultures, rodents, wolves, and stags. He does so through the employment of one of the best-loved meters of Tibetan *gur* and a unique expressive poetic device.

I used technical Latinate terms for classifying the meter of this *gur* in my book *The Inescapable Nation* (stating that each line consists of four feet: three trochees with catalexis in the first foot, and the fourth foot a dactyl).[12] I believe I was wrong to employ such vocabulary for explaining the Tibetan arrangement of rhythm. After reading Ted Hughes's brilliant essay "Myths, Meters and Rhythms,"[13] and given that even great English-language poets disagree over what a certain poem's meter is, I have no idea how to classify this Tibetan verse according to the English metrical system. To say it simply, this *gur* excerpt is a syllabic verse written in four-line stanzas with each line consisting of eight syllables. When scanning a line for rhythm, the first and last syllables are read on their own. A slight pause of breath follows the first syllable and precedes the last syllable of a line. The six syllables in the middle are read in pairs. To put it another way, within each line two monosyllables frame three dissyllables. For example, the breakdown of syllables in the first stanza could be rendered:

མེང་ སྣ་མ་ ཆེན་པོའི་ གྲགས་པ་ ཅན།།

ཕྱུགས་ ནི་སྐྱས་ གཏད་པས་ བཞགས་དུས་ མེད།།

མཚོ་ དགུང་སྔོན་ བསྐྱོད་པའི་ བྱ་ཁྱོད་ དེ།།

ཕོ་ ཤྭབ་བེ་ ཤྭབ་བེ་ རོ་ལ་ འཕོར།།

It is quite impossible to translate the metrical pattern, cadence, alliteration, and other sound-based qualities of a Tibetan poem into English. Foregrounding the musical dimension, Edgar Allan Poe defines "the Poetry of words as the Rhythmical Creation of Beauty."[14] Alas, as you can see in my translation of this *gur* above, I impair that sound-forged "Beauty" by failing to mirror the Tibetan arrangement of rhythm. A more accomplished translator with a musical ear and a deeper knowledge of English prosody might be able to transport the musical mode of this Tibetan verse into English. However, as André Lefevere notes, such "metrical translation" might only be achieved at the expense of the poetic text as a whole.[15] Thus, in this translation I took the advice of John Dryden and varied "the dress" in an effort "not to alter or destroy the substance."[16] It must be said that although no metrical translation is attempted here, the English rendering might still have faint echoes of the rhythm and cadence of the Tibetan original—which after all still serves as a source of inspiration even in a subtle metrical sense.

Another fundamental element of this *gur* poem is the use of an ancient and prevalent Tibetan poetic device that embellishes the last line of each stanza. It is formed of phrases that are visually, aurally, kinetically, and rhythmically descriptive in an untranslatable way. Here are the last lines of each stanza from the *gur* translated above:

ཕོ་ཤྭབ་བེ་ཤྭབ་བེ་རོ་ལ་འཕོར།།

———

མཆུ་མོ་རེ་མོ་རེ་དགལ་དུས་མེད།།

———

མཚན་གུག་གི་གུག་གི་ད་མཐའ་ཞུལ།།

———

ཁོ་གྲབ་བེ་གྲབ་བེ་འདུག་དུས་མེད།།

Commenting on the archaic songs in the Dunhuang manuscripts, Roger Jackson identifies these rhetoric traits as "reduplicated or trebled ono-matopoetic phrases."[17] In his analysis of a subversive recitation by the Bhutanese wandering bards Michael Aris calls these figures "that well-known poetic device of reduplicated syllables having no lexical value, em-ployed to describe specific appearances or situations."[18] However, these poetic phrases are not just for conveying rhythmic sound or producing alliterative pattern and syllabic meter. They are lexically rooted and are a nuanced imagistic representation of both abstract and concrete entities. On top of the onomatopoeic quality, they add visual images of the action, scene, and object in question. These include highly perceptive and vivid descriptions of specific sense, motions, or movements that breathe life into the entities being portrayed. Within them one finds the heightened sensibility of the poet and the impressionable and vivid imagination of the reader.

These turns of phrase are some of the distinctive Tibetan linguistic features Gedun Choepel (1903–1951) singles out for their poetic qual-ity. In his གཏམ་རྒྱུད་གསེར་གྱི་ཐང་མ།, *Spread-Out Gold Tales*, he laments the fact that they hardly feature in formal *kāvya*-influenced Tibetan verse. These image-laden onomatopoeic figures busy with action, sound, and sense form part of what Gedun Choepel calls པ་མེས་ལུགས་ཀྱི་ཚིག་སྒྲ, "the ancestral dic-tion," or བོད་སྐད་རང་དབང་བའི་སྒྲ་ཀུན, "the diction according to the natural free-dom of the Tibetan language."[19] Gedun Choepel advances the notion of a flexible Tibetan poetic diction naturally inherent within the Tibetan language (བོད་སྐད་རང་གི་གཤིས་ལ་ཡོད་པ) that is unrestricted by the artificial style of the Indian *kāvya*-influenced Tibetan literature. This is something very similar to what Ted Hughes calls poets' use of words according to their "natural quantity."[20] That is the observation of "the emphasis and time-value given to [each syllable] in natural conversational speech."[21]

My translation here captures the action-packed aspect of these phrases, but it doesn't quite manage to convey their evocative descrip-tions of a movement or an appearance. For instance, the line "Circles over the corpse with its wings—flap, flap" doesn't reproduce that ungainly, awkward, and desperate flight of the vulture distilled in ཀླབ་ཐེ་ཀླབ་ཐེ. This clumsy, macabre flight contrasts sharply with the masterful flight of the white vulture that cuts through the high heavens, which I cited at the start of this essay. Although my translation is nowhere near adequate regarding the importation of this poetic device, I believe it does relay Shangton Tenpa Gyatso's critical spirit and a bit of his zesty style. However, our challenge is to find a way of translating these poetic turns of phrase that does justice—even a modicum—to their expressiveness, rhythmic beauty, and visual intensity. A list of 124 such poetic epithets just for the color white compiled by my beloved cousin and mentor the late Tibetan poet and essayist Dhatsenpa Gonpo Tsering (1963–2013) offers a blizzard of images, actions, and sounds dressed in white.[22] It is clear that we, as translators, have our translation work cut out for us.

Kāvyic Style

This leads me to a closely related issue: the difficulties we encounter when translating the Tibetan poetic image. Both Tibetan written and oral poetry are obsessed with similes, metaphors, and all kinds of figurative speech. Not only does the Vorticist dictum that the image is "the primary pigment" of poetry[23] apply to Tibetan poetry but the Tibetan fixation upon it results in poems bursting with imagery. Such poetic compositions don't lend themselves easily to translation. For example, here is a *kāvya* verse by the Great Fifth Dalai Lama (1617–1682), which overflows with images:

དབྱངས་གསལ་སྦྱོར་གྱིས་སྲ་བར་བཅིངས་པའི་ལྕགས་རིའི་ཁོར་ཡུག་དབུས་ན་མཐོན་མཐོ་གླེགས་བུའི་རིན་ཆེན་རྡུལ་མང་
བརྩེགས་པའི་བ་གམ་ན།།
འགལ་བའི་ཁྱུར་མང་གྱ་གྱུའི་ཚུལ་སྤངས་ལེགས་བཤད་ཁམས་ཀྱི་དྭངས་མ་ཀུན་བསྡུས་ཚར་དུ་དངར་བའི་དེབ་ཐེར་རི་དྭགས་
མིག་ཅན་མ།།
ཉམས་འགྱུར་འཛེ་ཟླིག་གར་གྱི་རྣམ་རོལ་བཅད་ལྷུག་སྤེལ་མའི་དབྱངས་བདུན་ལྷུར་ལེན་ཚིག་དོན་མ་འདྲེས་ཟུར་མིག་དབང་
གཞུ་ལྟར་འཁྱུག་ཅིང་།།
མངོན་བརྗོད་ཤུ་དུམ་ལྷ་རའི་འཕྲེང་མཛེས་གཏམ་རྒྱུད་མགོ་སྐྱེས་གཡོན་འཕྱང་མ་འདི་བློ་ལྡན་བརྒྱ་བྱིན་དག་ལས་གཞན་གྱི་
སྤྱོད་ཡུལ་མིན།།

Inside the towering, heavenly mansion of heaped jewel dust books,
amid an encircling bulwark bound and reinforced by the fusion of
vowels and consonants,

Resides the wild animal-eyed beauty of a well-structured annal that
   abandons the coquetry of heavy inconsistencies and deceptions
   and distills all the essences of the finest writings.
Her beautiful dances of emotional expression embrace the seven
   melodies of verse, prose, and their blend while sidelong glances of
   words and their meaning, unmixed, flash like the rainbow,
And this woman adorned with an *udumbara* garland of *kāvya*
   kennings, with the tresses of tales cascading on her left, can be
   relished by none but the Indras of wisdom.[24]

This is how the Great Fifth concludes his history of Tibet, which he
likens to the call of the cuckoo: བོད་ཀྱི་དེབ་ཐེར་དཔྱིད་ཀྱི་རྒྱལ་མོའི་གླུ་དབྱངས།, *The Tibetan
Annals: Song of the Spring Queen.* In this verse the Great Fifth eschews
his usual utterances of humility and eulogizes his history for its poetic
language, consistency, truthfulness, orderly structure, semantic clarity,
wealth of references, and sheer intellectual force. He identifies these note-
worthy features of his book through, to borrow a phrase from John Stu-
art Mill, "an exuberance of imagery."[25] The profusion of imagery seems
to be both a strength and a weakness of the Great Fifth's poetry. In these
lines, a heavy heap of metaphors and similes borrowed from classical In-
dian literature and mythology almost suffocates the meaning. The whole
stanza is an example of what Tibetan *kāvya* poetics calls མཐའ་དག་གཟུགས་ཅན་གྱི་
རྒྱན་, "the adornment of total metaphor." In such an instance, the principal
metaphor—here the beautiful woman—is further adorned throughout
the stanza with subsidiary metaphors, such as her graceful dance, flashing
eyes, and cascading hair, that correspond to the history book and each of
its perceived qualities.

My translation imparts the overall meaning but loses the polished yet
somewhat labored meter as well as some of the complex Indic allusions.
Maybe Walter Benjamin is right when he states that translations "prove
to be untranslatable not because of any inherent difficulty, but because
of the looseness with which meaning attaches to them."[26] This verse
by the Great Fifth contains Tibetan translations of Sanskrit terms and
concepts—some of them serving as images—such as "towering," "heav-
enly mansion," "the wild animal-eyed beauty," "emotional expression,"
"verse, prose, and their blend," "the seven melodies," "rainbow [the bow of
Indra]," "*udumbara* garland of *kāvya* kennings," "tresses [lit., "that grows
on the head" or "the head born"], and Indra, མཆོན་མཐོ། བ་གཨ། རེ་དགའ་མིག་ཅན། ཅུམས་

འགྱུར། བཅད་ལྷུག་སྟེ་མ། དབྱངས་བདན། དབང་གཟུ་ མཚན་བརྗོད་ཤུ་དུན་སྐྲ་ར། མགོ་སྐྱེས་ བརྒྱ་བྱིན། In a way, the *kāvyic* style itself is also a form of translation. After all, *kāvya* is a mode of formal poetic expression imported from classical India and Tibetanized with great éclat and creativity by Tibetan scholars for many a century. Despite these aspects being hard to translate, my rendition brings out the bulk of the imagery, albeit in a stilted, awkward metrical vehicle lacking the contrived majesty of the original.

CULTURAL SENSIBILITY

Let me present another contrasting Tibetan poetic composition that also explodes with an excess of conceits. In འདབ་ཆགས་མི་ཆོས་སུ་བཤད་པ་རིག་པའི་གཏེར་མཛོད།, *The Treasury of Intellect: Narrating the Worldly Tale of the Winged Ones,* a beautiful narrative belonging to the genre of Tibetan bird stories, the villain, Mr. Sparrow, comes across the nest of the Swallow family. He sees Mrs. Swallow asleep within it. To him Mrs. Swallow appears something like this:

དེ་ཡང་མིའི་བུ་མོ་མི་འདུག་སྟེའི་སྲས་མོ་འདུག་པ། གྲང་ལྷགས་ལ་ལ་བསྐྱེན་ན་འཁད་ལ་ཁད། དྲོ་ཉི་མ་ལ་བསྐྱེན་ན་ཞུ་ལ་ཁད། དེ་ གྲིབ་མཚམས་ཀྱི་སོ་ལེ་མ། ཡ་ཐོད་ལ་ཏ་བཀྲ་རེ་བ། མ་ཐོད་ལ་འབྲི་བཀྲ་རེ་བ། སོ་ཆོ་ལ་ལུག་བཀྲ་རེ་བ། སྨིན་མ་ལ་ར་བཀྲ་རེ་བ། མཛུར་ཆོས་གཡས་ལ་གསེར་སྦྲང་དང༌། གཡོན་ལ་གཡུ་སྦྲང་འཕོར་བ། ཞན་སྐོང་ཡན་ཆད་ལ་ཏ་བོང་འདྲེན་པ་སུམ་བརྒྱ་སུམ་ ཅུ་ཐམ་པ་ཚམ་རེ་བ། ལྷ་ཁང་ཁྲ་མོ་དང་འདྲ་སྟེ་གང་ན་འདུག་ཀྱང་མཆོད་སྟིང་འདོད་པ། མཆོད་རྟེན་དཀར་ཆུང་དང་འདྲ་སྟེ་ གང་ན་འདུག་ཀྱང་སྐོར་སྟིང་འདོད་པ། དངུལ་དཀར་མེ་ལོང་དང་འདྲ་སྟེ། གང་ན་འདུག་ཀྱང་བལྟ་སྟིང་འདོད་པ། འདི་རིག་ཏ་ བོ་དང་འདྲ་སྟེ། གང་ན་འདུག་ཀྱང་ཆེན་སྟིང་འདོད་པ་ཞིག་འདུག

She appears not like the daughter of a human but like the daughter of a god. When in cold wind she is about to freeze, when in warm sunshine she is about to melt, and in-between the shade and sun she sparkles. Her upper brow is worth a hundred horses. Her lower brow is worth a hundred *dris*.[27] Her white teeth are worth a hundred sheep. Her eyebrows are worth a hundred goats. Over her right cheek circles a golden bee. Over her left cheek circles a turquoise bee. Her neck is worth three hundred and thirty horses and donkeys mixed. She is like the shimmering temple: wherever she is one wants to pay homage to her. She is like the little white stūpa: wherever she is one wants to circumambulate her. She is like the white silver mirror: wherever she is one wants to look at her. She is like a fine steed: wherever she is one wants to mount her.[28]

I hope my translation manages to reflect the fast pace, the lively tone, and the stream of imagery that conveys a sense of delicate beauty and irresistible attraction. I may have even caught something of the "tempo of its style"—which Friedrich Nietzsche believes is the most difficult quality to translate.[29] However, it does not transfuse the alliterative Tibetan sound patterns or the propelling rhythm and heighten the subtle cultural references that underpin the images. In this passage, set expressions and images are piled up not just to hammer home a single message or to enhance overall rhythm and rhetoric function but to bring into relief a Tibetan notion of beauty by exposing wider cultural perspectives and values. For instance, the evaluation of Mrs. Swallow's beauty in terms of different types of livestock communicates her stunning looks as well as the esteemed value of domestic animals in that specific community.

The finding of her irresistible charm in "the shimmering temple," "the little white stūpa," "the silver mirror," and "the fine steed" is revealing about the prominent role of these entities in Tibetan society. These similes unveil Mrs. Swallow's charm and also make us explore the holy, beautiful, and priceless things she is compared to. Through these things we discover a wider cultural world that feeds both aesthetic and moral attitudes. I tried to be as faithful to the original as possible and did not add interpretative words or adjectives such as *sacred, precious,* and *brilliant* to magnify the cultural significance of the images to the target language readers. This literalism still imparts the relentless flow of poetic images but does not enhance a reader's cultural sensibility for a more complex appreciation of the Tibetan original.

Cultural Untranslatability

Serious linguistic obstacles the translator encounters are interconnected with and compounded by aspects of what J. C. Catford identifies as "cultural untranslatability."[30] When faced with such challenges I try to strike a balance between extreme literalism and absolute liberty in an effort to capture the cultural nuances. If I believe a word or a concept is quite untranslatable then I—to coin a new verb—"Tibetan" the English by prioritizing the Tibetan cultural references or keeping the Tibetan term untranslated. Let me cite a free-verse poem called "A Realm," by one of the most celebrated contemporary Tibetan poets, Kyabchen Dedrol (b. 1977).

ཞིང་ཁམས་ཤིག
བདུད་རྩིར་ལྷུང་བ།

སྤང་གི་གཞུང་གཤོང་ནས་གློག་འཁྱུག
དྭ་བའི་རྗེག་རྗེས་ལ་ཆུ་འཁྱིལ
སྨུག་པའི་ནང་ལ་འཇའ་ཤར
མིང་མེད་པའི་ཁ་དོག་གཅིག་རེ་མང་ལ་སོང
འབྲོག་མོ་མཛེས་མའི་ལན་བུའི་ནང་ལ་ཟིལ་པ་ཆགས

ཐག་རིང་གི་གངས་རིའི་རྩེ་ན
ཞི་བའི་སྤྱན་དང་སྐར་ཚོགས་ཁྲ་ལམ་ལམ

འུར་རྡོག་ཅིག་གིས་མུན་པ་མར་ཐབ་སྟེ
མཚམས་སྤྲིན་བསུབ་པར་རྩོམ་དུས
བསང་དུད་ཀྱི་སྐོང་ན་དཔའ་བོ་གོ་ཁྲབ་ཤིག་ཞེ
གསོས་ཟེའུ་ཡི་ནང་དུ་འོ་མའི་དུང་མདའ་ཕག་ཕག

སྐབས་དེར་བདུད་རྗེའི་སྐུ་སྙད་ཀྱིས
སྨྲ་ནང་དགར་གསལ་ལེར་བཅད
ཕུལ་གྱུར་བ་དྲན་པའི་གདུང་བ་རེ་ཟིར་སོང
སྒོག་གིས་ཁྲ་བའི་སྐྱིད་སྡུང་ཡང་རེ་ཟིར་སོང

A Realm
Dedicated to Dubhé

Lightening streaked out of the dimpled meadow
Water swirled in the hoof prints of the deer
A rainbow came out in the mist
And gained one more nameless color
Dewdrops formed on the plaits of beautiful nomad women

On the summit of the distant snow mountain
The hallowed eyes of peace and stars—twinkling

When a crack of the sling brought down the dark
And began erasing the crimson twilight clouds
Amidst the *sang* smoke were warriors in their armor—bristling
Inside the cedar pail were conch-white arrows of milk—pulsing

At that moment Dubhé's voice
Brightened the inside of the yak-hair tent with brilliant light
The longing for the exiles became heavier
The seeming joy borne by the life force too became heavier[31]

This is a tribute poem to the famous Tibetan *dunglen* singer Dubhé, who is affectionately known to Tibetans as གངས་ལྗོངས་ལུ་བྱུག་སྔོན་མོ, "The Blue Cuckoo of the Snowland."[32] In a sense, he became the contemporary Tibetan cuckoo, thereby perpetuating the Tibetan archetypal significance of the cuckoo. This is the cuckoo that sung the Bön and Buddhist teachings and the very same cuckoo that narrated Tibetan history for the Great Fifth Dalai Lama. Kyabchen Dedrol's poem contextualizes Dubhé's birth by embedding it within Tibetan imperial history and martial spirit, nomadic culture, and dark contemporary times. It puts Dubhé's birth within long, complex historical and cultural contexts. The poem locates Dubhé's arrival in a Tibetan nomadic tent at a critical juncture in Tibetan history, a point in time bracketed by the Tibetan empire born of military might ("warriors in their armor") and dark contemporary times. The sublime wonders of nature gracing Tibetan pastoral life welcome Dubhé into the world. The grassland greets him, as do the snow mountain, the yak-hair tent, the Tibetan wilds and climate, nomad women and warriors. But a descending darkness also threatens to erase the Tibetan civilization.

I have left one word partially untranslated and another translated in a strictly literal sense in order to reflect the poem's historical and cultural context. Firstly, the word བསང་དུད could be rendered loosely as "sacred smoke," "purifying fire smoke," or something along those lines, but such a translation would not convey the history, ritual, and cultural significance enmeshed within the term. I left བསང as an alien object so as to whet the reader's cultural appetite for the original text, believing that it would serve as a portal to the Tibetan cultural world. Secondly, ཤོ་མའི་དུང་མདའ could be rendered more smoothly and aptly as "conch-white *darts* of milk." However, this does not get across the bold martial imagery hearkening back to the Tibetan imperial military might. "The conch-white *arrows* of milk" is more literal, but it hasn't got that smooth, flawless effect in English. On the other hand, the image of arrows does bring forth the Tibetan military spirit that imbues the preceding line and that is attributed to the hero of the poem, Dubhe, who sings to and of the contemporary Tibet with such valor and passion.

Cultural Invisibility

In his seminal work *The Translator's Invisibility*, Lawrence Venuti recommends foreignization as a strategy for countering "the illusion of transparency" that makes the translator and the conditions under which he or she operates disappear.[33] My concern is with the linguistic and cultural invisibility of the Tibetan original texts in highly fluent, transparent translations, translations that appear as if they were written in the target language, leaving not even the faintest traces of the original. I believe that occasional foreignization—in my case Tibetanization—would help the English reader be conscious of the source language and appreciate its cultural matrix. Let me briefly demonstrate my point through two excerpts from an extraordinary poem on the theme of March 10, Tibetan National Uprising Day, called "The Anniversary and the Melody," by another acclaimed contemporary Tibetan poet, Sangdhor (b. 1982):

ཡོང་མི་ཚང་མ་འགྲོ་མི་རེད་དོ་ལོ། །
འཇིག་རྟེན་འདི་ན་སྐྱ་གཤོང་མང་དོ་ལོ། །
ཁ་ཆེའི་ཕ་ལུའི་དབྱངས་དེ་རྒྱང་ལ་འཐེན། །
གནམ་མཐའི་མཚམས་ནས་ནི་ཅི་ཞིག་ཕྱག་ཚར་འཁོར། །

འདི་ནས་ཉི་མ་ནུབ་ཀྱི་ཕྱོགས་རོལ་ཏེར། །
སྔར་གྱི་ཆོས་ཚན་གཅིག་ན་དེ་སྐད་བྲིས། །
བྱ་རྒོད་སྐྲག་སྐྱེབ་འཁོར་བ་རེ་ཆད་རེད། །
རྒྱ་ཐག་ལྷ་ཐེར་འཐེན་པ་ཐབས་ཉེས་རེད། །

"All the people who come are people who must go;
This perishable world has many a high and a low."
Sing the tune of *Khaché Phalu* far into the distance,
From the horizon something bounces back as an echo.

———

"From here over towards the region where the sun sets,"
Thus, is it written in a passage of an early dharmic text.
Despair is the circling of vultures with wings flapping,
Defeat is the spreading of *muthak* with tassels flipping.[34]

Sangdhor's poem on Tibetan National Uprising Day is composed of thirty stanzas, and these two are selected from different parts of it.[35] They therefore do not reflect the overall fluidity and coherence of the poem. As one can tell in these excerpts, two Tibetan terms are left untranslated. Through these and other similar instances I want to reveal the complex cultural setting of the poem and its highly intertextual nature. These foreign terms maintain a Tibetan presence in the English translation as well as drawing our attention to Terry Eagleton's belief that translation entails going beyond the text as a given datum. Eagleton states:

> Every text is a set of determinate transformations of other, preceding and surrounding texts of which it may not even be consciously aware; it is within, against and across these other texts that the poem emerges into being. And these other texts are, in their turn, "tissues" of such pre-existent textual elements, which can never be unravelled back to some primordial moment of "origin."[36]

The untranslatable and untranslated words in my translation serve as doorways to the tangled web of literary texts and sociocultural "tissues" that make up the poem. For instance, in the first excerpt Sangdhor draws on Tibetan literary and oral traditions by borrowing the memorable meter, cadence, and wisdom of the *Khaché Phalu*, a famous eighteenth-century lyrical and popular aphoristic work.[37] Thus "the tune of *Khache Phalu*" is employed to discover, fathom, and augment the surge of a deep melody the poet detects in contemporary Tibet.

In the second cited stanza the Tibetan word རྨུ་ཐག (*muthak*) introduces an intriguing foreign presence. I suppose one could translate it loosely as "sky rope" or "soul rope," but this would lose or dilute the symbolic richness of *muthak*, and it would also fail to inject that "spirit of the foreign works" recommended by Rudolf Pannwitz.[38] *Muthak* is a long cord of loosely spun predominantly white wool with tassels running along the entire length of it. *Muthak* has great mythic and symbolic significance, and it is believed that it bridges death and the afterlife as well as the earth and the sky. Indeed, old Tibetan historical texts often state that some of the earliest Tibetan kings used *muthak* to travel to the heavens after their death, thus leaving no corporeal remains. To this day such mysterious ropes are stretched out on the ground when performing sky burials for the dead. Here Sangdhor is referencing this funereal function to highlight the despair, death, and defeat that characterize today's Tibet, but the mythic cord stretches back and beyond the immediate text into preexisting textual and cultural elements.

Retaining such multivalent words and images in the English transla-
tion moves the reader closer to the language of the poet as well as miti-
gating that "obliterating violence" that translation sometimes inflicts. In
his illuminating play *Translations*, Brian Friel shows how the nineteenth-
century English translation of Irish place names—their Anglicization—
erases Irish history, cultural memory, and identity. The foreignization
strategy—even the transliteration of a single word or a name—is some-
times effective for highlighting the continued life of the original language
and the past historical and cultural forces and meanings that have shaped
it and remain submerged within it. Leaving culturally loaded terms un-
translated or bracketing original words or phrases within the translated
text might be necessary for the survival of the Tibetan original in a dif-
ferent tongue. A failure to convey the historical and cultural complexities
of a poem might mean that the act of translation has not borne fruit and
the poetic consciousness is still lost in *bardo*.

CONCLUSION

Despite my best endeavors to relay as much as possible, something of
the originals remains uncaptured in my translations. This might be an
indication of my own incompetence, but it is also a reflection of that
time-immemorial human struggle for expression. Gedun Choepel writes:

ཇི་ལྟར་དངོས་པོའི་གཞིས་ལ་ཉེ་གྱུར་བ། །
དེ་ལྟར་མཁས་པའི་ཚིག་ནི་སྨྱུགས་འགྱུར་བས། །
རང་བཞིན་ཞིང་གྱིས་ཕྲ་བའི་ཆོས་རྣམས་ཀུན། །
སྨྲ་བསམ་བརྗོད་པའི་ཡུལ་ལས་འདས་པར་བཤད། །

The closer one gets to the nature of things
The more mute the words of the learned get.
Thus, it's said that all phenomena subtle by nature
Are beyond the reach of expression, thought and speech.[39]

Here Gedun Choepel is specifically talking about the ineffability of the
ultimate nature of reality དངོས་པོའི་གཞིས or ཆོས་ཉིད (Skt: *dharmatā*). He is ad-
dressing that age-old human conundrum of how we can truly communi-
cate in words things that are beyond speech and thought. If we apply this
profound statement to the task at hand, the act of translation faces this
challenge in at least two ways.

Firstly, the translator needs to work out what the writer is really saying or what ineffable thing they are trying to describe in words. The translator endeavors to draw ever closer to the reality of what is being expressed. Secondly, the translator must make a tremendous effort to faithfully reproduce the foreign language of the writer. However, the words of the translator decrease in number—and decline in felicity— the closer one gets to the original language. Because of this twofold challenge something might always be lost in translation or left in *bardo* between the two languages. Still, like José Ortega y Gasset's "good utopian," we must continue to translate for the sake of enabling communication across linguistic and cultural boundaries.[40] Until the day humanity gains enlightenment—which we are told is beyond language and contemplation (ཐ་སྙད་དང་རྟོག་ལས་འདས་པ)—or discovers Walter Benjamin's "pure language," we translators must toil on in our task, blending cultures, languages, and minds by effecting rebirths of both poetry and prose.

Notes

1. The *bardo* (Tib: *bar do*) is an intermediate state, the term often referring to the transition between death and rebirth.
2. Benjamin, "Task of the Translator," 82.
3. གཙང་མཁའ་འབྱམས་དང་བཀྲ་ཤིས་རྒྱལ་མཆོག [The immaculate divine material: A matrimonial speech], 3–4.
4. Schopenhauer, "On Language and Words," 33.
5. Shelley, "Defense of Poetry," 107–8.
6. Coleridge, *Coleridge's Table Talk and Omniana*, 73.
7. *Kāvya* refers to the classical style of Tibetan poetry, based on a Sanskrit literary model that became prevalent after the thirteenth-century translation of the *Kāvyādarśa* by Daṇḍin.
8. John Dryden, quoted in Stokes, introduction, xxv.
9. Ishikawa, *Critical Edition of the sGra sbyor bam po gnyis pa.*
10. Shelley, "Defense of Poetry," 107.
11. ཞང་སྟོན་བསྟན་པ་རྒྱ་མཚོ [Jeweled rosary of advice], 286–87.
12. Lama Jabb, *Oral and Literary Continuities*, 62.
13. See Hughes, "Myths, Meters and Rhythms," 320.
14. Poe, "Poetic Principle," 222.
15. Lefevere, *Translating Poetry.*
16. Dryden, "On Translation," 20.
17. Jackson, "'Poetry' in Tibet," 371.
18. Aris, "'Boneless Tongue,'" 150.

19. དགེ་འདུན་ཆོས་འཕེལ། [Spread-out gold tales], 277–92.
20. Hughes, "Myths, Meters and Rhythms," 320–26.
21. Hughes, "Myths, Meters and Rhythms," 320.
22. མདན་ཚན་པ། [Singing about nouns].
23. Pound, "Vortex. Pound," 154.
24. རྒྱལ་དབང་ལྔ་པ་དག་དབང་རྒྱ་མཚོ། [Tibetan annals of the Spring Queen Songs], 195.
25. Mill, "Thoughts on Poetry," 361.
26. Benjamin, "Task of the Translator," 81.
27. Female yaks (Tib: འབྲི།).
28. རྣ་འབྲི་ཚེ་རིང་གིས་ལེགས་སྦྱར་སྒྲ་བཞིན། [The treasury of intellect: Narrating the worldly tale of the winged ones], 61.
29. Nietzsche, "On the Problem of Translation," 69.
30. Catford, Linguistic Theory of Translation.
31. ཞིང་ཁམས་ཞིག [A realm].
32. Dunglen, literally "to strum and sing" (Tib: རྡུང་ལེན།), is a contemporary popular musical form from the Tibetan region of Amdo consisting of vocals accompanied by the mandolin. On the life and songs of Dubhé (also featuring the cited poem by Kyabchen Dedrol), see Lama Jabb, "Wandering Voice of Tibet," 387–409.
33. Venuti, Translator's Invisibility.
34. མེ་ཏོག [The anniversary and the melody], 97, 99.
35. For an English translation of this poem in its entirety and an analysis of it, see Lama Jabb, "Mingled Melody."
36. Terry Eagleton as quoted in Bassnett, Translation Studies, 108–9.
37. For the Khaché Phalu, see ཁ་ཆེ་ཕ་ལུ། [Khaché Phalu].
38. Rudolf Pannwitz as quoted in Benjamin, "Task of the Translator," 81.
39. དགེ་འདུན་ཆོས་འཕེལ། [Selected works of the great scholar Gedun Choepel], 420.
40. Ortega y Gasset, "Misery and the Splendor of Translation," 98–99.

Tibetan Sources

གཉའ་མཁའ་འབུམ་དང་བཀྲ་ཤིས་རྒྱལ་མཚན་གྱིས་རྩོམ་བསྒྲིགས་བྱས། བག་སྟོན་བཤད་པ་ཏེ་མེད་ལྟ་བུ། [The immaculate divine material: A matrimonial speech]. In ཁྱིན་བཤད་ཚོ་པ་ཀུན་དགའའི་ལམ། [All pleasing wedding speeches], 1–10. Ziling: Qinghai Nationalities, 1996.

སྐུབས་ཆེན་བདེ་གྲོལ། ཞིང་ཁམས་ཞིག [A realm]. Posted 28 February 2016. མཆོད་མེ་བོད་ཀྱི་རྩོམ་རིག་དྲ་བ། [Butter lamp: Tibetan literature website]. https://www.tibetcm.com/news/2016-02-28/8003.html.

དགེ་འདུན་ཆོས་འཕེལ། ཁྲུལ་ཁམས་རིག་པས་བསྐོར་བའི་གཏམ་རྒྱུ་གསེར་གྱི་ཞང་ས། སྤྲོ་ཁ། [Spread-out gold tales of exploring the world by intellect]. In ཌགེ་འདུན་ཆོས་འཕེལ་གྱི་གསུང་རྩོམ་དེབ་དང་པོ། [The collected works of Gedun Choepel]. Lhasa: Tibet's Tibetan Ancient Books, 1994.

དགེ་འདུན་ཆོས་འཕེལ། ⁄སྨྲས་དབང་དགེ་འདུན་ཆོས་འཕེལ་གྱི་གསུང་རྩོམ་ཕྱོགས་སྒྲིག ⁄ [Selected works of the great scholar Gedun Choepel]. Chengdu: Sichuan Nationalities, 1988.

རྒྱལ་དབང་ལྔ་པ་བློ་དབང་རྒྱ་མཚོ། ⁄ཕོད་ཀྱི་དེབ་ཐེར་དཔྱིད་ཀྱི་རྒྱལ་མོའི་གླུ་དབྱངས། ⁄ [Tibetan annals of the Spring Queen Songs]. Beijing: Nationalities,1988.

ཏུ་མགྲིན་རྟ་རིང་གིས་ལེགས་སྦྱར་བགྲིགས། ⁄འདབ་ཆགས་མི་ཆོས་སུ་བཀོད་པ་རིག་པའི་གཏེར་མཛོད། ⁄ [The treasury of intellect: Narrating the worldly tale of the winged ones]. Lanzhou: Gansu Nationalities, 1993.

མདའ་ཚན་པ། མིང་དང་མིང་གི་ཁྱད་ཆོས་སྒྱུ་རུ་ལེན། [Singing about nouns and their descriptive qualities]. ཨབས་མཆན་པ། ⁄ ཁ་བརྡ་རྩོམ་སྒྲིག ⁄ [Conversation Website]. 2010. https://www.khabdha.org/?p=10595.

མིག་དམར་ཀྱིས་རྩོམ་བསྒྲིགས་བྱས། ⁄ཁ་ཆེ་ཕ་ལུ། ⁄ [Khaché Phalu]. Lhasa: Tibetan People's, 1992.

ཞང་སྟོན་བསྟན་པ་རྒྱ་མཚོ། བསླབ་བྱ་ནོར་བུའི་ཕྲེང་བ། [Jeweled rosary of advice]. In ཞང་སྟོན་བསྟན་པ་རྒྱ་མཚོའི་གསུང་འབུམ་བཞུགས་སོ། ⁄ ཕོད་བཞི་པ། ⁄ [The collected works of Shangton Tenpa Gyatso], 279–87. Lanzhou: Gansu Nationalities, 2004.

མེ་ཏོག ⁄ དུས་དྲན་དང་རོལ་དབྱངས། ⁄ [The anniversary and the melody]. In ⁄ རྩོམ་རྩོལ་ཐག་དུལ་ལ་མོ། ⁄ ལས། ⁄ [Wild writings dragging a lasso], 96–106. Ziling: Sangdhor Website Editorial Board, 2011.

ADDITIONAL SOURCES

Aris, Michael. "'The Boneless Tongue': Alternative Voices from Bhutan." *Past and Present* 115.1 (1987): 131–64.

Bassnett, Susan. *Translation Studies*. 3rd ed. London: Routledge, 1994.

Benjamin, Walter. "The Task of the Translator." In *Illuminations*, 70–82. London: Pimlico, 1999.

Catford, J. C. *A Linguistic Theory of Translation*. London: Oxford University Press, 1965.

Coleridge, Samuel Taylor. *Coleridge's Table Talk and Omniana*. London: Humphrey Milford, Oxford University Press, 1917.

Dryden, John. "On Translation." In Schulte and Biguenet, *Theories of Translation*, 17–31.

Friel, Brian. *Translations*. London: Faber & Faber, 1981.

Hughes, Ted. "Myths, Meters and Rhythms." In *Winter Pollen: Occasional Prose*, 310–72. London: Faber & Faber, 1995.

Ishikawa, Mie, ed. *A Critical Edition of the sGra sbyor bam po gnyis pa: An Old and Basic Commentary on the Mahāvyutpatti*. Studia Tibetica, no. 18. Tokyo: Toyo Bunko, 1990.

Jackson, Roger R. "'Poetry' in Tibet: *Glu, mGur, sNyan ngag* and 'Songs of Experience.'" In *Tibetan Literature: Studies in Genre*, edited by Jose Ignacio Cabezon and Roger R. Jackson, 368–92. Ithaca, NY: Snow Lion, 1996.

Lama Jabb. "The Mingled Melody: Remembering the Tibetan March 10th Uprising." *Revue d'Etudes Tibétaines* 48 (April 2019): 50–98.

———. *Oral and Literary Continuities in Modern Tibetan Literature: The Inescapable Nation.* Lanham, MD: Lexington Books, 2015.

———. "The Wandering Voice of Tibet: Life and Songs of Dhube." *Life Writing* 17.3 (2020): 387–409.

Lefevere, André. *Translating Poetry: Seven Strategies and a Blueprint.* Amsterdam: Mouton, 1975.

Mill, John Stuart. "Thoughts on Poetry and its Varieties." In *English Critical Essays,* edited by Edmund D. Jones, 341–67. London: Oxford University Press, 1968.

Nietzsche, Friedrich. "On the Problem of Translation." In Schulte and Biguenet, *Theories of Translation,* 69–70.

Ortega y Gasset, José. "The Misery and the Splendor of Translation." In Schulte and Biguenet, *Theories of Translation,* 93–112.

Poe, Edgar Allan. "The Poetic Principle." In *The Complete Poetical Works of Edgar Allan Poe with Three Essays on Poetry,* edited by R. Brimley Johnson, 213–39. London: Henry Frowde, Oxford University Press, 1909.

Pound, Ezra. "Vortex. Pound." *Blast,* edited by Wyndham Lewis, 1 (20 June 1914): 153–54.

Schopenhauer, Arthur. "On Language and Words." In Schulte and Biguenet, *Theories of Translation,* 32–35.

Schulte, Rainer, and John Biguenet, eds. *Theories of Translation: An Anthology of Essays from Dryden to Derrida.* Chicago: University of Chicago Press, 1992.

Shelley, Percy Bysshe. "A Defense of Poetry." In *English Critical Essays,* edited by Edmund D. Jones, xxv–xxx. London: Oxford University Press, 1968.

Stokes, Richard. Introduction to *The Penguin Book of English Song: Seven Centuries of Poetry from Chaucer to Auden.* London: Penguin Classics, 2016.

Venuti, Lawrence. *The Translator's Invisibility: A History of Translation.* London: Routledge, 1995.

Devotional Poetry and Songs from Tibet

1

An Ocean of Melodies

INTRODUCED AND TRANSLATED BY
GEDUN RABSAL AND NICOLE WILLOCK

WHILE JÉ TSONGKHAPA LOZANG DRAKPA (1357–1419) is widely celebrated today for his contributions to Buddhist philosophy, "An Ocean of Melodies" highlights another side of his erudition, that of language and poetry. Jé Tsongkhapa claimed himself to be "the lone *kāvya*-savant in the Land of Snows."[1] The two praise poems presented here show how he makes this claim by calling forth Yangchenma (Skt: Sarasvatī), the goddess of music, poetry, and language, in a performative mode of writing that garners the power of speech for himself to invoke Yangchenma. These poems exemplify fourteenth-century Tibetan *kāvya* or *belles-lettres*.[2] These eulogies serve to remind readers not only of Jé Tsongkhapa's polymathic erudition but also of the crucial role translation played in Tsongkhapa's transmission of different fields of Buddhist knowledge, including philosophy, ritual, and poetics.

By the time that Tsongkhapa wrote these two praise poems, translations of Sanskrit treatises on language, especially on poetics, had made their way into Tibetan discourse alongside Buddhist philosophy as subjects in a system of knowledge commonly referred to as Indo-Tibetan classical learning.[3] Sakya Paṇḍita (1182–1251) is generally credited with introducing this system to Tibet; however, it took another generation for a seminal manual of poetic theory, Daṇḍin's *Kāvyādarśa* (Looking glass of poetics), to be translated into Tibetan. This was completed by Shongtön Dorjé Gyaltsen (1234?–1282?) around 1270 under the patronage of Sakya Paṇḍita's nephew Drogön Chögyel Phakpa (1235–1280). Shongtön Dorjé Gyaltsen's younger brother Shong Lodrö Tenpa[4] gave instructions on the *Kāvyādarśa* to Lochokpa (13th century),[5] who then transmitted these teachings to Pang Lotsawa Lodrö Tenpa (1276–1342).[6] Panglo taught the *Kāvyādarśa* and composed its first major Tibetan-language commentary.

Interestingly, this lineage includes not only Jé Tsongkhapa, posthumously recognized as the founder of the Geluk tradition, but also Longchen Rabjam Drimé Özer (1308–1364), the great master of the Nyingma tradition. Longchenpa studied with Panglo directly and also composed his own short commentary on *kāvya*. Panglo's nephew Lochen Jangchub Tsemo (1315–1379) translated Kālidāsa's *Meghadūta* into Tibetan around 1353 and like his uncle was active in transmitting teachings on *kāvya* in Tibet.[7] One of his students, Namkha Sangpo (1333–1379),[8] is credited with teaching the *Kāvyādarśa* to Tsongkhapa.[9] The Fifth Dalai Lama's *Record of Received Teachings* (*Gsan yig*) mentions a Yangchenma lineage whereby Tsongkhapa received some teachings from Jé Tsultrim Pelzang, about whom no other information is currently available.[10]

Biographies of Tsongkhapa provide clues as to when he may have composed the two eulogies to Yangchenma translated below. The biographer and direct disciple of Tsongkhapa, Tokden Jampel Gyatso (1356–1428), writes:

> In such places as Olkha, Jé Tsongkhapa studied Sanskrit language books, e.g., *Kalāpasūtra*, *Candravyākaraṇasūtra*, etc., and although he was an expert in these texts, he didn't acknowledge himself as such. Again, he received teachings [from Namkha Sangpo] on poetic treatises, such as *Kāvyādarśa*, and then practiced *kāvya* and became a profound expert. At that time, he composed a "Verse in Praise of Yangchenma," and henceforth this poem became famous for its aesthetic value. In the following year, Chennga Drakpa Jangchub (1356–1386) passed away. Requested by local leaders to write Chennga's biography, Tsongkhapa wrote a biographical *avadāna* (*rtogs brjod*). Since then, it has been well known that no other poems surpass this.[11]

Although little is presently known about the teacher-student relationship between Namkha Sangpo and Tsongkhapa, the larger context of Tsongkhapa's biography suggests that he wrote "Verse in Praise of Yangchenma" (the first poem presented here) shortly after he began studying *kāvya*, that is, prior to 1386, when Chennga passed away. Another biography of Tsongkhapa suggests that he composed this piece when he was twenty-four years old, in 1380, in Bodong É monastery in Tsang, and then continued to study *kāvya* poetics with Lotsawa Namkha Sangpo in Central Tibet.[12] "Verse in Praise of Yangchenma" is generally understood to be one of his earliest compositions. Its charm earned Jé Tsongkhapa the reputation of being Tibet's greatest *kāvya* poet within his lifetime, and it remains popular to this day.[13]

Tokdenpa's biography also indicates when Tsongkhapa wrote "Homage to Yangchenma," the second poem presented here. Tokdenpa elaborates on Tsongkhapa's visualization practice of Yangchenma, stating:

> Later on, due to his accomplishment of Yangchenma practice, she came to him in a vision at Sangphu in Central Tibet. From that point on, Yangchenma looked after him, and his works on teaching, debating, and composition flourished. His composition of religious songs and other melodious verses of deities in Highest Yoga Tantra are superior to all others.[14]

Given that "Homage to Yangchenma" is a detailed visualization of Yangchenma, and considering its length and its deployment of numerous literary devices, we deduce that this eulogy was written later, most likely after his visionary accomplishment at Sangphu. The colophon states that it was written during a break from a dharma session while in Jayul, which is in the Lokha region. Tsongkhapa wrote four titles on Yangchenma: the two eulogies presented here and two *sādhanas,* all of which are found in his *Collected Works.*[15]

Tsongkhapa wrote these two poems within a century after the Tibetan translation of the *Kāvyādarśa.* The poems mark a point in time when Tibetan lamas began to build on the first stanza of the *Kāvyādarśa,* a verse of praise to Yangchenma, to write their own eulogies of her,[16] and they indicate that Tsongkhapa was at the forefront of this tradition. Other writings point to how he simultaneously established links with the Indic tradition of *kāvya.* For example, he referred to himself as Tibet's equivalent of the fourth-century Indian savant Āryaśūra, the author of *Jātakamālā,* claiming, "I, the glorious Lozang Drakpa, the lone *kāvya*-savant in the Land of Snows, am [Tibet's] illustrious Āryaśūra, the Noble Land's greatest king of speech, who traveled from India and composed this."[17] The composition referred to here was Tsongkhapa's biographical *avadāna* of Chenngapa, which, similar to his renowned "Four Great Praises" (*bstod chen bzhi*),[18] displays his mastery of *kāvya.* The last two verses of "Homage to Yangchenma" directly draw attention to the use of *kāvya* as the art form most suitable for calling forth this goddess.

In our translation of both poems, we paid particular attention to the form of literary embellishments (Tib: *rgyan*, Skt: *alaṃkāra*) found in these praise poems, because according to *kāvya* theory, these make a poem "tasteful" (Skt: *rasa*)[19] or aesthetically pleasing. We suggest that *kāvya* theory based on Tibetan-language commentaries of the *Kāvyādarśa* can aid in translating Tibetan texts because literary embellishments have specific purposes. That said, frequently they can also operate in more than one way. While many *kāvya* masters do not identify the particular figures they use in their writings, Buddhist scholars such as Tseten Zhabdrung Jigmé Rigpai Lodro (1910–1985), hereafter Tseten Zhabdrung, frequently make an effort to identify them and use them appropriately. This is especially the case when they compose texts on "expressions of examples" (*dper brjod*), which practice literary forms in the *Kāvyādarśa*.[20] Attuned to this tradition, we as translators attempted to identify which literary embellishments stood out to us as readers of the Tibetan and then to play with poetic freedom within the form of literary devices, such as simile, metaphor, kennings, and wordplay.

For example, Tsongkhapa makes ample use of simile (Tib: *dpe rgyan*, Skt: *upamā*). Like English similes, Tibetan similes require the use of a word such as *like* or *as* to make a comparison; however, in Tibetan there are more than seventy different "terms to clarify congruence" (*mtshungs pa gsal byed kyi sgra*).[21] Simile is one of the most ubiquitous literary devices. Based on the *Kāvyādarśa*, Tseten Zhabdrung's *General Commentary on Poetics* (*Snyan ngag spyi don*) identifies more than thirty different subtypes of simile, each with a slightly different focus.[22] In this work, he notes Tsongkhapa's use of simile in the last stanza of "Verse in Praise of Yangchenma" but doesn't mention which subtype.[23] As translators, we paid attention to the use of this literary device in both poems and rendered these in English accordingly.

An established body of cultural references, including Indic stories, can make some similes difficult to understand for those unfamiliar with them. For example, when we read the line in "Homage to Yangchenma" that begins with the words "like a white goose playing in a lotus-lake," it is clear from the context that Yangchenma is likened to a white goose. This raises the question why this goddess is compared to a goose. To answer this, it's necessary to have background cultural knowledge. In Indic iconographic depictions from the seventh century onward, Yangchenma, like her spouse, Brahmā, mounts a *haṃsa*, which is similar to a white goose. Known for its beautiful voice and its discriminating ability to separate milk from water (or in some cases, ambrosia), this bird is a metaphor for Yangchenma.[24] In the context of this poem, this simile could indicate Tsongkhapa's visualization of Yangchenma with her appearance in his mind. More straightforward similes are created when Yangchenma's body, speech, and mind are likened to a mountain, a dragon's roar, and the sky, respectively.

Tsongkhapa also draws upon metaphors to express Yangchenma's allure. In "Verse in Praise of Yangchenma" the conventional metaphors he uses to describe beauty include a lotus and bees. A lotus represents an attractive round face, and bees signify eyes because of their shape. As a bee is drawn to a lotus, eyes are alluring. In "Homage to Yangchenma," Tsongkhapa uses complex extended metaphors (*gzugs can 'phar ma*) to express her majesty.[25] In a particularly difficult section of this poem, he uses this type of metaphor to compare Yangchenma and Mount Meru of Buddhist cosmology.[26] Each line of this stanza is constructed around this metaphorical relationship. He cleverly employs attributes and verbs that can be used to describe both the goddess and the mountain (wearing celestial raiment, wrapped in multiple layers, bejeweled with topknots, and possessing majesty). These in turn are likened to various aspects of writing poetry: grammar, composition, poetics, and kennings. This stanza also has to be read together with the following one because the extended metaphor is the principal subject for the main idea in this section of the poem:

> You goddess are Mount Meru,
> draped in a glowing celestial raiment: grammar and logic;
> wrapped with a band of four layers: composition;
> beautified with a bejeweled topknot: poetics;
> possessing majesty: kennings;
>
> having gloriously expanded the depths of my mind, an ocean,
> moved by waves of compositions, teachings, and debates,
> inspired by thousands of great scholars, the Nāga kings;
> please delight in this pure vast sea for a long time!

The second stanza clarifies that the goddess expands the depths of Tsongkhapa's mind, which is another indication of his successful visualization. This stanza simultaneously lauds previous Buddhist scholar-practitioners and expresses the intention of maintaining this visualization.

In Tibetan classical learning, a kenning (*mngon brjod*) is technically not considered a literary embellishment (*alaṃkāra*) but rather is one of the five minor subjects of language study. Based on Sanskrit synonymy, Tibetan kennings are derived from combining terms, frequently nouns; interestingly, this technique is also found in ancient Norse poetics. Because kennings frequently represent a semantic meaning that is not readily transparent, they are notoriously difficult to translate, as the translator often is forced to choose between a literal translation, which might maintain some poetic sense but loses sensibility in the target language, and a translation that expresses solely the semantic value. Sometimes, however, the capaciousness of English wordplay allows both poetry and meaning to align. For example, in the first stanza of "Verse in Praise of Yangchenma," we translate the Tibetan *chuzin* (*chu-'dzin*, lit. "water-holder") as "rain-holder," which refers to clouds. For the most part, kennings need to be memorized, as is indicated from kennings in the second poem, "Homage to Yangchenma." In these cases, the combinations of nouns are so obscure that we had to take a different approach to their translation. So we combined the kenning, for example, the "night-air-maker," with its semantic value, in this case "moon," to create a poetic phrase, "night-air-maker moon." This approach retains the kenning but also provides a semantic value for Anglophone readers unfamiliar with its meaning.

The final literary acrobatic act that we will highlight is that of phonetic wordplay. Both verses draw upon a technique of repetition known as *yamaka* in Sanskrit (Tib: *zung ldan*), which involves the duplication of syllables in specific positions in a line and in a stanza. In the third verse of "Verse in Praise of Yangchenma," Tsongkhapa uses *yamaka*, so that the final syllable of each of the first three lines (all of them distinct from one another) is repeated in the first syllable of the following line. In our translation, we decided to focus on this wordplay to mirror the Tibetan, so that "doe-eyed" at the end of the first line becomes "eyes" at the beginning of the second line, and so forth. In other stanzas, this type of word play involves repeating the same first word in each line of a stanza, which we similarly attempt to replicate in the translation.

Although the style is ornate, the message of both poems is simple. Tsongkhapa draws upon the literary devices available to him to evoke Yangchenma. Her alluring charm and his belletristic verse work in tandem so that his visualization of the goddess of speech and poetry empowers his compositions. While these literary figures evoke sensuality, this is also met with restraint, as indicated in verse five of "Homage," whereby the poet himself wears the garments of "pure conduct with two wings of logic and scripture."

Verse in Praise of Yangchenma
Jé Tsongkhapa Lozang Drakpa

White rain-holders catch lattices of light,
like an adornment for the sky, the Diva
among youthful *gandharva*, enchantress,
ever-loving goddess, please come forth now!

A lotus face with dancing-bee eyes,
a white halo crowns your bluish-black braids,
Yangchenma poised in a playful dance;
please grant me greater power of speech!

Playful dancing postures, doe-eyed;
eyes, hungry to glance at such a divinity.
Divine-motherly love, give me the words,
words of power, like yours, goddess!

Lovelier than the glorious harvest moon,
outshining Brahmā's mellifluous tones,
profundity as difficult to measure as the ocean's depth,
I pay homage to Yangchenma's body, speech and mind!

The Poet of the Northern Land, Lozang Drakpai Pel [a.k.a. Tsongkhapa], composed this piece to call forth Yangchenma, the Goddess of Music, in prayer and praise.

Homage to Yangchenma
Jé Tsongkhapa Lozang Drakpa

To you,
seated on the night-air-maker moon, a splendid Kailash white,
atop a lake bank like a whorl of dissolved emeralds,
poised cross-legged, and
delighting in the music of an azure lute,
I bow.

With a topknot adorned by a white flower garland,
bedecked by a moon at its peak and
tassels of blue-black hair covering your torso,
you, Brahmā's daughter, a captivator,

like the-lord-of-stars, the moon, in the sky path-of-gods, or
like a white goose playing in a lotus-lake of a
vast and pure garden of my mind,
please stay for a while and bestow upon me ultimate confidence!

Your body like moonlight on a cloudless autumn night
falling on the whitest peak of an earth-holder mountain;
your body, an ocean of milk, I gaze insatiably upon such
luminous whiteness.

Wearing the feathery garments of pure conduct,
with two wings of logic and scripture, I soar
to enjoy the sky of vast knowledge, and
my lucid, clear mind is captivated by joy!

Very majestic Mount Kailash touches the sky path-of-gods, like a
very beautiful top-knot while glancing sideways and playing a
very melodious lute; only that
verily compares to you, luminous white goddess with

soft nimble fingers strumming and
lotus-blue eyes making sideway glances to
touch the surface of the beautiful lute
and provide an acoustic feast of mellifluous melodies.

With shining golden earrings like a thousand
shiny golden rays of sun in a lotus garden and a
perfect string of pearly whites like
perfectly twinkling stars in the sky,

your visage, a pure crystal mountain,
illuminated by the colors of Indra's bow;
all parts of your body, without exception,
enchanting adornments, scintillate.

Snow-mountains covered with a blanket of
trees, the color of sapphires;
your body is as lovely as this in all respects.
An azure lute decorates your left side.

The one who strings together sixteen vowels, Sarasvatī,
your body at the center, the lotus of my heart, is like
a young flash of lightning, captivatingly radiant,
swirling in white cotton-clouds.

Say that your speech is so pure that even in its slightest segment,
say that it merely falls upon the pathway of one's ear,
say that it cuts through the ignorance of the obscured mind.
Say, that is your speech, the melody of Brahmā.

Like a divine wish-fulfilling tree for divinities,
you bestow fruits to whomever wants whatever.
With great loving-kindness for as long as saṃsāra is saṃsāra
your mind remains unobstructed for all always.

A perfect body as white as a snow mountain,
a captivating voice as majestic as a dragon's roar,
a clear mind as unshakeable as the sky,
you, the great treasure of virtues, please protect me!

You goddess are Mount Meru,
draped in a glowing celestial raiment: grammar and logic;
wrapped with a band of four layers: composition;
beautified with a bejeweled topknot: poetics;
possessing majesty: kennings;

having gloriously expanded the depths of my mind, an ocean,
moved by waves of compositions, teachings, and debates,
inspired by thousands of great scholars, the Nāga kings;
please delight in this pure vast sea for a long time!

With this eulogy by me, the one who roars with intense yearning,
may you, Drayang Lhamo, the fulfiller of all wishes,

you, the goddess of song and melodies,
never be separated from my heart in all future lives!

In this way, tasteful excellences of *rasa* and *bhāva*,
adorned with colorful, astounding *alaṃkāra*—
these words of praise, a flowing ambrosia, are
a joyous feast only for those well-acquainted with poetics!

This art form was articulated with ethical wealth
at the especially special request
of a wholeheartedly kind-hearted nephew and
composed with poetic words according to a treatise on poetry.

These stanzas praising the goddess of sound and melody, Yangchenma, were composed by the Poet of the Northern Land, Lozang Drakpai Pel [a.k.a. Tsongkhapa] during dharma retreat in Jayul.

Notes

1. Tsong kha pa blo bzang grags pa, "Byin rlabs kyi lhun po," 495.
2. Contemporary scholars recognize Tsongkhapa's compositions as marking an important milestone in the development of Tibetan *kāvya*-style compositions. See, for example, Tshe tan zhabs drung, *Snyan ngag spyi don*, 22.
3. See Dorje, introduction; and Gold, *Dharma's Gatekeepers*.
4. His exact dates are unknown, but he was active in the late thirteenth century.
5. He is also known as Chokden Legpai Lodrö (Mchog ldan legs pa'i blo gros).
6. Gedun Rabsal, *Rig pa'i khye'u* [Birth of the literary arts], 207–58.
7. Gedun Rabsal, *Rig pa'i khye'u* [Birth of the literary arts], 261–62.
8. He is also known as Drapa Namsang (Sgra pa nam bzang).
9. Rtogs ldan 'jam dpal rgya mtsho, "Rje btsun tsong kha pa'i rnam thar chen mo'i kha skong legs bshad," 1:17.
10. Furthermore, the Fifth Dalai Lama traced Yangchenma teachings to Sumpa Lotsawa in the thirteenth century. Cf. Ngag dbang blo bzang rgya mtsho, "*Zab pa dang rgya che ba'i dam pa'i chos kyi thob yig gang ga'i chu rgyun*." We note that Tsongkhapa could have received teachings on Yangchenma from Lochen Jangchub Tsemo and Dratsadpa Rinchen Namgyel (1318–1388) among others.
11. Rtogs ldan 'jam dpal rgya mtsho, "Rje btsun tsong kha pa'i rnam thar chen mo'i kha skong legs bshad," 1:17.

12. Ye shes don grub bstan pa'i rgyal mtshan, "Rje btsun bla ma tsong kha pa chen po'i rnam thar dad pa rgya mtshor rol pa'i 'jug ngogs," 70.

13. For example, the contemporary Tibetan filmmaker and musician Ngawang Choephel added music to this poem for the soundtrack to the movie *Ganden: A Joyful Land* (2020).

14. Rtogs ldan 'jam dpal rgya mtsho, "Rje btsun tsong kha pa'i rnam thar chen mo'i kha skong legs bshad," 1:17; see also Thupten Jinpa, *Tsongkhapa*, 53–55.

15. The two *sādhanas* are grouped together in Tsong kha pa blo bzang grags pa, "Lha mo dbyangs can ma'i sgrub thabs rje tsong kha pas mdzad pa dang dbyangs can ma'i sgrub thabs rje gnang ba gzhugs so."

16. Dimitrov, *Mārgavibhāga*, 154–55; see also Dan Martin's translation of *Praise of Sarasvati* in "Indian Kāvya Poetry on the Far Side of the Himālayas," 574–78.

17. Tsong kha pa blo bzang grags pa, "Byang chub sems dpa' chen po grags pa byang chub dpal bzang po'i rtogs pa brjod pa'i snyan dngags byin rlabs kyi lhun po," 2:495.

18. These are "Praise to the Buddha for his teachings on Interdependent Origination," "Praise to Maitreya," "Praise to Mañjuśrī," and "Praise to Namgyalma."

19. Martin, "Indian Kāvya Poetry on the Far Side of the Himālayas," 579n31, mentions five different Tibetan terms for *rasa*.

20. Pema Bhum and Janet Gyatso identify this genre as a pedagogical tool that is foundational to writings inspired by the *Kāvyādarśa*. See their "Mirror on Fire." We are grateful to Janet Gyatso for sharing a draft of this chapter.

21. Tshe tan zhabs drung, *Snyan ngag spyi don*, 44.

22. Tshe tan zhabs drung, *Snyan ngag spyi don*, 42–43.

23. Tshe tan zhabs drung, *Snyan ngag spyi don*, 70.

24. Ludvik, *Sarasvatī*, 133–35.

25. Cf. Tshe tan zhabs drung, *Snyan ngag spyi don*, 72.

26. In the original Tibetan, the metaphor is found in the last line of the stanza. Because of the complexity of this stanza and the requirements of English syntax, we placed the metaphor "the goddess, Mount Meru" in the first line of our translation. The Tibetan reads: *sgra tshad nyi zla'i 'od kyi gos bzang bgos / sdeb sbyor bang rim bzhi yi ska rags bcings / snyan dngags nor bu'i cog gi thod kyis mdzes / mngon brjod gzi ldan ri dbang lha mo de.*

Tibetan Source

Tsong kha pa blo bzang grags pa. "Sgra dbyangs lha mo dbyangs can ma la bstod pa" [Verse in praise of Yangchenma] and "Sgra dbyangs lha mo dbyangs can ma la phyag 'tshal lo" [Homage to Yangchenma]. In *Rje tsong kha pa chen po'i gsung 'bum* [Collected works of Jé Tsongkhapa], 2:259–62. Beijing: Krung go'i bod rig pa dpe skrun khang, 2012. BDRC: W29193.

ADDITIONAL SOURCES

Bhum, Pema, and Janet Gyatso, with contributions by Jonathan Gold, Shenghai Li, and Vesna Wallace. "Mirror on Fire: The Tibetan Reception of Daṇḍin's *Kāvyādarśa*." In *A Lasting Vision: Dandin's Mirror in the World of Asian Letters*, edited by Yigal Bronner, 308–61. Oxford: Oxford University Press, 2023.

Dimitrov, Dragomir. *Mārgavibhāga: Die Unterscheidung der Stilarten, Kritische Ausgabe des ersten Kapitels von Daṇḍins Poetik Kāvyādarśa und der tibetischen Übertragung Sñan ṅag me loṅ nebst einer deutschen Übersetzung des Sanskrittexts*. Marburg: Indica et Tibetica Verlag, 2002.

Dorje, Gyurme. Introduction to *The Treasury of Knowledge: Indo-Tibetan Classical Learning and Buddhist Phenomenology*, by Jamgön Kongtrul, translated by Gyurme Dorje, 8–30. Boston: Snow Lion, 2012.

Dung dkar blo bzang 'phrin las. "Snyan ngag la 'jug tshul tshig rgyan rig pa'i sgo 'byed" [Opening the door to an awareness of the rhetoric of poetics]. In *Mkhas dbang dung dkar blo bzang 'phrin las kyi gsung 'bum* [Collected works of the great scholar Dungkar Lozang Trinle], edited by Ngag dbang phun tshogs, vol. 1. Beijing: Mi rigs dpe krun khang, 2004.

Gedun Rabsal (Dge 'dun rab gsal). *Rig pa'i khye'u* [Birth of the literary arts]: *Papers on the Arrival of Literary Field of Knowledge in Tibet during the 13th Century and Beyond*. Dharamsala: Library of Tibetan Works and Archives, 2017.

Gedun Rabsal (Dge 'dun rab gsal) and Nicole Willock. "Dictums for Developing Virtue." In *A Gathering of Brilliant Moons: Practice Advice from the Rimé Masters of Tibet*, edited by Holly Gayley and Joshua Schapiro, 83–96. Boston: Wisdom, 2017.

Gold, Jonathan. *The Dharma's Gatekeepers: Sakya Paṇḍita on Buddhist Scholarship in Tibet*. Albany: SUNY Press, 2007.

Jackson, David P. *The Entrance Gate for the Wise (Section III): Sa-skya Paṇḍita on Indian and Tibetan Traditions of Pramāṇa and Philosophical Debate*. Vienna: Arbeitskreis für tibetische und buddhistische Studiene Universität Wien, 1987.

Kapstein, Matthew. "The Indian Literary Identity in Tibet." In *Literary Cultures in History: Reconstructions from South Asia*, edited by Sheldon Pollock, 747–802. Berkeley: University of California Press, 2003.

Kilty, Gavin. *Splendor of an Autumn Moon*. Somerville, MA: Wisdom, 2001.

Ludvik, Catherine. *Sarasvatī: Riverine Goddess of Knowledge from the Manuscript-carrying Vīṇā-player to the Weapon-wielding Defender of the Dharma*. Leiden: Brill, 2007.

Martin, Dan. "Indian Kāvya Poetry on the Far Side of the Himālayas: Translation, Transmission, Adaptation, Originality." In *Innovations and Turning Points: Toward a History of Kāvya Literature*, edited by Yigal Bronner, David Shulman, and Gary Tubb, 563–608. Oxford: Oxford University Press, 2014.

Ngag dbang blo bzang rgya mtsho. "*Zab pa dang rgya che ba'i dam pa'i chos kyi thob yig gang ga'i chu rgyun*" [The flow of the Ganges River: A record of the teachings of the profound, extensive, and sacred dharma]. In *Rgyal dbang lnga pa ngag dbang blo bzang rgya mtsho'i gsung 'bum* [The collected works of the Fifth Dalai Lama], 1:119–22. Beijing: Krung go'i bod rig pa dpe skrun khang, 2009.

Pollock, Sheldon. *A Rasa Reader: Classical Indian Aesthetics.* New York: Columbia University Press, 2016.

Rtogs ldan 'jam dpal rgya mtsho. "*Rje btsun tsong kha pa'i rnam thar chen mo'i kha skong legs bshad kun 'dus bzhugs so*" [Compendium of eloquent expressions: Supplement to the biography of Jé Tsongkhapa]. In *Rje btsun tsong kha pa chen po'i rnam thar phyogs bsgrigs* [Collected biographies of Jé Tsongkhapa], 1:11–28. Beijing: Krung go'i bod rig pa dpe skrun khang, 2015.

Thupten Jinpa. *Tsongkhapa: A Buddha in the Land of Snows.* Boulder, CO: Shambhala, 2019.

Tshe tan zhabs drung 'Jigs med rigs pa'i blo gros. *Snyan ngag spyi don* [A general commentary on poetics]. 1957; reprint, Lanzhou: Gan su'u mi rigs dpe skrun khang, 2005.

Tsong kha pa blo bzang grags pa. "*Byang chub sems dpa' chen po grags pa byang chub dpal bzang po'i rtogs pa brjod pa'i snyan dngags byin rlabs kyi lhun po*" [A mountain of blessings: Avadāna poetry of Chennga Drakpa Jangchub, 1356–1386, the Great Bodhisattva]. In *Tsong kha pa'i gsung 'bum* [Collected works of Tsongkhapa], vol. 2. Bylakuppe: Ser byes rig mdzod chen mo'i rtsom sgrig khang, 2021. Available at https://www.serajeyrigzodchenmo.org/du-rab-14/item/50-sjrb-0026.

———. "*Lha mo dbyangs can ma'i sgrub thabs rje tsong kha pas mdzad pa dang dbyangs can ma'i sgrub thabs rjes gnang ba gzhugs so*" [A *sādhana* to Yangchenma written by Tsongkhapa and *sādhana* of Yangchenma bestowed by Tsongkhapa]. In *Rje tsong kha pa chen po'i gsung 'bum* [Collected works of Jé Tsongkhapa], 11:515–19. Beijing: Krung go'i bod rig pa dpe skrun khang, 2012. BDRC: W29193.

Willock, Nicole. *Lineages of the Literary: Tibetan Buddhist Polymaths in Socialist China.* New York: Columbia University Press, 2021.

Ye shes don grub bstan pa'i rgyal mtshan. "*Rje btsun bla ma tsong kha pa chen po'i rnam thar dad pa rgya mtshor rol pa'i 'jug ngogs*" [Entryway to joy: The ocean of pure faith, the biography of Jé Tsongkhapa]. In *Rje btsun tsong kha pa chen po'i rnam thar phyogs bsgrigs* [Collected biographies of Jé Tsongkhapa], 4:1–444. Beijing: Krung go'i bod rig pa dpe skrun khang, 2015.

2

Milarepa Meets the Huntsman

INTRODUCED AND TRANSLATED BY ANDREW QUINTMAN

A MONG THE many stories associated with the acclaimed Tibetan master Milarepa (c. 1028–1111) in the compilation known as *The Hundred Thousand Songs*, the yogin's encounter with the huntsman Gönpo Dorjé is perhaps the most memorable. With notes of pathos and high drama, this tale reveals contours of the human condition marked by pride, fear, rage, jealousy, and longing for release from suffering. It also demonstrates the transformative power of the dharma to counteract even the strongest afflictive emotions. More strikingly, the episode presents Milarepa as a consummate teacher, capable of instructing, and liberating, humans and animals alike. In the process, it highlights the significant role that devotion to a qualified master plays within the Tibetan religious world.

The best-known version of this encounter, recorded in the late-fifteenth-century anthology edited by Tsangnyön Heruka (1452–1507), opens with Milarepa sequestered in a high mountain retreat, traditionally located in the region of Manang in northern Nepal.[1] His meditation is disrupted first by the appearance of a terrified deer, then by a fierce hunting dog, and finally by the dog's hot-tempered owner, the huntsman Gönpo Dorjé. Milarepa teaches each figure in turn by reciting the spiritual song-poems known as *gur* (*mgur*) for which he was famous. One by one his interlocutors are converted to the dharma. The episode concludes with Gönpo Dorjé offering Milarepa his quarry and his hunting dog, laying down his arrows and bow, confessing his sinful deeds, and renouncing his life as a hunter. He pledges to become Milarepa's disciple and, in the fashion of his new master, adopts the single robe of an ascetic practitioner for which he became known as Khyira Repa, the "cotton-clad huntsman." He was later counted as one of the yogin's eight foremost heart-disciples.

The narrative prose and song-poems that constitute Milarepa's en-
counter with the huntsman exemplify many themes for which *The Hun-
dred Thousand Songs* is best known: the pleasures of solitude, the natural
beauty of mountain retreats, renunciation of worldly affairs, the exhor-
tation to practice dharma, and the profound experience of meditative
realization. In particular, the story highlights the pacifying nature of
devotion to one's spiritual master, an attitude capable of transforming
an irascible killer into a reverent religious practitioner. Indeed, expres-
sions of devotion lie at the heart of both *The Life of Milarepa* and *The
Hundred Thousand Songs*, where Milarepa's unwavering faith in his guru,
Marpa the Translator, leads him to begin many of his verses with tradi-
tional expressions of heartfelt longing for his teacher. In this story, for
example, Milarepa sings, "I bow at the venerable guru's feet," and "Father,
king of translators, splendor of compassion, / Consider me quickly and
protect me with compassion." Such words of supplication convey both
a palpable sense of the teacher's absence and the concomitant longing
for the teacher's presence even as they model appropriate attitudes to be
emulated by Milarepa's own followers.

The Hundred Thousand Songs is divided into several distinct sections
that narrate the yogin's encounters first with nonhuman spirits and
later with women and men of all stripes. In some accounts, Milarepa
tames and then converts malevolent demons to serve as protectors of
the dharma. The Five Sisters of Long Life, goddesses associated with
the mountainous border region between Tibet and Nepal, express their
faith in Milarepa and become devoted followers. One sister serves as
Milarepa's consort and practice partner. Later in the text, Milarepa en-
counters a great diversity of human characters: arrogant monks, lay-
men, and laywomen from nearby villages, practitioners of Indian and
pre-Buddhist Bön traditions, as well as roving gangs of bandits, brig-
ands, murderers, and thieves. In most cases, the meeting concludes with
expressions of religious commitment, devotion to the yogin, and faith
in his exemplary dedication to a life of solitary meditation. The hunts-
man episode clearly follows this paradigm, but it adds an additional
twist. In scenes reminiscent of the life of St. Francis of Assisi, Milarepa
also preaches to animals—here a wild deer and hunting dog—who re-
spond as did their human and nonhuman counterparts, with displays
of faith and devotion. Once they have heard Milarepa's instructions,
both deer and dog circle the master three times in a wordless gesture of

"respect and devotion" that mirrors the traditional Buddhist practice of circumambulation.

The story culminates with the huntsman's own expression of devotion to Milarepa. The spiritual connection shared by this pair, the yogin and the huntsman, is highlighted from the outset, where Milarepa's dreams are filled with miraculous signs that lead him to wonder, "Is this a disciple with a previous connection on his way?" The huntsman echoes this idea near the cycle's conclusion when he wonders to himself, "Don't we have some karmic connection from the past?" Gönpo Dorjé, for his part, undergoes a shift in emotional tenor from jealousy and rage to an overwhelming sense of admiration for the yogin. The story makes clear that this transformation is not based on blind faith or simple hearsay. Rather, the huntsman and the yogin engage in a set of repartee songs, with the huntsman inquiring, "Who are you?," to which the yogin responds with a biographical song narrating his spiritual lineage and religious training. Next the huntsman asks, "What is your practice like?," and the yogin replies with a detailed review of his religious life concluding with the "dharma view, meditation, and conduct." These expressions are reminiscent of the traditional Buddhist practices buddhānusmṛti, "recollection of the qualities of the Buddha," and guruyoga, "meditation on the guru" or, more literally, "union with the guru," in which the teacher's deeds, qualities, and attainments are systematically noted and taken to heart. This leads the huntsman to offer all the worldly possessions that are remnants of his former life.

The translation here presents the second of two early accounts of Milarepa's encounter with the huntsman preserved as a single chapter in a version of The Black Treasury (Mdzod nag ma), the informal name given to a series of literary compilations incorporating both the Life and the Songs of Milarepa that predate Tsangnyön Heruka's better-known composition.[2] The author or editor is unknown, although the text identifies the Third Karmapa Rangjung Dorjé (1284–1339) as a principal contributor to what may have been an even earlier compilation.[3] This text, perhaps assembled between the last quarter of the fourteenth century and the middle of the fifteenth, is poetically titled A River of Blessings Relieving the Tormenting Heat of the Mental Afflictions (Byin brlabs kyi chu rgyun kyis nyon mongs pa'i tsha gdung sel bar byed pa) and records a somewhat abbreviated form of the "standard" version, which is preceded by an "alternate" account purportedly drawn from the oral tradition. A systematic literary study and critical comparison of these two accounts with the later standard version would be instructive but lies beyond the scope of the present essay. Only the alternate account appears below.

This version is of interest for a number of reasons. As told here, the encounter takes place not in Nepal but at the well-known religious site of Tsibri in Western Tibet. We also find additional songs attributed to Milarepa and the huntsman that are absent in the later work. The poetic language appears less polished and only lightly edited; many verses have lines of irregular length. Perhaps the most interesting divergence from the standard account is the appearance of Gönpo Dorjé's wife at the end of the story, where she makes a dramatic entrance with an axe in her belt and lasso in hand, mirroring the huntsman's own appearance at the opening. She derides Milarepa and threatens to kill the deer, which leads the huntsman to shout: "You want to kill this deer? I'd like to chop off your head with this axe." But after listening to an extended song on the suffering of ordinary life, she too gains faith in the yogin, through which she "realized the meaning of Mahāmudrā" and attains the state of an accomplished meditation master.

In the translation that follows I have tried to preserve the style and rhythm of the original verses even when they appear somewhat unpolished. My overall aim is to capture the vivid emotional registers within which the characters interact, while also evoking the theatrical nature of the entire story. I have paid particular attention to repetitions and parallelisms in structure frequently witnessed in the spiritual songs of Milarepa and other masters. These are seen, for example, in Milarepa's songs inspiring the deer and the dog to practice, which incorporate both parallel themes and repeated lines ("Deer, the time's come to practice sublime dharma" and "Dog, the time's come to practice sublime dharma"). We also find unusual parallel compound constructions used as names for the story's main characters:

You, creature with antlered head on a deer's body,
Deer-body antler-head listen to me here.

and

You, creature with a wolf's head on a dog's body,
Dog-body wolf-head listen to me here.

and

You, sentient being with a demon's face on a human body,
Human-body demon-face listen to me here.

Another example of formal parallelism appears in Milarepa's exhortation
to the huntsman in the song that repeats "come follow me." In this case,
each stanza begins with a triplet of items related to Milarepa's practice:
nettles, wild garlic, and hemp (practice provisions); and slate caves, snow
caves, and rock caves (meditation spots).

An Oral Account about Khyira Repa
Attributed to the Third Karmapa Rangjung Dorjé

Next, the Jetsün and his disciple practiced meditation on the mountain
called Nyishar (Snyi shar),[4] to the south of Gyalgi Tsibri (Rgyal gyi rtsib
ri). While staying there the Jetsün thought, "Although I have practiced
meditation in many places, realization such as I've gained here never oc-
curred anywhere else. I should offer a song of praise to this spot." And
then he sang this song:

I bow at the venerable guru's feet.

At the blessed site of Tsibri
five hundred arhats dwelled.
Now it's Mila's meditation spot.

At the blessed site of Tsibri
water is far but the path is near,
wood is scarce but instructions are plenty.

At the blessed site of Tsibri
provisions are scarce but absorption grows,
yidam Cakrasaṃvara dwells,
the deity bestowing supreme *siddhi*.

At the blessed site of Tsibri
brother and sister protectors dwell,
the dharma protectors who clear away obstacles.

A remote place at the wrong time is the cause of desire and hatred;
I, Mila, great meditator, am off to meditate,
off to meditate in the six fortress retreats.

In the lower part of that valley, called Nishang (Sni shang), lived a hunter named Gönpo Dorjé (Mgon po rdo rje), who was killing all the deer in the area. One evening, many miraculous signs about him appeared in the Jetsün's dreams. "Is this a disciple with a previous karmic connection on his way," he wondered, "or is it a demon's trick?" In the morning, to relax he sat atop a cliff and looked off into the ten directions.

While he sat there, a stag appeared with its mouth agape. The Jetsün thought, "This deer lives alone in the mountains. It seems that over there, he's not threatened even for a moment, while over here there's not much of a threat apart from me. His present state is due to his previous bad actions and were he to die it seems he'd be bound for the hells. Now if I were to say a few helpful words, and he had some good karma left, he might understand them. The cause of enlightenment lies in the mind streams of all such creatures, and since I am a person engaged in dharma, perhaps I should implant a teaching in this deer's mind." Then binding it with a lasso of concentration, he sang this song to the deer:

Father, king of translators, splendor of compassion,
consider me quickly and protect me with compassion.

You, creature with antlered head on a deer's body,
Deer-body antler-head listen to me here.

Flesh and blood flee but can't escape out there.
The time's come for mind itself to flee within.

Your mind has hope upon hope, fear upon fear.
Hope is the hope of freedom in flight,
fear is the fear of capture by dogs.
Hope and fear keep you wandering through life's round.

Life's round stems from instability and pain,
great happiness, from authentic dharma.
Deer, the time's come to practice sublime dharma.
The time has come to rely on yourself.

The deer understood what Milarepa said, approached his right side, and listened as he again sang this song:

You, antlered head on an animal's body,
escaping beast with antlered head listen to me here.

A man last year living he now has passed on.
Don't birth and death make you afraid?
If birth and death frighten you, here's what to do—
perk up a little bit more.

A fleeing illusory body out there won't free you.
The time's come to let your mind flee within,
yes, the time's come to let your mind flee.

A thunderclap is a mighty roar but still an empty sound.
A rainbow has a lovely design but still it fades away.
Among a hundred heads in Tibet, your own you value most.
Among your ten fingers, it's the one that's cut that hurts.

Deer, the time's come to rely on yourself.
Happiness in this life is sublime dharma.
Happiness in the next life is sublime dharma too.
Out there, the sea of life's round is vast and deep.
If you want to escape it, practice sublime dharma.

With an attitude of respect and devotion, the deer circumambulated Milarepa three times, and three times it bent its legs on the ground before him. Then it rested there as if listening to the dharma, feeling completely at ease, its mind still and clear. Just then a red she-dog with a red and white yak-hair collar appeared. Her mind was filled with hatred; she barked out through the heavens and let forth a growl so menacing that it terrified all living beings. At the mere glimpse of the Jetsün, her pride was pacified. Upon seeing the deer, however, her pride was reignited, and she repeatedly tried to seize it by the hair.

The Jetsün thought, "Alas, she has taken a dog's body now due to her practice of bad actions in the past. She's bound for the hells when she dies. Since she spent a long time in the company of humans, she should

understand more than did the deer. If I could do one thing to help her,
I should lead her to the path to enlightenment." Then he addressed this
song to the dog:

> You, creature with a wolf's head on a dog's body,
> Dog-body wolf-head listen to me here.
>
> Don't go killing the deer out there.
> The time's come to kill off your pride within.
>
> Your mind has hope upon hope, fear upon fear.
> Hope is the hope of killing the deer,
> fear is the fear of him slipping away.
> Hope and fear keep you wandering through life's round.
>
> Life's round stems from instability and pain,
> great happiness, from authentic dharma.
> Dog, the time's come to practice sublime dharma.
> The time's come to take hold of your mind.

The she-dog also understood what was said, approached his left side,
and sat there listening as he sang this song:

> You, wild beast's head on a hungry ghost's body,
> hungry ghost beast-head listen to me here.
>
> A man last year living he now has passed on.
> Don't birth and death make you afraid?
> If birth and death frighten you, here's what to do—
> perk up a little bit more.
>
> Chasing illusory bodies out there, you won't reach them.
> The time's come to catch mind itself within,
> yes, the time's come to catch mind itself within.
>
> A thunderclap is a mighty roar but still an empty sound.
> A rainbow has a lovely design but still it fades away.

Among a hundred heads in Tibet, your own you value most.
Among your ten fingers, it's the one that's cut that hurts.

You dog, the time's come to rely on yourself.
Happiness in this life is sublime dharma.
Happiness in the next life is sublime dharma too.
Consider your karma, you she-dog.

With an attitude of respect and devotion, the dog circumambulated
three times and then rested her muzzle upon outstretched paws to the
deer's left side. She remained there as if listening to the dharma with a
content mind.

After this happened, a young man, thirty years old, arrived. He wore
an antelope-skin coat draped with white cloth and tied with a wide sash,
full trousers about his legs, blue felt boots, and a white cap on his head.
Five arrows were tucked into his waist. In his right hand he clutched an
arrow, in his left a bow. He carried a multicolored lasso as a shoulder
sling and tucked a small silver-tipped dagger into his belt. He looked at
the Jetsün and said, "You yogins beg for butter and cheese in the summer
and beg for wine in the winter. You, vagabond who begs all autumn and
spring seasons long, listen here. I chased this deer from the upper end of
the valley and you put it under your spell, I chased it in the lower end
and you put it under your spell, so I couldn't kill it. You, yogin, when I
was on the upper reaches of three high mountains you had already gone
there. When I chased it through three low valleys, you had gone there
too. Now you've gotten yourself in the middle of the fight between my
dog and the deer. I've got military service, taxes, and forced labor, plus
a family of seven with this dog to feed, so I am looking for food. If you
release the deer to us unhindered, then my dog Lokchang Barma could
give up running near and far, and when I carried the load to my village
they'd be satisfied. Yogin, why have you hindered my deer and my dog?
I've drawn up an arrow from my quiver and nocked it. If I don't loose an
arrow at you today, I'll end up just like them."

He fired an arrow at the Jetsün's heart, but the tip of the arrowhead
bent like a hook. The Jetsün thought, "Alas, it doesn't appear that a sen-
tient being like him understood the purpose of a human body, even
though he's attained one. Since he took birth in the body of a hunter, he's
bound for the hells when he dies. I should do something to help him. The

dog and deer understood human words even though they are animals. He's human and so should be able to understand something."

"Hunter, listen here to my song for a while," he said and then sang this song.

> You, sentient being with a demon's face on a human body,
> Human-body demon-face listen to me here.
>
> Your hope is the hope that you'll slay the deer sitting here,
> your fear is the fear that the deer sitting here slips away.
>
> Between hope and fear, right there, you wander life's round.
> Between hope and fear, right there, go ponder it now.
>
> You, don't grasp your dog's prey,
> for the time's come to grasp mind itself within.
>
> Son, the time's come to grasp your own mind,
> the time's come to practice clear light meditation.
>
> Hunter, that's happiness in this life and bliss in the next.
> Practice sublime dharma, happiness in this life and the next.

The hunter thought, "What's this? The dog and deer are mortal enemies, but it seems they are resting together." Then he prostrated and sat down in front of the Jetsün. At that moment through the blessings of the Lama Jetsün, he cultivated love and compassion and his pride was pacified. The Jetsün then sang this song:

> You, Yama's head on a human body,
> Human-body Yama-head, you listen to me here.
>
> A man last year alive he now has passed on.
> Don't birth and death make you afraid?
> If birth and death frighten you, here's what to do—
> perk up a little bit more.

Slaying illusory bodies out there won't kill them.
The time's come to slay mind itself within,
Apa, the time's come to slay mind within.

A thunderclap is a mighty roar but still an empty sound.
A rainbow has a lovely design but still it fades away.
Among a hundred heads in Tibet, your own you value most.
Among your ten fingers, it's the one that's cut that hurts.

You, the time's come to rely on yourself.
Happiness in this life is practicing sublime dharma.
Happiness in the next is sublime dharma too.
You, think about this and practice sublime dharma.
Later keep this in mind, you fortunate one.

The hunter was filled with intense faith and made numerous prostrations and circumambulated many times. He thought, "It's said that there is a man named Milarepa, lord and king of realized beings who gained mastery in subtle-energy-mind at Drok Lapchi Gangirawa ('Brog la phyi gang kyi ra ba), showed no fear of the element water, and elicited sustenance from gods and demons of the phenomenal world. Could this be him? He certainly is of the same caliber as one of his disciples. I'll ask him who he is." Then the hunter offered this song of inquiry:

I prostrate to the venerable gurus.
I seek refuge in the protector of beings.

Lama, what lineage do you have?
Please tell me, don't keep it secret.

What ancestors do you have?
Please tell me, don't keep it secret.

What gurus do you have?
Please tell me, don't keep it secret.

What sort of person are you?
Please tell me, don't keep it secret.

What sublime dharma do you know?
Please tell me, don't keep it secret.

What meditation place do you have?
Please tell me, don't keep it secret.

What chosen deity do you practice?
Please tell me, don't keep it secret.

In response to that, the Jetsün sang this song:

If you ask me, this man, what is my lineage,
my lineage is that of the great Vajradhara.
It's not a bad dharma lineage, it's an excellent lineage.

If you ask me, this man, who are my ancestors,
my ancestors are Telo and Naro.
They're not bad ancestors, they're excellent ancestors.

If you ask me, this man, who are my gurus,
my gurus are both Marpa and Ngok.
They're not bad gurus, they're excellent gurus.

If you ask me, this man, what sort of person I am,
I am Milarepa.
I'm not a bad yogin, I'm an excellent yogin.

If you ask what are my instructions,
my instructions are the *ḍākinī* aural transmissions.
They're not bad instructions, they're excellent instructions.

If you ask what is the sublime dharma,
sublime dharma is Mahāmudrā.
It's not bad dharma, it's excellent dharma.

If you ask what is my meditation place,
my meditation place is Jagyal Tsibri.
It's not a bad place, it's an excellent place.

If you ask what is my chosen deity,
my chosen deity is Cakrasaṃvara.
It's not a bad deity, it's an excellent deity.

The hunter thought, "He really is the famous adept Milarepa. He certainly possesses the narrow path that would lead a sinner like me to the higher realms. So, I should by all means follow this accomplished master as his attendant." He then offered this song:

Once more, please listen, Jetsün with great compassion.

The accomplished master Milarepa
renowned here in the snow lands of Tibet—
today I've met him, how fortunate I am.

Master, to follow as your attendant and then
practice authentic dharma wholeheartedly, that's my intent, so
Master, what sort of home do you have?

Since I wish to practice authentic dharma sincerely,
Master, what sort of firewood do you have?

Since I wish to practice authentic dharma sincerely,
Master, what sort of food do you have?

Since I wish to practice authentic dharma sincerely,
Master, what sort of drink do you have?

Since I wish to practice authentic dharma sincerely,
Master, what sort of wealth do you have?

Since I wish to practice authentic dharma sincerely,
Master, what sort of neighbors do you have?

Since I wish to practice authentic dharma sincerely,
Do you, Master, have all those things?

The lama replied, "It's excellent if you follow me. A human body is most difficult to obtain. If you can now practice austerities, that is excellent too, and if you follow me, it's possible you have some good karma left."

The hunter was filled with intense faith and said, "Now I will follow you as your attendant."

Mila replied, "Son, listen to me for a moment without your ears wavering," and then sang this song:

Son, listen here, fortunate faithful one.

Slate mountains, rock mountains, and snow mountains three:
these three are Mila's meditation spots.
If these three meditation spots suit you, come follow me.
If these three meditation spots suffice, practice sublime dharma.

Slate water, rock water, and glacial water three:
these three are Mila's drinking water.
If these three drinking waters suit you, come follow me.
If these three drinking waters suffice, practice sublime dharma.

Cotton wool, brushwood, and tamarisk three:
these three are Mila's tinder.
If these three kinds of tinder suit you, come follow me.
If these three kinds of tinder suffice, practice sublime dharma.

Nettles, wild garlic, and hemp three:
these three are Mila's practice provisions.
If these three practice provisions suit you, come follow me.
If these three practice provisions suffice, practice sublime dharma.

Vultures, grouses, and blackbirds three:
these three are Mila's house birds.
If these three house birds suit you, come follow me.
If these three house birds suffice, practice sublime dharma.

Deer, wild sheep, and antelope three:
these three are Mila's domestic animals.
If these three domestic animals suit you, come follow me.
If these three domestic animals suffice, practice sublime dharma.

Slate caves, snow caves, and rock caves three:
these three are Mila's meditation spots.
If these three meditation spots suit you, come follow me.
If these three meditation spots suffice, practice sublime dharma.

Channels, subtle winds, and essential drops three:
these three are Mila's garments.
If these three garments suit you, come follow me.
If these three garments suffice, practice sublime dharma.

Foxes, wild dogs, and wolves three:
these three are Mila's watchdogs.
If these three watchdogs suit you, come follow me.
If these three watchdogs suffice, practice sublime dharma.

Flint, striker, and tinder three:
these three are Mila's neighbors.
If these three neighbors suit you, come follow me.
If these three neighbors suffice, practice sublime dharma.

Skull cup, leather sack, and staff three:
these three are Mila's attendants.
If these three attendants suit you, come follow me.
If these three attendants suffice, practice sublime dharma.

Dharma view, meditation, and conduct three:
these three are Mila's practices.
If these three practices suit you, come follow me.
If these three practices suffice, practice sublime dharma.

Happiness in this life, joy in the next—
if you practice like this, liberation you'll gain.
Fortunate one, keep this in mind.
Practicing sublime dharma is bliss all the time.

The hunter thought, "The great Jetsün's words of advice are true. Don't we have some karmic connection from the past? Now I've met this lama. I'll give up killing. I should also take vows. Previously, having fallen under the sway of bad karma, I would have taken the life of this creature. It

occurs to me that I've been speaking a lot of nonsense to the lama. Now
I should follow this accomplished master as his attendant, whether I live
or die, and then practice dharma by giving up concern for this life."

He took his coat, boots, hat, arrows, bow, dagger, lasso, deer, and dog,
all nine together, and offered them to the lama. He put on his boots once
again and offered this song in the theatrical dance style called *shon:*

> This white hat I wore on my head,
> a hat adorned with a peacock feather brim,
> when worn keeps you free from rain and snow.
> I offer this hat complete for the lama's head.
> In general, please keep sinners from falling to the lower realms.
> Please lead the she-dog Lokchang Barma on the path to enlightenment.
> Please lead this deer on the path to liberation.
> Please keep the hunter Gönpo Dorjé from being sent to the hells.
>
> This coat of antelope skin I wore on my body,
> a coat adorned with silk trim on its edges,
> when worn keeps you warm on the highest mountain glaciers.
> I offer this coat complete for the lama's body.
> In general, please keep sinners from falling to the lower realms.
> Please lead the she-dog Lokchang Barma on the path to enlightenment.
> Please lead this deer on the path to liberation.
> Please keep the hunter Gönpo Dorjé from being sent to the hells.
>
> These blue boots I wore on my feet,
> boots adorned with four blue bootstraps on their edge,
> when worn keep you free from thorns and blisters.
> I offer these boots complete for the lama's feet.
> In general, please keep sinners from falling to the lower realms.
> Please lead the she-dog Lokchang Barma on the path to enlightenment.
> Please lead this deer on the path to liberation.
> Please keep the hunter Gönpo Dorjé from being sent to the hells.
>
> These arrows I held in my right hand,
> arrows adorned with vulture feathers and pointed tip at their ends,
> when fired slay your most hated enemies.
> I offer these arrows complete for the lama's hands.
> In general, please keep sinners from falling to lower realms.

Please lead the she-dog Lokchang Barma on the path to enlightenment.
Please lead this deer on the path to liberation.
Please keep the hunter Gönpo Dorjé from being sent to the hells.

This bow once held in my left hand,
an "excellent white" bow adorned with acacia twine on its ends,
when snapped roars like a celestial dragon.
I offer this bow complete for the lama's hands.
In general, please keep sinners from falling to the lower realms.
Please lead the she-dog Lokchang Barma on the path to enlightenment.
Please lead this deer on the path to liberation.
Please keep the hunter Gönpo Dorjé from being sent to the hells.

This dagger I had tucked in my belt,
a dagger adorned with a conch-white ring at its end,
when struck cuts through even dark armor plate.
I offer this knife complete for the lama's hands.
In general, please keep sinners from falling to the lower realms.
Please lead the she-dog Lokchang Barma on the path to enlightenment.
Please lead this deer on the path to liberation.
Please keep the hunter Gönpo Dorjé from being sent to the hells.

This lasso that snaps to life in movement,
a multicolored lasso adorned with a ring at its end,
when flung holds even wild yaks of the northern steppe at bay.
I offer this lasso complete for the lama's hands.
In general, please keep sinners from falling to the lower realms.
Please lead the she-dog Lokchang Barma on the path to enlightenment.
Please lead this deer on the path to liberation.
Please keep the hunter Gönpo Dorjé from being sent to the hells.

This deer with ten-point antlers before me,
a ten-point deer adorned with conch-white antlers,
if slain would keep you from hunger for seven days.
I offer this deer complete before the lama.
In general, please keep sinners from falling to the lower realms.
Please lead the she-dog Lokchang Barma on the path to enlightenment.
Please lead this deer on the path to liberation.
Please keep the hunter Gönpo Dorjé from being sent to the hells.

This red she-dog adorned with a yak-tail collar,
when loosed catches even birds in the sky.
I offer her too as the lama's watchdog.
In general, please keep sinners from falling to the lower realms.
Please lead the she-dog Lokchang Barma on the path to enlightenment.
Please lead this deer on the path to liberation.
Please keep the hunter Gönpo Dorjé from being sent to the hells.

I the hunter Gönpo Dorjé, who has no beasts of burden,
I have faith but little wealth.
If I had riches and hid them, the lama would make me ashamed.
Search for riches I lack, they won't turn up here.

These nine things offered in a single group
I present before the lord guru.
My previous bad actions I regret and confess,
and from now on I promise to do them no more.
Even if death falls upon me I'll do no evil deeds.
Please hold me, your son, with kindness in your heart.
Wherever you go I'll follow to serve.
Hold me with compassion that I'm freed through instructions on
    the path.

After he said this, while he was kneeling before the Jetsün with his
palms pressed together, the hunter's wife appeared, an axe tucked into
her belt, a basket on her back, and holding a lasso in her hand. She said,
"These realized yogins are everywhere. When you go to the mountain-
top, there they are. When you go down the valley, there they are. When
you go up the valley, there they are too. Why have you have seized my
man and dog? I have seven in my family, men and dog. Are you going to
feed them? If I tie up its neck with this rope and chop off its head with
this axe, then we'll have something to eat."
    The Jetsün sang this song to her.

You, a demoness face on a dark female body,
Dark-body demon-face, listen to me here.

Your hope is the hope of slaying the deer,
your fear is the fear of the deer slipping away.

Between hope and fear, right there, you wander life's round.
Between hope and fear, right there, go ponder it now.

You'd slay the deer but don't kill it,
the time has come—grasp your own mind within.
Daughter, the time's come to grasp your own mind.
The time's come to meditate on clear light meditation.

Dark lady, that's happiness in this life and bliss in the next,
practice sublime dharma that's bliss in both.
Practice sublime dharma that's bliss in both.

The woman replied, "All your dharma is incomprehensible, and it looks like your practicing sublime dharma has made you a beggar. You might say you stole my dog and deer."

Her husband shot back at her, "You always come where you shouldn't. The deer is listening to dharma, let it be."

"If you say do it, I'll kill the deer and carry away the pieces." Having said this, she tied the rope to the deer's head and fixed it by winding it around a dead tree.

The woman's husband kicked her, screaming, "You want to kill this deer? I'd like to chop off your head with this axe."

At that point, the Jetsün sang her this song of impermanence.

You demoness mind in a dark female body,
Lady evil-karma listen to me here.

We are impermanent worldly beings.
Looking out at people in the world
don't you feel they're perpetually tossed
by waves of the four seas of suffering,
the four seas of birth, aging, sickness, and death?
They have not a moment of happiness.

To explain the suffering of birth a little:
ground consciousness traversing the intermediate state
enters the womb of a mother. All the while
it rests in the middle of blood and pus,
using filth as its mattress and pillow.

Through its bad karma it takes an ugly body,
through its bad state it experiences suffering.
It remembers past and future lives but knows not how to speak.
It suffers intensely but cannot call out.
Due to all sorts of hot and cold miseries
it burns in hell for nine months.
When it takes birth from the womb
it's like its body being cast into thorns.
When pulled into the lap of its mother
it's like a hatchling being snatched by a hawk.
When the mother gives her baby its first taste of butter
it's like eating a powerful poison.
When wrapped up in swaddling clothes
it's like being locked in a dungeon.
So, if you don't realize the sole unborn meaning,
the suffering of birth is unimaginable.

To explain the suffering of aging a little:
of the head, chief of limbs, and the rest,
the ears, ruler of sounds, go deaf.
The hair, leaves of the skin, turns white.
Wrinkles appear on one's handsome face.
Clarity of the faculties such as sight are dimmed.
The nose, chief of features, breaks down.
The cheeks, ruler of ruddy flush, dry up.
The teeth, ruler of bones, fall out.
You give good advice on the way things are
but nobody listens to a word you say.
In the heat you wear light clothing, but
in the cold you're forced to put on heavy garments.
The body born straight hunches over.
Hunched with a cane, the gait turns unsteady.
Lice and debts are wiped out but pile up.[5]
The food and friends you hope to gather all scatter.
Such is the suffering of aging.

If one period of sickness befalls you
then sudden visceral physical pain
like a tortuous enemy emerges.

Wind, phlegm, and bile fall prey to demons.
Blood and pus flow out before you.
When you succumb to a physical ailment,
you have comfortable thick cushions but feel cold underneath.
You rest on high pillows but your head still hurts.
You're presented with delicious, sweet food,
but just seeing it makes you feel nauseous.
You're surrounded all around by loving friends,
but none of them can share your pain.
You rest your head in someone's lap
while being served food with a spoon
and sucking drinks through a straw,
but nothing can remedy your illness.
A hundred come, a thousand come, but none see you.
You call a thousand, you call ten thousand, but none hear you.
Such is the suffering of sickness.

When one day your hour of death arrives,
riches can't ransom you.
Eloquent stories can't pardon you.
The heroic can't stay around forever.
The timid can't escape like a fox.
The evil can't insist on staying.
The clever can't fool it with food.
The evil can't cut it away.
A beautiful lady can't deceive it with her appearance.
Trunk and limbs are pulled in from the side
and you're laid on the road in a bundle to be carried.
Your flesh and bones, guarded as so essential,
become food for all the birds and dogs.

When such an hour arrives for you,
though you have much wealth and belongings, they're enjoyed by others.
Though you have many friends and children, you pass on alone.
Though you have a fine household and home, you're carried out
   through the door.

Can you bear all that, my fortunate one?
Your body is nourished with care but

some are burned up in fire,
some are tossed in the water,
some are buried with earth in a pit,
some are eaten by birds and wolves.

Think about it, my fortunate one.
Worldly riches have power but
can't ransom your life for even a moment.
What use is there in being stingy?

When the time comes to depart all alone
who for a spouse can accompany you on your way?
Who can you visualize as you go on your way?
What can you carry on your back as you go on your way?
Who can you have as companion or counselor?

Be blind to it or be at ease.
Without authentic sublime dharma
there's nothing at all that can help you.
The mirror of karma is clear
and reflects all the virtue and sin that you do.

The dharma king Yama is a fearsome figure.
Bull-headed Awa has no compassion.
You're plunged into a pit of molten copper.[6]
Black marks are drawn on your body,
which is then cut with a poisonous saw.
You're forced to drink boiling molten metal
and forced to roast in a pit of hot coals.
The armies of dharma king Yama
will assail your body with weapons.
One moment you die and the next you're revived.

When the time for such things arrives
a lord has not even the help of a child.
You can't even take your wealth and possessions.
Except for authentic sublime dharma
there's no one to help or protect you.

Therefore right now, in this time of comfort,
take refuge in the venerable Triple Gem.
Make prayers to the venerable gurus.
Be persistent in the deity's generation and completion.
Between sessions cultivate love and compassion.
Do this with confidence for the time of your death.

She also gained faith and then her seven family members requested dharma, through which they realized the meaning of Mahāmudrā and then attained accomplishment. The hunter shaved his head, received a new name, took lay vows, and then practiced meditation, for which he was called the excellent meditator and accomplished master Khyira Repa. It is said that from among the eight great disciples of the Jetsün, the champion of beings, he developed an excellent practice of supporting some five hundred monks.

Notes

1. See the recent translation in Gtsang smyon Heruka, *Hundred Thousand Songs of Milarepa*. *The Life of Milarepa*, companion to *The Hundred Thousand Songs*, has been translated by Quintman.
2. For a survey and history of these collections, see Quintman, *Yogin and the Madman*, chap. 3.
3. See the discussion in Quintman, *Yogin and the Madman*, 104–7.
4. Nyishar (Snyi shar) is likely a manuscript misspelling of Nyishang (Snyi shang), the region of Manang in which the story is traditionally set and where Khira Repa remains a cultural hero. The toponym Nishang (Sni shang) appears later in this text.
5. Unsure reading: *shig dang bu lon bsad kyang 'du*.
6. Unsure reading: *zang dmar kha sbyor yang shong* (var. *shang*) *che*.

Tibetan Sources

The two manuscripts used for this translation, DNM-I and DNM-S, frequently differ in syntax and the spelling of words, especially grammatical particles. They also occasionally diverge through the addition and omission of words, phrases, or lines. I have drawn on both editions in order to create a coherent translation and have occasionally referred to DNM-D, which appears to have drawn on DNM-I/S or a common source, as well as BC-N, which have occasionally helped clarify the meaning of the text. However, I have not attempted to create a critical edition or note intertextual relationships with other *Mdzod nag ma* versions.

BC-N. *Rje btsun chen po mid la ras pa'i rnam thar zab mo* [The profound life of the great Jetsün Milarepa]. Unpublished manuscript in the collection of the Newark Museum of Art, Tibetan Book Collection, Folio 36.280. IIB R 16.

DNM-D. *Mi la'i gsung mgur mdzod nag ma* [The Black Treasury songs of Milarepa]. 2 vols. Khren tu'u: Si khron mi rigs dpe skrun khang, 2008.

DNM-I. "Khyi ra ras pa la gsung tshul ma'i 'dra gnyis kyis bskor." In *Rnal 'byor gyi dbang phyug mi la bzhad pa rdo rje'i gsung mgur ma mdzod nag ma zhes pa karma pa rang byung rdo rjes phyog bcig* [The songs of the lord of yogins Mila Zhepa Dorjé called the Black Treasury, compiled by Karmapa Rangjung Dorjé], 1:518, 2:26. 2 vols. Dalhousie: Damchoe Sangpo, 1978.

DNM-S. "Khyi ra ras pa la gsung tshul ma'i 'dra gnyis kyis bskor." In *Rje rnal 'byor gyi dbang phyug dpal bzhad pa'i rdo rje'i 'gur 'tshogs tshad phyogs gcig du bsgrig pa lo rgyus kyis spras pa* [The collected and compiled songs of the powerful lord of yogins glorious Zhepa Dorjé, embellished with stories], 2:3–22. Unpublished manuscript in the collection of E. Gene Smith. 2 vols. BDRC: MW4CZ45235.

Gtsang smyon Heruka. "Khyi ra ras pa dang mjal ba'i skor." In *Rnal 'byor gyi dbang phyug chen po mi la ras pa'i rnam mgur* [The life and songs of the powerful lord of yogins Milarepa], 430–42. Zi ling: Mtsho sngon mi rigs dpe skrun khang, 1981.

Additional Sources

Gtsang smyon Heruka. *The Hundred Thousand Songs of Milarepa: A New Translation.* Translated by Christopher Stagg and Dzogchen Ponlop. Boulder, CO: Shambhala, 2017.

———. *The Life of Milarepa.* Translated by Andrew Quintman. New York: Penguin Classics, 2010.

Quintman, Andrew. *The Yogin and the Madman: Reading the Biographical Corpus of Tibet's Great Saint Milarepa.* New York: Columbia University Press, 2014.

3

A Sarcastic Song

INTRODUCED AND TRANSLATED BY TRUNGRAM
GYALTRUL RINPOCHÉ AND LARA BRAITSTEIN

"YOU RASH little monks" begins the refrain of a delightfully humorous song attributed to the yogin known as Rechungpa, "The Junior Cotton-Clad One" (c. 1084–1161). Rechungpa gained this moniker in respectful contrast to his teacher, the great Milarepa, who is Tibet's most famous wandering cotton-clad yogin (*repa*) and poet. Rechungpa's full name was Dorjé Drakpa (shortened to Dordrak in this song). As with many Tibetan figures from the eleventh and twelfth centuries, we find a number of different versions of Rechungpa's life. The broad outline, however, is quite consistent, and tells the story of a boy whose father dies when he is young (perhaps around 8 years old) and whose mother is unusually cruel. Unwanted and neglected by his mother and stepfather, he is eventually either kicked out or abandoned. He happens upon Milarepa in the mountains one day when he is herding animals (somewhere between the ages of 10 and 13), and hearing his voice, he spontaneously enters meditative absorption. Milarepa accepts the boy as his disciple and adopts him, raising him to adulthood. Rechungpa finds in Milarepa not only care and protection but a tough and effective guide toward enlightenment.

Rechungpa has a strong character and often rebels against his teacher, so he tends to be recalled as headstrong and proud. This reputation should not be permitted to eclipse his extraordinary accomplishments as a practitioner and teacher in his own right, however. His determination and strength were very likely what permitted him to survive an abusive family, leprosy, two journeys by foot to India and back, and a life largely spent wandering the rough countryside of Tibet clad in his white cotton robe. Not to mention the extraordinary diligence and persistence—even stubbornness—required to master the difficult yogic practices taught to him by Milarepa.

Rechungpa adopted Milarepa's method of teaching by uttering spontaneous songs in response to specific situations. These songs of realization, known as *gur*, are the poetic genre that came to be associated most closely with the expression of realization and personal experience. The phenomenon of singing in verse to express spiritual accomplishment and experience was imported from the Indic context, in which Tibetans like Milarepa's teacher, Marpa, were trained to compose yogic songs called *dohās*. *Dohās*, or pithy couplets, were the chosen mode of expression of the great accomplished ones (*mahāsiddhas*), the antinomian Buddhist tantric poet-saints generally situated in the eighth to twelfth centuries CE. Tibetans already had a rich poetic culture, and this blended beautifully with the *dohā* tradition. The Tibetan touch, lent to the tradition of singing yogic songs, makes them deeply personal; the inclusion of life events, earthy metaphors, and deep emotional experiences gives *gur* an especially relatable flavor.

Gur may be composed in a number of styles, and the one translated here is typical of the time and context from which it derives. The song opens with an homage to Rechungpa's guru, Milarepa. Devotion to one's teacher is fundamental to the tantric view of reality, and an opening homage is a consistent feature of these songs of experience. In the homage, Rechungpa refers to Milarepa as his father, which is true in both a spiritual and a mundane sense. He then qualifies Milarepa as the father of the Kagyu (special transmission) lineage and the teacher of the practice lineage and the realization lineage.[1] Following the homage are a short verse that sets the scene and then nine stanzas of three couplets each, the last of which is a repeating refrain, which contributes to the folksy, down-to-earth rhythm of the song.[2]

The first couplet in each stanza highlights a point of ignorance in the monks whom he is addressing. Rechungpa points first to something the monks misunderstand (e.g., "Not knowing your body is a deity") and then to the outcome of their mistaken belief ("You hope to get enlightened by wearing yellow clothes"). The mistakes have to do with view (e.g., not grasping that in a tantric context one's form is the form of the meditational deity and is thus perfect as it is), and the outcomes have to do with outer practices maintained to give the appearance of being a good Buddhist (i.e., wearing monastic robes). In the second couplet,

Rechungpa holds up a (metaphorical) mirror to show the monks that their unwarranted arrogance is founded in ignorance of their own errors.

In each stanza, Rechungpa contrasts the meaningless rote practices and rituals performed by the monks whom he is addressing with his own sincere practice, which is grounded in a tantric view of reality. He uses sarcastic language to mock the monks' attitudes and in each stanza reveals their errors in view and practice. This song is not only humorous but quite revealing of the tension in those early times between the freewheeling spirituality of yogic adepts and the institutionalized religion of monks. The song creates a set of contrasts between monks and adepts, book learning and experiential learning, and outer displays of virtue and impartial virtue based on realization. Importantly, Rechungpa emphasizes—and criticizes—their pride.

Another important aspect of Rechungpa's *gur* is that contextualization is an important part of the song. This is exactly the same as in the case of his teacher, Milarepa. Their songs take place as part of a *mise-en-scène*; we are always introduced to the physical setting, the audience, and the reason the audience needs to be taught something. In this case, the context enhances our understanding of the tension between yogic and monastic lifestyles during Rechungpa's lifetime. This tension between the more hermit-like ascetic lifestyle and practice of the adepts and the more organized monastic communities of monks and nuns ran deep in the eleventh and twelfth centuries.

As a teacher, Rechungpa—a cotton-clad, long-haired yogin who often dwelt in mountain retreats—developed the habit of wandering into monasteries. There, the monastic inhabitants would be clean-shaven, neatly dressed in their robes, and engaged in a regular schedule of practice and ritual as part of their community life. The reactions of the monks provided the perfect grist for Rechungpa's teachings. In this song, we see that Rechungpa is being forcibly kicked out of a monastery on the orders of the abbot. The orders are carried out by two overzealous young monks who roughly shove Rechungpa out of the monastery and then close the gate on his foot, causing him excruciating pain. It is in this context that Rechungpa sings them this magnificently sarcastic song. It is the repeated refrain that ties the whole song together: *"Ow! Ow! Ow! You rash little monks, don't crush this leg! / Let this leg go!"* The refrain is an ingenious device that brings the reader's mind back to the context, back to the audience, and back to Rechungpa, all the while giving a humorous tone to this otherwise deeply critical piece.

Our source for the song is the hagiography of Rechungpa, compiled by Lhatsun Rinchen Namgyal in 1503. We had two editions to work from, both of which are rife with spelling errors. Some of the errors appear to be due to the great number of homophones in Tibetan, others to simple human error. We have done our best to emend the text on the basis of the context, meaning, and the rules of Tibetan grammar.

The Unobstructed Nature, a Sarcastic Song
Rechungpa Dorjé Drakpa

Then the yogin Rechungpa arrived at Chayul monastery. He found monks in the main hall reciting prayers, led by the Abbot. Rechungpa sat at the end of the rows of monks. The Abbot said, "There is a saying that [even] a white billy goat cannot fit in with a flock of sheep. So, go and expel that *repa* from this place!"[3] To that end, one young monk dragged him to the gate from the front, and another pushed him from behind. They slammed the gate so quickly that one of his feet got caught. [They held the gate closed on his foot,] causing unbearable pain to arise.

So he sang this song, *The Unobstructed Nature, a Sarcastic Song*:

I bow to the feet of the Great Repa, my father Mila:
Precious father, teacher of the Kagyu lineage,
Blessed teacher of the practice lineage,
Awakened teacher of the realization lineage.

I, Rechung Dordrak from Gungthang region,
Have been all over, but never seen this behavior before!
Oh, monks of the Jowo Kadam, listen carefully to this song for a while:

Not knowing your own body is a deity,
You hope to get enlightened by wearing yellow clothes.[4]
I see you haven't noticed that you slipped into thinking of your body
   as mundane,
Braggarts in robes!

Ow! Ow! Ow! You rash little monks, don't crush this leg!
Let this leg go!

Not knowing food and drink are a tantric feast,
You hope to get enlightened by skipping dinner.
I see you haven't noticed that you insult the deities
As you brag about your austerities.

Ow! Ow! Ow! You rash little monks, don't crush this leg!
Let this leg go!

Not knowing all speech is mantra,
You hope to get enlightened by simple ritual recitation.
I see you haven't noticed that you are just wasting your breath[5]
As you brag about your endless mumbling.

Ow! Ow! Ow! You rash little monks, don't crush this leg!
Let this leg go!

Not knowing your own mind is awakened,[6]
You hope to get enlightened through words and terms.
I see you haven't noticed that your mind is running wild
As you brag about your knowledge of the "true dharma."

Ow! Ow! Ow! You rash little monks, don't crush this leg!
Let this leg go!

Not purifying your mental stains,
You hope to get enlightened simply by washing your face in the
    morning.
I see you haven't noticed that you are soiled by habitual stains
As you brag about your purity.

Ow! Ow! Ow! You rash little monks, don't crush this leg!
Let this leg go!

Not knowing the unborn mind is self-liberated,
You hope to get enlightened from sitting up straight.
I see you haven't noticed that your defilements are growing coarser
As you brag about your virtuous practice.

Ow! Ow! Ow! You rash little monks, don't crush this leg!
Let this leg go!

Not knowing nondiscriminative virtue,
You hope to get enlightened from biased tenets.
I see you haven't noticed that your giving is part of a transaction
As you brag about accumulating merit.

Ow! Ow! Ow! You rash little monks, don't crush this leg!
Let this leg go!

Not practicing for buddhahood in one lifetime,
You hope to get enlightened in three countless eons.
I see you haven't noticed that your mind is just wandering in saṃsāra
As you brag about the duration of your practice.

Ow! Ow! Ow! You rash little monks, don't crush this leg!
Let this leg go!

The bandits and raiders of Ngamshö,
The barmaids of the four quarters of Lhasa,
And the young pea-headed Kadampa monks—
I swear, none of them has compassion.

Ow! Ow! Ow! You rash little monks, don't crush this leg!
Let this leg go!

In general, the leg is very essential to all.
And it is particularly essential to vagabonds.

The young monks were distracted by his words and relaxed their grip on
the gate just long enough to allow him to pull his leg out. Swiftly running
about a quarter mile away, he sat there rubbing his feet.

Notes

1. These three lineages are very closely associated and often used interchange-
   ably but have different emphases. The Kagyu is the lineage of the special
   transmission teachings (*bka' babs bzhi*, four special transmissions of teach-
   ings); the practice lineage specifically emphasizes the way of practicing the
   teachings, particularly regarding meditation; and the realization lineage em-
   phasizes the result or meaning.

2. The first two couplets in each stanza notably do not follow any repeating pattern of number of syllables; in fact no two stanzas have the same distribution of syllables. There are patterns in the structure and vocabulary, however, which tie the stanzas together in different ways.

3. Goats make a nice metaphor for yogic adepts, with their propensity to climb high into the rocky mountains and with their beards. Sheep in this context are considered superior to goats, and the sense of this statement is that no matter how white (pure) the goat may be, it will never measure up to sheep. The meaning is that a yogin can never measure up to the monks.

4. Literally "yellow clothes [*gos ser mo*]," but it refers to monks' robes. It is often used together with "gray clothes [*ser skya*]," which refers to the lay people.

5. *Srog rtsol*, meaning control of the vital breath (Skt: *prāṇayama*). The multiple layers of meaning expressed in the Tibetan are impossible to capture in English.

6. The reference here is to *dharmakāya*.

Tibetan Sources

The song is found in two versions of the hagiography of Rechungpa (Ras chung pa), a text first printed by Lha brtsun rin chen rnam rgyal in 1503 at Brag dkar rta so.

Lha brtsun rin chen rnam rgyal. "Tshe gcig la 'ja' lus brnyes pa rje ras chung pa'i rnam thar rags bsdus mgur rnam rgyas pa" [The abundant songs and a summary of the exemplary life of Lord Rechungpa who attained the rainbow body in one lifetime]. In *Bka' brgyud pa Hagiographies: A Collection of rnam thar of Eminent Masters of Tibetan Buddhism*, compiled and edited by Khams sprul Don brgyud nyi ma, 1:677–80. Palampur, Himachal Pradesh: Sungrab Nyamso Gyunphel Parkhang, Tashijong, 1972.

———. "Tshe gcig la 'ja' lus brnyes pa rje ras chung pa'i rnam thar rags bsdus mgur rnam rgyas pa" [The abundant songs and a summary of the exemplary life of Lord Rechungpa who attained the rainbow body in one lifetime]. Photograph of a rare old blockprint text, TBRC (BDRC) collection, image 105–7. Brag dkar rta so: Brag dkar rta so'i par khang, 1503.

Additional Sources

Bhum, Pema. "Heartbeat of a New Generation: A Discussion of the New Poetry." Translated by Ronald Schwartz. In *Modern Tibetan Literature and Social Change*, edited by Lauran R. Hartley and Patricia Schiaffini-Vedani, 112–34. Durham, NC: Duke University Press, 2008.

Don sgrub rgyal. "Mgur glu'i lo rgyus dang khyad chos" [The history and features of *gurlu* (songs)]. In *Dpal don grub rgyal gyi gsung 'bum* [Pal Döndrup Gyal's collected works], 3:316–601. Beijing: Mi rigs dpe skrun khang, 1997.

Gtsang smyon Heruka. *The Life of Milarepa.* Translated by Andrew Quintman. New York: Penguin Books, 2010.

Jackson, Roger R. "'Poetry' in Tibet: Glu, mGur, sNyan ngag and 'Songs Of Experience.'" In *Tibetan Literature: Studies in Genre,* edited by José Ignacio Cabezón and Roger R. Jackson, 368–92. Ithaca, NY: Snow Lion, 1996.

Lama Jabb. *Oral and Literary Continuities in Modern Tibetan Literature: The Inescapable Nation.* New York: Lexington Books, 2015.

Mi la ras pa. *The Hundred Thousand Songs of Milarepa: A New Translation.* Translated by Christopher Stagg and Dzogchen Ponlop. Boulder, CO: Shambhala, 2017.

Quintman, Andrew. *The Yogin and the Madman: Reading the Biographical Corpus of Tibet's Great Saint Milarepa.* New York: Columbia University Press, 2015.

Roberts, Peter Alan. *The Biographies of Rechungpa: The Evolution of a Tibetan Hagiography.* London: Routledge, 2007.

4

Longchenpa's Lineage Prayer

INTRODUCED AND TRANSLATED BY RENÉE L. FORD

IN HIS LINEAGE prayer from the *Lama Yangtik*,[1] the Nyingma master Longchen Rabjam (abbreviated Longchenpa, 1308–1364) reflects tantric meditational and philosophical frameworks that rely on nonconceptual techniques like imagination and rhythm. The purpose is to connect to a matrix of student, teacher, lineage figures, and landscapes in which a reader already has a connection. The relationship is strengthened through reciting the prayer translated in this chapter, "Cloud Banks of Nectar: Prayers of the *Lama Yangtik*"[2] (*Bla ma yang tig gi gsol 'debs bdud rtsi'i sprin tshogs*),[3] which intensifies and strengthens devotion. As devotion is understood to be the key ingredient for tantra in general, including Dzogchen, or the "Great Perfection," any medium that builds devotion is crucial.

Longchenpa's prayer to the lineage is one example of the Dzogchen emphasis on prayer to elicit devotion and blessings. Devotion (*mos gus*) in Tibetan is a combination of two terms, *möpa* (*mos pa*) and *güpa* (*gus pa*), where the former can be translated as "interest" and the latter as "respect." As a way to incorporate the felt sense, or affective component, of *mögü*, I interpret respect as "heartfelt." From this perspective, *mögü* can be understood as a "heartfelt interest." This alternative translation allows for a broader understanding of how *mögü* operates within Tibetan Buddhism and specifically of how Longchenpa's prayer implements the disposition of *mögü*. The translation "heartfelt interest" points to a connection being forged between the reader and the object of that interest, here lineage figures of the *Lama Yangtik*. This is a special relationship that allows for transformation, in this case in the practitioners who might recite this prayer in liturgical practice.[4] Longchenpa expresses his "heartfelt interest" in the poem, and interest is performed by others as a means for transformation.

In the Nyingma tradition, especially for Longchenpa, Dzogchen moves away from conceptual frameworks as the basis of transformation. Instead of relying on concepts and reasoning that engage conceptual thought, tantric meditation practices emphasize the relationship between a student and a teacher. Tantric liturgies and meditational practices encourage a student to cultivate devotion, in particular toward their teacher. Devotion to one's teacher also relates to figures in the Nyingma lineage, such as historical figures and tantric deities. For example, a common feature of *guruyoga* practices is to imagine one's teacher as Padmasambhava, who is an embodiment of wisdom. Additionally, a student might be asked to imagine an entire environment of nonhuman female beings[5] called *ḍākinīs*, or "sky-goers," rainbows streaming throughout, and entire continents that have islands, mountains, and oceans. All these elements are emanations of wisdom and are not perceived as separate from oneself, nor from one's teacher and the historical lineage. In this way, a student creates a subtle visualized matrix as a way to cut through conceptual dualism. Instead of using analysis and reasoning that direct a student to recognize emptiness, tantra offers instructions on nonconceptual sensorial means to arrive at an understanding of nondualism.

"Cloud Banks of Nectar" operates within this matrix of a nonconceptual, nondualistic, and creative format in which the recitation of the prayer allows one to tap into one's devotion, offering an avenue to connect to that lineage and wisdom at large. The first stanza of the poem begins with calling out to the primordial buddhas (male and female) Samantabhadra and Samantabhadrī in order to realize "self-arisen mind nature," luminosity. This realization is the goal of the Nyingma path, and straight away Longchenpa (and anyone else who recites the prayer) asks to receive blessings as an aid to realization. This request to Samantabhadra and Samantabhadrī is not an ordinary request, since according to esoteric understandings, Samantabhadra, Samantabhadrī, the self-arisen nature, and practitioners are not separate.

This poem has a simple and straightforward form, featuring repeated requests for blessings. This form is the basis of the poem's success. The stanzas cultivate a recursive rhythm, which bolsters the mood being engendered through the words. The rhythm of "please love me. / Bless me" (*gsol ba 'debs so thugs rje'i spyan gyis gzigs*) conjures devotion as affect. My translation of this poem attempts to re-create this rhythm by consistently translating two particular repeated lines. While it may seem to be a simple move, and perhaps not the most creative choice on my part, it allows the affective mood to develop as the reader recites the words.

To understand what love means in this context, I turn to how we understand the term *thukjé* (*thugs rje*), which is usually translated as "compassion." The repeating phrases in the text, "please love me. / Bless me," is a request that is typically translated as "please look upon me with compassion." I chose to translate the first phrase as "please love me" to express Longchen Rabjam's request to the lineage masters to "see him with compassion" in an affective manner that expresses how tantra and Dzogchen understand the student-teacher relationship in experiencing the nature of mind. This poem invokes Longchen Rabjam's devotion to the lineage as well as his recognizing the qualities that he is asking to experience throughout the poem. Moreover, the term *thukjé* is understood differently depending on the context. In Dzogchen, *thukjé* is (1) a description of the *nirmāṇakāya* (manifest body) as responsiveness; (2) an act of compassion between subject and object such as in the student-teacher relationship; and (3) the heart-mind of a practitioner. In this poem, I believe, *thukjé* touches on all three of these. Lastly, in reference to the "four boundless states" (*tshad med bzhi*), love refers to the wish that all beings be happy, while compassion refers to the wish that no being experience suffering.

Additionally, I tried to use the historical names of persons found within the poem to allow readers to recognize that the figures are significant to the Nyingma lineage. Longchenpa supplicates lineage figures like Mañjuśrīmitra, Śrī Siṃha, and Vimalamitra, all of whom are considered lineage holders because they transmitted the teachings through symbols, one of three modes of transmission according to the Nyingma tradition. Historical figures like Nyang Tingdzin Zangpo (8th to 9th century), Dangma Lhungyel (11th century), and Chetsün Sengé Wangchuk (11th to 12th century) were all part of the oral transmission lineage. Additionally, these three illuminate the treasure (*gter*) tradition. Nyang Tingdzin Zangpo created treasures, which were sealed and hidden until other Buddhist masters, such as Lodrö Wangchuk, revealed them later.[6] These figures created various connections that prevented teachings from being lost or diluted over time.

Lastly, it is important that the requests made by those who recite the prayer align with the philosophical frameworks and definitions found in the Nyingma tradition. Since Longchenpa is asking to receive qualities of wisdom, such as freedom from saṃsāra and nirvāṇa, great bliss, luminos-

ity, and the inseparable kāyas and wisdoms, it is important to understand
how he discusses these descriptions in his other seminal works, such as
The Treasury of Philosophical Systems and *The Treasury of Basic Space*. I
chose to translate Tibetan terms from a context based upon Longchenpa's
other writings so that the English translation upholds Longchenpa's view
of the Buddhist path according to the Nyingma tradition.

Cloud Banks of Nectar: Prayers of the *Lama Yangtik*
Longchen Rabjam

Oṃ Āh Hūṃ

Beginningless protectors, Samantabhadra, Samantabahdrī,
    please love me.
Bless me so I may now realize
    the self-arisen mind nature, luminous essential meaning.

Infinite peaceful and wrathful spontaneous conquerors,[7]
    please love me.
Bless me so I may now see
    the self-luminous wisdom, great light.

Dechen Gyalpo, Dorjé Chang,
    please love me.
Bless me so I may now realize
    the dharmakāya, mind nature, naturally freed from saṃsāra and nirvāṇa.

Illusory manifestation wisdom, Vajrasattva,
    please love me.
Bless me so I may now go
    to changeless, spontaneous, great bliss, the highest pure land.

Lord of the maṇḍala, Vajrapāṇi,
    please love me.
Bless me so I may now proceed as
    the Victor of Secret Mantra, the instant Buddha path.

Emanation of victors, Garab Dorjé,
    please love me.
Bless me so I may now liberate
    this flesh and bone into a wisdom-light body.

Wisdom emanation, Mañjuśrīmitra,
    please love me.
Bless me so I may be now released
    from karma and afflictions, the ocean of suffering.

Supreme awareness, Śrīsiṃha,
    please love me.
Bless me so I may now go on
    the way of dharma, ocean of scriptures, land of jewels.

Supreme siddha, Jñanasūtra,
    please love me.
Bless me so I may now accomplish
    wish-fulfilling clouds, the common and extraordinary feats.

Great learned Vimalamitra,
    please love me.
Bless me so I may now develop
    the luminous three manifestations and the four aspects of appearances.

Great self-arising Lotus-Born,
    please love me.
Bless me so I may now pacify
    all hindrances, wrong guides, and obstacles.

Mind itself, empowerment received, Tingzin Zangpo,
    please love me.
Bless me so I may now develop
    a non-dual great luminous, timeless disposition.

Perfect two accumulations, dharma-king Tri Songdetsen,
    please love me.
Bless me so I may now attain
    the seven noble riches just like the great Tha Okchö Gyalpo.[8]

Illuminating the land of liberation, Dangma Lhungyel,
    please love me.
Bless me so I may now go
    to the ground of Buddha essence, a support for all beings.

Lord Lion, clear-light body, Jetsün Wangchuk,
    please love me.
Bless me so I may now enter
    into basic space, beginningless ground, where mistaken appearances
        self-exhaust.

Spontaneous conqueror King Zhangtön,
    please love me.
Bless me so I may now realize
    the meaning of the inseparable kāyas and wisdoms.

Treasury of excellent speech, Drupchen Khepa Nyima Bum,
    please love me.
Bless me so I may cleanse the collection of ignorance's darkness
    with the sun of wisdom.

The expounder of excellent dharma, Guru Jober
    please love me.
Bless me so I may now accomplish
    great waves of activities, which completely benefit others.

Mistaken subject, object destroyer, Trülzhik Senggé Gyappa,
    please love me.
Bless me so I may now extinguish
    all attachments, which are deluded appearances of cyclic existence.

Drupchen Melong Dorjé,
    please love me.
Bless me so I may go to
    the state of luminous reality itself—spontaneous twofold benefit.

Great awareness-holder, Kumarādza,
    please love me.

Bless me so that there is a dawning of
    supreme cloud banks of compassion, brilliant realization.

Luminous, illusory Tulku Natsok Rangdrol,
    please love me.
Bless me so I may now appear
    for the illusory universe of possibilities.

Great learned Deleg Gyatso,
    please love me.
Bless me so I may now master
    this supreme Buddha heart-mind of love and compassion.

Lord of space, Chatral Chojé,
    please love me.
Bless me so there is an increase
    of these luminous, indestructible essential teachings.

Great renunciate, Sangyé Tashi,
    please love me.
Bless me so that I now perceive
    all-accomplishing life, without essence.

Great ascetic, Guṇaśrī,
    please love me.
Bless me to now realize
    the unique orb of all phenomena of saṃsāra and nirvāṇa.

Protector of all beings, Sangyé Gyaltsen,
    please love me.
Bless me to now realize
    the actual dharmakāya, undifferentiated luminous basic space and
        awareness.

The five stanzas above are found in the manuscript of the jeweled lotus.

Vimalamitra manifestation, Sangyé Gyaltsen,
    please love me.

Bless me to now go
    to where all phenomena are even, luminous, vast openness.

Great awareness-holder, Kunga Palzang,
    please love me.
Bless me to now purify
    mistaken dualistic thoughts into the primordial sky-expanse.

Embodied victorious-one, Jetsün Ratna,
    please love me.
Bless me to now accomplish
    the perfected four appearances, wisdom-light body.

Actual three-bodies manifestation, Prajñā,
    please love me.
Bless me to now attain
    ultimate truth, the way through the base, good qualities of basic space.

Great venerable Chatral Chojé,
    please love me.
Bless me to now go to
    a pure effortless three doors dwelling.

Liberation protector, Shenpen Dorjé,
    please love me.
Bless me to be liberated
    from the abyss of the mundane six realms.

Powerful lord, Namkha Dorjé,
    please love me.
Bless me to now destroy
    all karma, afflictions, and mistaken appearances of samsaric duality.

Ösal Loyang, manifesting reality,
    please love me.
Bless me to now be liberated
    from appearing objects, dualistic tendencies.

Dzogchen master, Sönam Rinchen,
    please love me.
Bless me to now realize
    the great complete exhaustion of mind and phenomena.

Garuḍa, lord of speech,
    please love me.
Bless me to now realize
    the expanse of wisdom-mind[9] uncontrived Samantrabhadra.

Lord of compassion, Sönam Wangpo,
    please love me.
Bless me to now realize
    final supreme grace-mind.[10]

Vimalamitra emanation, Namkha Jigmé,
    please love me.
Bless me to now reveal
    the vast luminous essence of the vajra supreme vehicle.

Completely learned Longdzog Thadrel,
    please love me.
Bless me to now accomplish
    all karmas through vast reality.

The thirteen stanzas above were composed by Nyima Drakpa.

Mahāsiddha Pema Rigdzin,
    please love me.
Bless me to now arrive
    in spontaneous, luminous basic space, primordial ground.

Luminous sky Samten Khenpo,
    please love me.
Bless me to now purify
    the dark mass of the two obscurations and habitual patterns.

Great scholar Pema Namgyal,
    please love me.

Bless me to now realize
   the essential instructions of the three classes and nine expanses.

Fortunate spiritual friend Gyaltsen Tsancan,
   please love me.
Bless me now to be guided
   to that supreme continent where all beings are liberated.

Vajra-holder teacher, Gyaltsen,
   please love me.
Bless me to now inherent
   the highest reality's purpose, free of bondage and liberation.

The three stanzas above were composed by Nyitrül Rinpoché.[11]

Embodied all-victorious, Ngedön Tenzin,
   please love me.
Bless me to now realize
   profound and manifest non-dual, all-pervasive, primordial wisdom.

All-pervasive of the Buddha-families, Kunzang Shenpen,
   please love me.
Bless me to now accomplish
   the great transference–rainbow body free from dissolution or destruction.

The two slokas above were added by Ngawang Lodrö.[12]

Furthermore, I devotedly pray to the entire spiritual heirs of the victorious
   ten directions,
hearers, solitary realizers, and monastics,
   please love me.
   Extend your hand of compassion to
   me who is deeply tormented
   with oppressed, long-lasting, unbearable karma and afflictions,
Now, I sincerely pray.

Please protect and be my refuge from this
exhausting illusion-like cycle of confusion,

wandering in this existence by ignorance,
which even the Buddha thought to be an endless condition.

I pray that all infinite beings and I be liberated
from the river of suffering through
unsurpassable great wisdom,
as it is difficult to cross the boundless ocean of saṃsāra.

I pray that the habitual patterns I have long grown accustomed to,
the massive mountain of dualistic mistaken appearances,
be completely liberated by indestructible wisdom.

I pray that I now clear away
this great dense dark ignorance
and examine obstruction with rays of wisdom,
great waves of clear-light heart essence
which has no borders.

I pray that I now transcend the cause of afflictions and suffering,
from the world where no essence exists, through great effort,
and perfectly reverse the mind that grasps itself[13]
through the dharma, every day and night.

I pray that I now pacify the waves of scattered mind,
chasing after the five sense objects with the varieties of thought,
and all affiliated with the eight groups of cognitions, latent dispositions
    and the ālaya
into the basic space of reality.

I pray that I will now purify everything
that comes from the latent predispositions of the worldly mind
of the luminous realm of form, the non-conceptual formless realm,
or the afflicted conceptual mind of the desire realm.

I pray that I will now accomplish benefit for others and great waves
abiding on the path of the outer, inner, and secret supreme dharma,
even though my intention was to meditate for myself and
reverse my karma for mere peace.

I pray that I will proceed as a support without exception to
the city of liberation, fulfilling all mind's wishes and
completely purify the karma, afflictions, and predispositions
of all beings on limited and wrong paths.

I pray that you, kind one, stay forever and
usher in our own liberation from
those faulty oceans of obstructions.

I pray to be protected from afflicted mind, whose power is difficult to endure,
to rise up from the torment of existence with its many sufferings
and from fear or carelessness, conditioned phenomena, and laziness.

I pray wholeheartedly to always overcome
through definitive weariness and
definitively realize the deception of the illusionary
transitory impermanence without essence.

Through accomplishing awareness, direct perception and meditative
    stabilization
on the pleasant and quiet mountainside of the noble ones,
I pray that I reach the sky-expanse in this lifetime
for the benefit for self and other, spontaneity, and great bliss.

I pray to delight the everlasting teacher
through endeavoring in one-pointed endurance,
not wavering for an instant,
and to finish the actual accomplishment, the supreme pursuit.

I pray to not waver day and night from the state of clarity-luminescence
and the two benefits for self and other by
not breaking pledges and vows
and through actual realization of the view, meditation, practice, and result.

I pray to accomplish the rain showers of the twofold siddhis
and the four kinds of activities
through completely purifying the aspects of apparent existence through
the creation and completion stages and
protected by sky-goers and oath-protectors.

I pray to accomplish the dawning of pure appearing unbiased devotion,[14]
uninterrupted love and compassion,
the blaze of good qualities—realization of view and meditation
equally and unlimited benefit for all beings.

I pray in this lifetime to go to the buddha-field of Samantrabhadra,
blissfully and spontaneously,
through my complete devotion and
through liberating and supporting all beings without exception.

NOTES

1. The *Lama Yangtik* is one section of the *Four-fold Heart Essence* (*Snying thig ya bhzi*). The *Four-fold Heart Essence* is Longchen Rabjam's collation and commentary on two collections of scriptures by Vimalamitra (9th century) and Padmasambhava (8th century), which are the *Vima Nyingtik* (*Bi ma snying thig*) and the *Khandro Nyingtik* (*Mkha' 'gro snying thig*), respectively. Longchen Rabjam's commentary *Lama Yangtik* (*Bla ma yang thig*) and the *Khandro Yangtig* (*Mkha' 'gro yang thig*) are referred to as "child texts" to their corresponding "mother texts."

2. Klong chen pa dri med 'od zer, *Snying thig ya bzhi*.

3. "Prayers of the *Lama Yangtik*: Cloud Banks of Nectar" is located between a collection of prayers to the lineage of the *Lama Yangtik* (*Bla ma yang tig*) and mandala offerings in the first volume.

4. The text as found in the *Four-fold Heart Essence* (*snying thig ya bzhi*) is an isolated work and not part of a larger liturgical sequence.

5. For a more detailed description and overview, *see* Cape, "Anatomy of a Ḍākinī."

6. Nyoshul Khenpo, *Marvelous Garland of Rare Gems*, 82–83.

7. *lhun grub rgyal ba*.

8. *Yon tan rgyal srid mchog*—one of the *sku lnga rgyal po*. https://www.thlib .org/reference/dictionaries/tibetan-dictionary/translate.php, accessed 7 January 2023.

9. *dgongs pa*.

10. *dgongs pa*.

11. *tshig bcad gsum nyi sprul rin po ches mdzad*. Klong chen rab 'byams, "Bla ma yang tig gi gsol 'debs bdud rtsi'i sprin tshogs," 59, line 2.

12. *shlo ka gnyis ngag dbang blo gros kyis kha bskang gyis pa yin*. Klong chen rab 'byams, "Bla ma yang tig gi gsol 'debs bdud rtsi'i sprin tshog," 59, line 8.

13. *bdag gi yid*. Klong chen rab 'byams, "Bla ma yang tig gi gsol 'debs bdud rtsi'i sprin tshogs," 60, line 4.

14. *mos gus phyogs med.* Klong chen rab 'byams, "Bla ma yang tig gi gsol 'debs bdud rtsi'i sprin tshogs," 61, line 13.

TIBETAN SOURCE

Klong chen rab 'byams. "Bla ma yang tig gi gsol 'debs bdud rtsi'i sprin tshogs" [Cloud banks of nectar: Prayers of the *Lama Yangtik*]. In *Klong chen rab 'byams kyi gsung 'bum* [Collected works of Longchen Rabjam], 9:53–62. Beijing: Krung go'i bod rig pa dpe skrun khang 2009.

ADDITIONAL SOURCES

Cape, Kali. "Anatomy of a *Ḍākinī*: Female Consort Discourse in a Case of Fourteenth-Century Tibetan Buddhist Literature." *Journal of Dharma Studies* 3 (2020): 349–71.

Dudjom Rinpoché, Jikdrel Yeshe Dorje. *The Nyingma School of Tibetan Buddhism: Its Fundamentals and History.* Translated and edited by Gyurme Dorje and Matthew Kapstein. Boston: Wisdom, 1991.

Klong chen pa dri med 'od zer, *Snying thig ya bzhi* [Four branches of the heart essence]. Delhi: M. M. Offset Press, 1975. BDRC: W12827.

Nyoshul Khenpo. *A Marvelous Garland of Rare Gems: Biographies of Masters of Awareness in the Dzogchen Lineage.* Translated by Richard Barron. Junction City, CA: Padma, 2005.

Rabjam, Longchen. *The Precious Treasury of the Basic Space of Phenomena.* Translated by Richard Barron. Junction City, CA: Padma, 2001.

5

The Mighty Siddha and the Arrogant King

INTRODUCED AND TRANSLATED BY JOSHUA BRALLIER

THE EIGHTH-CENTURY Indian tantric adept Padmasambhava, famed demon tamer and progenitor of the Nyingma tradition, commands an elevated status in Buddhist traditions across the Himalayas. To many from the region, he is known as Guru Rinpoché or the Lotus-Born One, Pema Jungné, who helped establish Buddhism in their lands and continues to play a vibrant role in Tibetan Buddhist ritual, art, and literature to this day. Amid the proliferation of stories about Padmasambhava's life, two versions stand out as the most substantial, enduring, and influential: *The Copper Island Biography of Padmasambhava*, by Nyangrel Nyima Öser (1124–1192), and *The Testament of Padmasambhava*, by Orgyen Lingpa (b. 1323). These works by Nyangrel and Orgyen are watershed moments in the creation and perpetuation of Padmasambhava's lore as a demon-taming tantric master, chronicling his subjugation of the unruly deities of the Tibetan landscape as Buddhism was first established on the Tibetan plateau. They offer visions of Padmasambhava that have endured through the centuries as a key element of the Nyingma imaginaire.

Although *Copper Island* preceded *The Testament* by two centuries, the narrative arcs of the stories are substantively the same, giving us a coherent vision of the lore relating Padmasambhava's journey from India to Tibet. To recap the lead-up to the episode featured in this chapter: Padmasambhava's renown as a ferocious tantric master capable of subduing demonic forces, a *mahāsiddha*, or "great accomplished one," has spread from India all the way to the Tibetan court of Emperor Tri Songdetsen (742–797). Tri Songdetsen aspires to convert his people to Buddhism with the help of the erudite Indian monastic scholar Śāntarakṣita by building Samyé, the first Buddhist monastery in Tibet. But their efforts are continually thwarted by the autochthonous spirits of Tibet, who resist the spread of Buddhism into their land. Śāntarakṣita tells the emperor of a famed demon tamer, an Indian siddha named Padmasambhava, who might be able to help them. Tri Songdetsen then invites Padmasambhava to his empire, hoping that the tantric master can prevail where he and Śāntarakṣita have failed.

When Padmasambhava arrives at Tri Songdetsen's court, we witness a quintessential masculine showdown between the emperor and the mighty guru in which the entire plot is halted by the unwillingness of either man to be the first to submit to the other's authority. As the emperor who invited the ritual specialist to his court, Tri Songdetsen is convinced that Padmasambhava should offer the first bow; such is the expected order within the hierarchy of political power—just as Śāntarakṣita bowed to the emperor first, so too should Padmasambhava. Padmasambhava, in his own right, balks at the king's arrogance, confident that because he is a supreme tantric master, it is the king who should first bow to him in order to acknowledge the hierarchy of spiritual power.

In this scene, Padmasambhava composes a spontaneous song (*mgur*) to resolve the duel decidedly in his favor, laying claim to mastery in every conceivable social category. From king to queen, gallant youth to vibrant maiden, *geshé* to lama, astrologer to sorcerer, Padmasambhava's mastery pervades all social distinctions—including gender. Indeed, in his own estimation, Padmasambhava's power cannot be contained by any category, but spreads capaciously across all boundaries, through all spaces, and among all people. The rhythmic repetition of the song gradually progresses in a steady crescendo, as the audience is washed over by the awesomeness of the tantric adept. This whirlwind tour de force has a strong impact on the listener or reader, who by the time the song is over can harbor no doubt of Padmasambhava's status as the superior man to whom the king must bow.

Upon completing his song, Padmasambhava lifts his finger to spray fire at Tri Songdetsen—burning off his clothes!—thereby literally laying bare the king's foolish arrogance for all the court to see. In this dramatic act, Padmasambhava highlights the consequences of misapprehending the guru's might: should one err in recognizing the mastery of the guru, one will not soon forget the consequences. This collision between the siddha and the king stalls the plot of the narrative, which advances only after the tension is resolved in favor of the tantric master. Once the siddha's superiority is firmly established and his place at the apex of all hierarchies is clearly demonstrated, the famed trio of tantric adept, Buddhist king, and monastic scholar (*mkhan slob chos gsum*) can undertake the work of spreading Buddhism throughout Tibet.

A compelling aspect of this song of defiance is that it ultimately persuades one of the most beloved emperors in Tibetan history to broadcast his submission to Padmasambhava in front of his entire court. This is no mere performance, however; Tri Songdetsen's humiliation inspires within him an awe of the terrifyingly capable *siddha*, whom he then takes as his guru and offers one of his prized brides, the Lady Yeshé Tsogyal. Thus, not only is Padmasambhava the decisive victor in this masculine showdown with one of the most powerful men in Tibetan history but he is also then able to inspire devotion in a king who has recognized his superiority. This illuminates an undertheorized aspect of devotion: how it can be deployed as a tool in the enactment of gender hierarchy. To what degree can someone's devotion be achieved through intimidation? How do the politics of fear and gender figure in a devotional framework? Padmasambhava opens the door to such questions with his compelling song.

The song translated here comes from Orgyen Lingpa's magnum opus, *The Testament of Padmasambhava*. I chose to translate this version of the song over that found in Nyangrel's *Copper Island* for two reasons: (1) it is quite a bit lengthier and more stylized than the version found in its predecessor, with a more formal structure that makes for compelling reading; and (2) Erik Pema Kunsang has masterfully translated *Copper Island* into fluent, pleasing English, whereas the only extant English version of this song is found in Kenneth Douglas and Gwendolyn Bays's *Life and Liberation of Padmasambhava*, which is itself a translation of Gustave-Charles Toussaint's 1935 French translation. Thus, with my translation from the Tibetan original I hope to bring the profundity and beauty of Padmasambhava's mastery to a fresh audience.

The "I Am Great and Mighty" Song
Orgyen Lingpa

Every buddha of past, present, and future has journeyed through the womb,
Accumulating wisdom and merit over three innumerable eons.
  I am the buddha Pema Jungné, born from a lotus.
  My dharma teaches the view that swoops down from above.

Trained in the scriptural authority of the sūtras and tantras,
I elucidate each vehicle wholly and distinctly.
    I am the sacred dharma Pema Jungné.
        My dharma teaches the conduct that rises up from below.

Outwardly bearing the articles of a saffron-robed monk,
Internally, I am a yogin of the unsurpassed secret mantra.
    I am the saṅgha Pema Jungné.
        My dharma teaches the union of view and conduct.

Though my realization is loftier than the sky,
My conduct is yet finer than barley flour.
    I am the lama Pema Jungné.
        My dharma teachings benefit whoever encounters them.

In the books of phenomena and sentient beings, saṃsāra and nirvāṇa,
I explain both provisional and definitive meanings.
    I am the geshé Pema Jungné.
        My dharma teachings distinguish virtue from vice.

Cloaked with the robe of the five wisdoms,
I carry the offering bowl of the five perfect buddha bodies.
    I am the abbot Pema Jungné.
        My dharma teachings catapult people to buddhahood.

Unifying calm abiding and penetrative insight,
I sustain non-meditation, the view of the Great Perfection.
    I am the meditator Pema Jungné.
        My dharma teaches meditative insight and subsequent attainment.

In saṃsāra and nirvāṇa, the victors' maṇḍala,
There is no generation or completion stage, no rejection or acceptance.
    I am the mantrika Pema Jungné.
        My dharma teachings unify generation and completion.

On the numerology table of the world and all its variety,
I flawlessly calculate the machinations of karma.
    I am the numerologist Pema Jungné.
        My dharma teaches the three inseparable vows.

All those laid low by the sickness of the five poisons,
I cure with the medicine of the uncontaminated dharma.
    I am the physician Pema Jungné.
        My dharma is a life-restoring nectar.

On the surface of all that appears,
I form the deities' bodies of non-duality.
    I am the statue forger Pema Jungné.
        My dharma teaches the clear-light expanse.

On the sheet of mind itself, the authentic state,
I write letters without meaning.
    I am the scribe Pema Jungné.
        My dharma teaches without words.

To all those born in the four continents,
I teach clairvoyantly through omniscience of the three times.
    I am the diviner Pema Jungné.
        My dharma teachings tame anyone with whatever means necessary.

Although the five poisons and five demons arise as enemies,
They are encased within the five wisdoms.
    I am the sorcerer Pema Jungné.
        My dharma teachings neutralize the five poisons into dharma.

I do not reject sense pleasures, but take them instead as the path,
Enjoying them as the five wisdoms.
    I am the Bönpo Pema Jungné.
        My dharma teaches that bad omens augur good fortune.

I bring joy to the six classes of sentient beings,
And take the eight classes of gods and demons as my servants.
    I am the king Pema Jungné.
        My dharma teachings captivate the three realms.

I clear out the filthy pit of saṃsāra: manifold karma,
And act according to the moment.
    I am the minister Pema Jungné.
        My teachings do whatever is necessary to advance the dharma.

Deeply interested in my future lives,
I set my gaze on the Three Jewels.
  I am the queen Pema Jungné.
    My dharma teachings secure buddhahood at the moment of death.

Guarding the aspirations of the pious,
I bring joy to people in their future lives.
  I am the chief Pema Jungné.
    My dharma teachings sever confusion at its root.

Wielding the weapons of bodhicitta and compassion,
I slay the enemy—discursive thought and wrong view.
  I am the hero Pema Jungné.
    My dharma teachings avert the warfare of saṃsāra.

By entrusting the wealth of the three generosities,
I settle my fortunate children in the dharma.
  I am the old man Pema Jungné.
    My dharma teachings are a male elder's pointing-out instructions.

Leading as a protectress of the three ethics,
I traverse the path of liberation in the higher realms.
  I am the old woman Pema Jungné.
    My dharma teachings are a female elder's pointing-out instructions.

Donning the armor of the three endurances,
I vanquish the enemies of delusion and affliction.
  I am the young man Pema Jungné.
    My dharma teachings carry the four māras to the path.

Adorned with the ornaments of the three exertions,
I process as bride to every sentient being.
  I am the maiden Pema Jungné.
    My dharma teaches both the indicative and definitive meanings.

Seizing the fortress of the three concentrations,
All the world is my playground.
  I am the child Pema Jungné.
    My dharma teachings dispel the allure of fantasy.

Gazing with the eye of the three wisdoms,
I drink the breastmilk of indivisible space-awareness.
  I am the infant Pema Jungné.
    My dharma teaches meditative stabilization and cuts through fatigue.

Though impermanent beings die in the three realms,
I have attained the glorious yoga of the immortal knowledge-holder.
  I am the deathless Pema Jungné.
    My dharma teaches the invincible longevity practice.

My external form is not of the four elements,
Neither do my insides rely on flesh and blood.
  I am the unborn Pema Jungné.
    My dharma teaches the Great Seal.

My diamond body is immune to old age and decline,
And the clarity in my awakening mind endures forever.
  I am the ageless Pema Jungné.
    My dharma teachings pacify afflictions.

Youthful bodies are overcome by sickness
And their radiance is stolen by time.
  I am the healthy Pema Jungné.
    My dharma teaches the Great Perfection.

Tibetan Source

O rgyen gling pa, Gter chen. *O rgyan gu ru padma 'byung gnas kyi skyes rabs rnam par thar pa rgyas par bkod pa padma bka'i thang yig* [The testament of Padma: The unabridged life story of Padmasambhava, the guru from Orgyen]. 2nd ed. Khreng tu'u: Si khron mi rigs dpe skrun khang, 2014.

Additional Sources

Doney, Lewis. "A Richness of Detail: Sangs rgyas gling pa and the *Padma bka' thang*." *Revue d'Etudes Tibétaines*, no. 37 (December 2016): 66–97.
Hirshberg, Daniel. *Remembering the Lotus-Born: Padmasambhava in the History of Tibet's Golden Age.* Somerville, MA: Wisdom, 2016.

Pakhoutova, Elena, ed. *The Second Buddha: Master of Time*. New York: Prestel, 2018.

Shelton, Joshua Brallier. "The Siddha Who Tamed Tibet: Padmasambhava's Tantric Masculinity." In *Buddhist Masculinities*, edited by Megan Bryson and Kevin Buckelew, 103–28. New York: Columbia University Press, 2023.

Tsogyal, Yeshe. *The Life and Liberation of Padmasambhava*, translated from the French by Kenneth Douglas and Gwendolyn Bays. Emeryville: Dharma Publishing, 1978.

———. *The Lotus-Born: The Life Story of Padmasambhava*. Translated by Eric Pema Kunsang. Boudhanath: Rangjung Yeshe, 2004.

6

Yeshé Tsogyal Laments

INTRODUCED AND TRANSLATED BY JUE LIANG

A S THE FIRST and foremost female saint in Tibet, Yeshé Tso-
gyal is remembered and revered by Tibetan Buddhists across
all traditions. She is known to be one of the most important
disciples of Padmasambhava, the Indian tantric master who
is said to have converted Tibet into a land of Buddhism in the eighth
century. She studied and practiced with Padmasambhava extensively, re-
ceived all his teachings and instructions, and served as his consort. And
when the master left Tibet, she was the single disciple entrusted with
the future transmission of his teaching lineage. In later centuries, she ap-
peared in the visions and dreams of tantric practitioners, guiding them
in their practice and leading them to continuous revelations of Padma-
sambhava's teachings.

Yeshé Tsogyal is an exemplar for devoted disciples. Her life stories
record many episodes that testify to her unwavering devotion. She faced
objections from her relatives when she expressed her wish to leave home
and practice. After trying to escape from her suitors, she was caught and
savagely beaten. She endured many more hardships in her years of prac-
tice. The songs translated in this chapter are drawn from one of her ear-
liest life stories, titled *The Extensive Liberation Account of Yeshé Tsogyal*.[1]
In this life story, the narrative is interspersed with songs of devotion and
conversations between her and Padmasambhava. The five songs selected
here are sung by her at a time when she is contemplating leaving home to
practice. This is when she first expresses her deep devotion to her teacher,
Padmasambhava, although they have yet to meet in person. The songs
provide vivid, idealized examples of a disciple's devotion to her guru and
the special karmic relationship that predestines their encounter.

The songs are called *gur* (*mgur*) in Tibetan, usually translated as "songs of religious experience" or "songs of enlightenment."[2] Although the content of such songs is Buddhist, they take the form of folk songs intended to inspire and edify their audience. In the case of these songs by Yeshé Tsogyal, their style remains unembellished, their rhetorical force strengthened by occasional repetition and simple yet powerful word choice. Most lines contain seven or nine syllables, some as many as eleven, forming three, four, or five and a half trochaic feet. In my translation, I present the lines in the order in which they appear in the original so as to reproduce the formal qualities of the metrical structure and to communicate their relatively unadorned style.

These songs convey a wide range of emotions expressed by Yeshé Tsogyal. They powerfully demonstrate the complexity of emotional states associated with devotion, adding to our understanding of what it means to be faithful and highlighting the gendered ways in which devotion is expressed in a Buddhist context. In these songs, Yeshé Tsogyal laments her unfortunate destiny of being born a woman, yet she distinguishes herself by asserting her perseverance and determination. It is implicitly stated that her relatives are less than enthusiastic at the prospect of her becoming a tantric consort—her brother, for instance, dismisses her aspiration as merely "a woman's dream" and therefore inauspicious. Nonetheless, Yeshé Tsogyal is shown to gladly embrace this identity.

In the first song, faced with objections from her parents and relatives, Yeshé Tsogyal expresses her resolution to leave home and practice. By skillfully repeating the same phrase, *donmachi* (*don ma mchid*)—which can mean both "meaningless" and "empty of true existence"—and playing with its many valences, she reveals that the mundane world is of no importance and ultimately insignificant if one does not seize the precious opportunity of a human rebirth and commit oneself to practice. Devotion and dharma practice are what elevates one from meaningless struggles in the cycle of life and death. Significantly, she also claims that the female body she inhabits is ultimately of no importance and that her family's objection to her renunciation based on her gender has no ground.

The second song takes place during a visionary encounter between Yeshé Tsogyal and Padmasambhava. Here she makes the bold statement that, as her dream the previous night indicated, she is to be his future companion. This assertiveness foreshadows her famed role as a consort to Padmasambhava and is highly unusual coming from a female voice. However, readers should be aware of the mediated nature of her voice:

while the biography is narrated by Yeshé Tsogyal, the text itself is discovered and recorded by a treasure revealer (most likely male). She also beseeches the master to appear and bestow teachings on her, stressing how important he is to her: "There is no way I can be without Padma!" This song imbues a prophetic quality to their relationship and evokes devotion as an affective sense of longing.

In the next three songs, readers get the full flavor of devotion, mixed with pride, confidence, discouragement, self-doubt, and longing. In the third and fourth songs, in comparing herself with other women, Yeshé Tsogyal prides herself for being earnest, faithful, and disciplined. Although she has not learned much, she aspires to practice with great determination. These two songs present an interesting contrast with the last song in this selection, where Yeshé Tsogyal embarks on her journey to meet with Padmasambhava. Inexperienced in travel, she laments the many difficulties on the road. She repeatedly mentions the impediments that come with her female body and how her determination and devotion are constantly shadowed by her inferior birth as a woman. Shortly thereafter, a miraculous intervention comes as an answer to her dejection: a rainbow appears in the direction of Samyé, where Padmasambhava resides, and Tsogyal's hair also becomes rainbow-colored. She continues her travel without further difficulty and finally meets Padmasambhava.

Considering contemporary concerns about gender and social injustice, the ambiguity of womanhood in relationship to enlightenment may lead us to ask, Is the female body an impediment to practice? Or is it a superior vehicle? More importantly, what is the role of devotion in transforming adverse circumstances into favorable ones? The following songs present a trajectory of devotion as Yeshé Tsogyal progresses on her path. From childhood, she longs for the Buddhist path, and she firmly rejects anyone who denies her the opportunity to practice because of her gender. The path is beset with external pressures as well as internal struggles. She must overcome not only objections and challenges from others but her own self-doubt and moments of weakness, as well as her "karmic lot" as a woman in a patriarchal society, facing significant social obstacles to obtaining the freedom to practice the dharma. In the end, it is devotion that lifts her up from a treacherous journey and delivers her to her predestined teacher and partner, Padmasambhava. The rest of Yeshé Tsogyal's life story, replete with both hardship and realization, affirms unequivocally the potential for enlightenment in a female body.

Songs of Yeshé Tsogyal
Attributed to Dorjé Lingpa

Song One

Since I wish for the teaching, Yeshé Tsogyal thought, when I think about practicing, I think about it day and night. I should just do it. Then she sang the following song:

How wonderful!
To be born in a degenerate country,
a degenerate continent, life must be impossible;
yet lucky I am, born in Kharchu, Upper Tsang!
Having heard the discouraging words, still
I think about practicing;
in the region endowed with timeless snow,
where is Tsogyal's dharma lot?

I am a girl who has practiced a bit;
I aspire to virtuous deeds
and cherish the supreme teaching.
My family belongs to the insignificant Kharchu lineage,
my body is this worthless female body.[3]
With this gross body, can I practice?

Living at a time when I have to act on my own,
without a friend whose views accord with mine,
as a girl, I have thought about practicing;
if the time comes, I shall take action!

Is it auspicious to be born in this Khar lineage?
My father, Prince Kharphub, is of no importance;
my mother, Bädron, the Lady from Tsang, is insignificant;
my younger brother, Tsodrön, remains unimportant;
my older brother, Pelgyi Wangchuk, too, is not worth mentioning.[4]

My foremost action should be to understand my situation—
overjoyed am I to have obtained a human body!
This body of mine is squandered meaninglessly
when I do not put it to use.
I cannot count the virtues of practicing![5]

Song Two

All the local people said, "This girl's smiling lips are like coral; her ability
to speak [at such a young age] is marvelous!" One night, the girl had a
dream. She dreamed about the rising sun, shaped like a conch shell, and
many stars spread across the sky. The next morning, Yeshé Tsogyal said,
"How wonderful! I had a dream last night, what auspicious occasion is
it?" Her brother Pelgyi Wangchuk said, "No pure karma will come out
of you dreaming a woman's dream."[6] Tsogyal meditated day and night.
Looking at the sky over the Khar region, where she considered practicing,
she sang:

In my previous lives, I did not have a gracious lama,
but now, through my meditation, there is the Lotus-Born One![7]
Holding on to what my dream last night indicates,
will there be a time when I am held by his compassion?

Happy am I around the preacher of dharma, Padma.
I think of his words, a continuously flowing lute song.
I recall Padmasambhava, the one endowed with supreme qualities.
I long for him day and night—
there is no way I can be without Padma!

If I get to practice, I will be content.
Upon hearing his name, now is the time for recollection!
Will I behold the face of Padma, who will look after me?
If I am to be his future companion,
May I have a vision of him!

Then a rainbow appeared in the sky and landed above her head. She
beheld Orgyen [Padmasambhava], who appeared in the sky. He said: "O
daughter of noble descent! Why are you calling for me? What has hap-

pened to you so that you have no way to cope? What are you planning to
do after calling me here?"

Tsogyal said: "I thought about devoting myself to practice, so I called
out to you."

I yearn for merit when I am close to you.
This teaching is like a triumphant hero in warfare;
because of my faith in it, my mind is at ease.
Just at the sight of you, I am perfectly liberated;
because of this realization, my mind is at ease.

Having weighed the pros and cons I called out to
you, the preacher of dharma,
for I am happy to receive the transmission!
Pray bestow the teaching on me,
A girl of good lineage, starved for it;
I will be thrilled to hear it and realize wisdom.[8]

Song Three

Orgyen vanished from the sky. Tsogyal thought that she had not gotten
to hear much teaching and lamented:

Alas!
This phenomenon called the cycle of impermanence!
Due to the magnificent force of karma,
I am deprived of the teachings.
Hindered by false appearances,
I have insufficient learning.

I am happy because of my faith in the teachings.
I am determined and have great diligence,
I am truly earnest and liberated from the unbearable:
These are the things that content me.

Other women want a householder life,
abandoning this life makes me happy.
While others prefer external beauty,
I see appearances as endless illusions.

Other women fall for wrongdoings,
I, a lady from Khar, am a believer in virtue.
While others falter in their conduct,
I closely guard my discipline.

Girls from the region of Ü or Tsang
are fickle-minded and tell lies;
I only aspire to practice the teaching
that liberates me in this life, with this body![9]

Song Four

Tsogyal expressed her intention to practice because of her faith, singing:

Alas!
Despite the magnificent force of karma,
I still think about the supreme teaching.
False appearances and birth as a girl
hindered my opportunity for learning.
I aspire to practice but haven't learned to voice my devotion.

Other women pay only lip service to the teaching;
my faith springs from the center of my heart.
While others want to dress up with baubles;
I long for the truth, which is timeless
and free from any characteristics.
Is my knowledge inferior?
Nevertheless, I have great determination.

Other women talk back and forth,
but I will not be married away by my relatives.
While others have faith in appearance and adornments
but not in the teaching,
I aspire to speak no dishonesty in this life.

Will I be held with compassion by the master,
who is the ultimate place of refuge?
I only want the unadulterated teaching.
With my great determination, may I study the dharma!

I am not ashamed that I haven't studied—
how could I act with any other intention?

Other women choose lofty status,
while I cultivate the mind that sees no distinction.
Pray bless me, O forefathers of the lineage,
with the teaching and spontaneous liberation.
For the sake of all beings, may I be naturally free!
May I complete the path of liberation for the Kharchu lineage![10]

Song Five

Yeshé Tsogyal left home. After a day's journey, she was without food or drink. Moreover, she was a young girl inexperienced in travel. Although she wanted to proceed, she was unable to; although she wanted to stay, she had no provisions. Tsogyal thought, What should I do? Feeling dispirited, she lamented:

Woe is me! A royal lady from Kharchu
has neither sustenance nor a suitable occasion to travel.
Although I am not faltering,
although I have much diligence—
I have a shameful, woman's body.
Still, I want to have this teaching!

Recalling Padma, where should this girl go?
Having come with the mind to benefit beings,
I, the lady from Khar, am stranded between Ü and Tsang.
I am young and don't know anything,
discouraged like this, how do I proceed?

She burst into tears.[11]

[After another such song of lamentation,] from the direction of Samyé a rainbow appeared. All the hair on Yeshé Tsogyal's body became rainbow-colored. Wondering what was happening, she stayed there. A man came from the direction of Samyé. Approaching her, he asked: "Girl! All of your hair is rainbow-colored. Where are you heading to?"

Yeshé Tsogyal replied: "I am going to meet Padma in Samyé."

That person asked: "Will he give you blessing?"

Yeshé Tsogyal replied: "There is no blessing for women whatsoever."
Then Tsogyal gave blessing to the man with the following prayer:

You, one with good karma and righteous birth!
Just by seeing and hearing me, you will become naturally liberated.
The miraculously born Padma will accept you with compassion.
I myself will give you blessing.
You will be reborn as my attendant!

[Then Yeshé Tsogyal parted ways with this man and arrived at Samyé.]

NOTES

1. I discuss the dating of this life story in Liang, "Branching from the Lotus-Born." For English translations of some of her other life stories see Gyalwa Changchub and Namkhai Nyingpo, *Lady of the Lotus-Born*; and Drime Kunga, *Life and Visions of Yeshé Tsogyal*.
2. For an extensive study on Tibetan *gur*, see Sujata, *Tibetan Songs of Realization*.
3. The preceding two lines can also be read as "My family, the Kharchu lineage, does not really matter; / My body is this illusory female body." Here and in the following verses, Yeshé Tsogyal plays with the semantically multivalent phrase *don ma mchis*. It can mean both "insignificant" or "unimportant" and "nonexistent" or "immaterial." The former conveys Yeshé Tsogyal's humility in talking about herself and her family members, while the latter emphasizes that the objection from her family and her own inferior female body are no real obstacles to her spiritual pursuit.
4. The preceding four lines can also be read as "My father, Prince Kharphub, is empty of true existence; / My mother, Bädron, the Lady from Tsang, is illusory; / My younger brother, Tsodron, exists not in the real sense; / My older brother, Pelgyi Wangchuk, too, is nonexistent."
5. "Ye shes mtsho rgyal gyi skyes rabs rnam thar rgyas pa," 5a–6a.
6. At the time Yeshé Tsogyal was only a 13-year-old girl.
7. This line can also be read as "But now, through my meditation, a lotus is born!" Here' the phrase *padma 'byung* could refer to the name of her master, Padmasambhava (*Padma 'byung gnas*), or literally mean "a lotus is born."
8. "Ye shes mtsho rgyal gyi skyes rabs rnam thar rgyas pa," 6b–7b.
9. "Ye shes mtsho rgyal gyi skyes rabs rnam thar rgyas pa," 8a–b.
10. "Ye shes mtsho rgyal gyi skyes rabs rnam thar rgyas pa," 9a–b.
11. "Ye shes mtsho rgyal gyi skyes rabs rnam thar rgyas pa," 14b–15a.

Tibetan Sources

There are two versions of this life story of Yeshé Tsogyal. Both claim to be revealed treasure texts (*gter ma*) by Dorjé Lingpa (Rdo rje gling gis phab). The catalog information given by the Buddhist Digital Resource Center likewise ascribes this life story to the treasure revealer Dorjé Lingpa (Rdo rje gling pa, 1346–1405). The first version is a handwritten manuscript from Kham. The second is included in a sixteen-volume collection of female lives in Tibet by the Āryatāre Publishing House at Larung Buddhist Academy. The translation prepared here is based on the manuscript, with occasional emendations made in consultation with the Āryatāre edition.

Rdo rje gling pa (?). *Ye shes mtsho rgyal gyi rnam thar rgyas pa* [The extensive liberation account of Yeshé Tsogyal]. BDRC: W8LS19260.

———. "Ye shes mtsho rgyal gyi skyes rabs rnam thar rgyas pa." In *'Phags bod kyi skyes chen ma dag gi rnam par thar ba padma dkar po'i phreng ba* [A garland of white lotuses: Liberation stories of great female lives in Tibet], edited by Bla rung arya tā re'i dpe tshogs rtsom sgrig khang, 6:5–179. 16 vols. Lhasa: Bod ljongs bod yig dpe rnying dpe skrun khang, 2013–14.

Additional Sources

Drime Kunga. *The Life and Visions of Yeshé Tsogyal: The Autobiography of the Great Wisdom Queen.* Translated by Chonyi Drolma. Boulder, CO: Snow Lion, 2017.

Gyalwa Changchub and Namkhai Nyingpo. *Lady of the Lotus-Born: The Life and Enlightenment of Yeshé Tsogyal.* Translated by Padmakara Translation Committee. Boston: Shambala, 2002.

Liang, Jue. "Branching from the Lotus-Born: Padmasambhava in the Extensive Life of Ye shes mtsho rgyal." In *About Padmasambhava: Historical Narratives and Later Transformations of Guru Rinpoché,* edited by Geoffrey Samuel and Jamyang Oliphant of Rossie, 169–85. Schongau, Germany: Garuda Verlag, 2020.

Sujata, Victoria. *Tibetan Songs of Realization: Echoes from a Seventeenth-Century Scholar and Siddha in Amdo.* Leiden: Brill, 2005.

7

A Singular Devotion

INTRODUCED AND TRANSLATED BY SARAH HARDING

IN THIS VAJRA song of realization, the great master Kunga Drolchok (1507–1566) focuses on a very unusual and singular devotion (*mos gus nyag gcig*),[1] which totally rejects the superficial iterations of Tibetan Buddhist party-line devotion. It reveals the unshakeable inspiration that he took from his spiritual master Gyagom Lekpa Gyaltsen (15th to 16th century), without the least concern for appearances or prescribed attitudes. He even overtly dismisses the prime directive of guru devotion, to see the guru as the Buddha, when he states "... whether [the guru] is a buddha or sentient being." It might even seem that Kunga Drolchok had eyes for no one else; that he was so dazzled by Gyagom that he felt there were "just the two of us" in the world.

And yet Kunga Drolchok is mainly known for his unflagging, lifelong (from the age of 7!) project of collecting as many transmissions as he could from all the lineages, often receiving and giving them multiple times, with multiple masters. The result of his endeavors is the collection known as *The One Hundred and Eight Guidebooks of Jonang*.[2] Whether or not this kind of accumulation is a sign of spiritual materialism, in the case of Kunga Drolchok it was more of a portent of things to come: the vast collection projects known as the Rimé (*ris med*), or eclectic, movement of the nineteenth century in Eastern Tibet, which culminated in the massive volumes compiled by Jamgön Kongtrul and Jamyang Khyentsé Wangpo. What are we to make of this seeming irony? Is there a way to resolve this tension of opposites?

Kunga Drolchok was born in Lo Montang, the capital of Mustang in present-day Nepal. His first teacher was his uncle, the Sakya master Drungpa Choje Kunga Chokdrup, from whom he received novice ordination at the age of 10 and heard many Sakya teachings. At the age of 13, in 1519, he traveled with his brother to Ü-Tsang to study Sakya doctrine further with Kunpang Doringpa (1449–1524) and Dönyö Drubpa (a.k.a. Amoghasiddhi, dates unknown). However, a smallpox epidemic claimed the lives of most of his cohort, including his brother. In an eight-month lockdown, which Buddhists like to call a "retreat," he studied the basic treatises of epistemology. However, his teacher Amoghasiddhi came into his retreat and warned him that scholarship alone did not result in enlightenment. When Kunga Drolchok emerged, he continued his Sakya studies for another five years and then returned to Mustang. There he took full ordination and received many more transmissions from his old teacher and other visiting masters.

At the age of 27, in 1534, he again traveled to Tibet, visiting the Karma Kagyu monastery of Tsurphu, where he received the complete transmission of Kagyu teachings. During this time, he also developed a special devotion to the Shangpa Kagyu teachings, which he received largely from Gyagom Lekpa Gyaltsen (the star of Kunga Drolchok's song). He was further inspired by a visionary experience of meeting the awareness ḍākinī Niguma, the primary progenitor of the Shangpa lineage some five hundred years earlier. Indeed, Kunga Drolchok himself transmitted the Six Dharmas of Niguma more than one hundred times and is considered an important lineage holder. He served as preceptor of the Jonang hermitage at Chölung Jangtsé and received the Six-Branch Yoga of Kālacakra from his relative Lochen Rinchen Zangpo (1489–1563). He mastered that instruction, which later became a trademark teaching of the Jonang lineage.

From 1546 until his death in 1566, Kunga Drolchok occupied the seat of Jonang Monastery as the twenty-fourth lineage holder.[3] It was there that he finally organized the meditation instructions that he had assiduously accumulated over thirty-one years. Although renowned as *The One Hundred and Eight Guidebooks of Jonang*, the majority of them hail from Kadam, Sakya, Kagyu, and Shangpa lineages. This collection has been recently translated by the late, great Gyurme Dorje, who notes that "the appellation 'Jonang' in this case points more toward the setting in which the anthology was eventually composed and its later transmission through Kunga Drolchok's illustrious reincarnation Tāranātha and the later Shangpa Kagyu succession."[4] And, one might add, it points also to Tāranātha's self-declared incarnation, Jamgön Kongtrul Lodro Thayé. Kunga Drolchok's collection is now safely nestled in the final (18th) volume of Kongtrul's anthology, *The Treasury of Precious Instructions*, a work that is certainly a conscious continuation of Kunga Drolchok's big project. The vajra song presented here is in volume 12 of the same anthology.

By his own account in "An Autobiographical Record of the One Hundred and Eight Guidebooks Received,"⁵ Kunga Drolchok was inspired by the introductory narrative given by a teacher named Sangyé Pal to seek out the respective lineage holders of these guidebooks, since they emphasized an approach that nurtured guidance rather than empowerments and transmissions. He received them mostly from twenty-eight named teachers belonging to different schools. Kunga Drolchok seemed particularly concerned right from the start with recording uncorrupted, original works that drew directly from sūtra, tantra, and treatise rather than from the commentarial tradition of, as he says in the song below, "random meanings led by personal ideas." He includes himself in this critique, as seen in another passage from the autobiographical record: "The definitive topics in all the profound guidebooks that I obtained in accordance with my good fortune are without even a single adulteration of mere discussion I had with teachers that are but the excellent imaginings, analyses, or inclinations of my own appraisal."⁶ He can therefore make the claim, so often echoed by his descendants in the Rimé tradition, that "since each individual may attain perfection by means of each of these guidebooks, the essential points firmly conveying beings to the state of buddhahood are unmistaken."⁷ For this reason also, Kunga Drolchok had sincere faith in all of them.

The song of realization presented here focuses on two Kagyu lineages. Here they are named Dakpo Kagyu, in reference to the early master Gampopa Sonam Rinchen (1079–1153) from Dakpo, and Shangpa Kagyu, founded first in the Shang area of Tibet by Khyungpo Naljor (1050/990–1127). These are two independent lineages, but when Kunga Drolchok mentions the sibling relationship of their respective Indian sources, Nāropa and Niguma, we are reminded of their closeness, which has carried through to the present. However, the song quickly moves on to prioritize the latter, seemingly because of the well-preserved state of its original intent: "Sister Ḍākinī's secret words of innermost potency were uncorrupted in the *Inventory*, [sealed by] a vajra knot."

The *Inventory* (*thems yig*) refers to texts written by Khyungpo Naljor,⁸ the only Tibetan recorded to have encountered Niguma in real time. It records the teachings and correct order of Niguma's Six Dharmas, more or less in outline form, and is praised repeatedly by the lineage holders as absolutely indisputable. This is in keeping, then, with Kunga Drolchok's predilection for authentic sources and might explain why he seems here to prefer the Shangpa teachings, even hinting that some compromise in the Dakpo Kagyu teachings might have crept in, using the classic example of watered-down milk sold in the market place. I could not access an actual copy of his *Garland of Songs*, mentioned here by Kongtrul. It is possible that he praised other masters similarly. But the words and style of this song seem to express Kunga Drolchok's unique devotion to his teacher Gyagom. In another verse in this collection of Shangpa vajra songs, in the genre known as "calling the lama from afar," Kunga Drolchok calls Gyagom "the refuge that I needn't seek for elsewhere."

Not much is known about Gyagom Lekpa Gyaltsen, even though he is counted as the seventh of the "latter seven jewels" of important Shangpa lineage holders. His biography is strangely missing from the collection of Shangpa biographies,[9] which veers off after his own teacher, Namkha Gyaltsen, and continues in a different direction. Other than his birthplace in Shang and his birthdate in a Dragon Year, possibly 1484, the two-folio biography by Tāranātha describes his received teachings and lists the various disciple lineages.[10] Kongtrul fashions a "biographical supplication" based on this,[11] and the one contemporary account basically rearranges those.[12] His fame seems to rest mainly on his being the source of Kunga Drolchok's Shangpa inheritance. And yet, of the 108 guidances, Kunga Drolchok received at most 6 from Gyagom, as opposed, for instance, to 41 received from his uncle Kunga Chokdrup. Some scholars have suggested that Lochen Rinchen Zangpo was actually the most important of his many teachers.

The brief song here tells the reader more about Gyagom Lekpa Gyaltsen than the above-named sources combined. I propose that Kunga Drolchok is expressing his devotion to him as an instructive example of two things: the kind of person to whom one should have devotion and the kind of meaningful devotion to have.

The first is easily discerned: a person who is worthy of our devotion is someone who holds the uncorrupted instructions of an authentic lineage and actually brings them into their own experience in a genuine way without fanfare. That is the sense here, and in those other brief narratives, of Gyagom's designation as a "hidden yogin," practicing in seclusion far from the stage of competitive religious status. He or she simply sits inside a distant hut, glowing with the radiance of enlightenment. Here that radiance is contrasted even with Buddha Vajradhara's radiance, which merely attracts the "small-minded."

The second is slightly more delicate, and it was a little tricky not to get carried away with an overly cynical translation. But it is pretty clear: all the directives on how to view the guru and the guru's conduct, the so-called "pure view" or "sacred outlook," are irrelevant unless devotion is real. The repeated refrain "They say . . ." seems, with more than a touch of irony, to dismiss the proper rules of devotion as more or less hearsay. Not only are they irrelevant unless coming from genuine devotion but they are not even the point. It doesn't matter whether the guru is a bud-dha or not. And all the promised results of holding those notions, the guaranteed powers and so forth, also don't matter. Those prescriptions even "agitate the hearts of formless gods and demons." For Kunga Drol-chok, even a vision of the *ḍākinī* Niguma was just an illusion. But when he fully understood what it meant to "see the guru's face," he could let go of all those ideas of devotion and experience what was real. That kind of devotion seems to be something that cannot be simulated or created. Kunga Drolchok may or may not have had that kind of experience with other masters, but at least in this case he shows the way.

Poems of devotion hold an important place in the literature of Tibet. They serve to support and express the crucial role that the spiritual mas-ter plays in the Vajrayāna Buddhism of Tibet, where the guru-disciple relationship is the very key to awakening. That relationship outshines all others, and while there are plenty of ordinary love songs outside the mon-asteries and hermitages, it is in spiritual songs of devotion that devotees can experience and express the exhilaration of a sanctified emotion. In this ubiquitous poetic genre, we see certain formulae again and again— the soaring praises, the comparison to gods and saints, the attribution of standard spiritual qualities such as beneficence and omniscience, and the humble plea for refuge. It is not unusual for the supplicants in such songs to portray themselves as wretched and foolish, particularly in the genre known as "calling the lama from afar," where the disciple suffers the separation from the guru in the manner of an orphaned child. Kunga Drolchok's song contains all these elements, and yet it stands apart in its derision of those very tropes. Perhaps the biographical events that he references, such as seeing light from his guru's meditation hut and his vision of Niguma, left him with an unassailable confidence in his own experience of devotion far beyond the acceptable formulae. It is this that makes his singular devotion so believable.

A Vajra Song of Singular Devotion
Kunga Drolchok Losal Gyatso; introduction by Jamgön Kongtrul

Niguma, Ḍākinī of Timeless Awareness, nurtured him with the transmission of a very direct lineage. Glorious Kunga Drolchok Losal Gyatso De was a gentle protector and heroic adept. From his *Garland of Songs* spoken in support of Niguma's teachings, these are vajra songs that express the connection with that dharma source.[13]

Śrī vajradhara sādhu pāda prāṇamayaṃ.

At the zenith of the noble Kagyu's midnight sky,
the guru adepts are as plentiful as the stars.
The brightest sun and moon unhindered by space
must surely be Nāropa and Niguma.

The river flow of practice lineages from those siblings
fully refreshes the fortunate ones even now.
That quenching gift of curative waters
is surely the teachings of Nāropa and Niguma.

The lord protectors of those two traditions
were glorious unrivaled emanated bodies,
single crown jewels of our many realized ones
in the two Kagyu lineages of Dakpo and Shangpa.

Formerly led by Tilo and Nāro,
later preserved by Marpa and Mila,
the profound vital teaching of Nāro's Six Dharmas
produced innumerable adepts with signs of success.

These days, as in the case of [watered-down] market milk,
the words are uncertain, like the babble of a lunatic,
random meanings led by personal ideas,
that left this man's mind somewhat dissatisfied.

Sister Ḍākinī's secret words of innermost potency
were uncorrupted in the *Inventory*, [sealed by] a vajra knot.
The meaning, the true nature of reality, fell into my heart
and gladdened my lowly mind, reviving the path to liberation.

If you have a mind to follow me,
don't think your painful tension is meditation.
Don't present your accomplishments for show.
I put this carefree heartfelt advice to song.

They say the root of spiritual powers is the guru.
They say the guru is the actual Buddha.
They say one must regard the guru's acts as good.
They say beautiful things, but it's just noise.

Whether or not I attain spiritual powers,
whether [the guru] is a buddha or sentient being,
whether good or bad deeds are displayed,
I personally have not an iota of egotistical doubt.

In the upper region, in the Akaniṣṭha palace,
dharmakāya is so-called Great Vajradhara,
deep blue in an effulgence of light rays.
This draws in the small-minded—how incredible!

In the lower region, in Mokchok of Shangpu,
inside the palace of a renunciant's thatched hut,
a human form blazes with light of melting bliss:
Great Vajradhara Gyagom dwells there.

You are inseparable from the primordial ground,
temporarily clothed as a hidden one of deliberate conduct.
But don't the fortunate ones see you clearly
as a lamp shining within a vase?

My past karmic propensity was not meager:
I understood illusion's own dynamic display from youth
and I saw Mother Ḍākinī's sublime face.
But I was still unsatisfied; it was just illusion's guise.

When I first discovered the visage of Father Lekgyal,
all my mental obsessions freed up by themselves.
A single certitude devoid of doubt was born,
which has not changed since that time.

Fixation on equipoise and subsequent attainment faded,
I forgot the distinction of meditation sessions and breaks,
let go of judgment whether "this is it," or "this isn't it,"
and lost the bias of self and other, close and distant.

When the great light of all-pervading empty clarity
arose in the mirror of my intrinsic awareness,
I gained the confidence that the terms of designations,
distinctions, and analyses would show up if needed.

Lord, if you are not possessed of knowledge,
how did you make a stupid fellow like me wise?
If you are not the one endowed with blessings,
how did I show signs of liberation upon arising?

Now, even if the buddhas of the three times arrived,
I would have no further issues to resolve.
Natural thought, like a bird's path in the sky,
travels freely without leaving a trace.

Even meditation is just the guru's natural appearance.
It would be well to rest in clarity and openness,
and to experience yoga and not sporadic practice.
Whether I go high or low, you will know.

Although supplications may be melodious,
if engaged with a hesitant divided mind,
in the long run, wouldn't it just be the song
of a prostitute to seduce the clueless?

Nonsensical words that speak indirectly
agitate the hearts of formless gods and demons.
Fervently recalling the guru and calling from afar;
how could your compassion not stir from basic space?

I, the father, those who have become my children,
and spiritual siblings joined in a single intention,
have no other place of hope or reliance than you:
Lord, please prolong your life of liberation.

This teaching supports guruyoga, which perfects the path by recollecting a singular devotion, expressed here in a song. Iti.

NOTES

1. *mos gus nyag gcig.* There was no actual title to this song in Jamgön Kongtrul's collection of experiential songs, which is known for short as *The Ocean of Songs of the Shangpa* (*Shangs pa mgur mtsho*). This title, "A Singular Devotion," is taken from the colophon.
2. Kunga Drolchok, *Jo nang khrid brgya.*
3. This biographical recap is taken from Stearns, "Kunga Drolchok"; and Gyurme Dorje, introduction, xvi–xix.
4. Gyurme Dorje, introduction, xvii.
5. Kunga Drolchok, "Autobiographical Record."
6. Kunga Drolchok, "Autobiographical Record," 136.
7. Kunga Drolchok, "Autobiographical Record," 135.
8. Two short texts together are referred to as the *Inventory*: "Clarification of the Root Verses of the Six Dharmas" (*Rtsa ba chos drug gi tshig gsal*) and "Clarifying the Six Dharmas" (*Chos drug gi tshig gsal*). *Gdams ngag rin po che'i mdzod*, 11: 6–10, translated by Sarah Harding in *The Treasury of Precious Instructions: Volume 11: Shangpa Kagyu, Part I*, 13–18.
9. These are found in the Shangpa texts (*Dpal ldan shangs pa'i chos 'khor gser chos rnam lnga'i rgya gzhung*) collected by Kalu Rinpoché and take up the first volume.
10. Tāranātha, *Rgyal ba'i bstan pa rin po che spyi'i rnam bzhag las 'phros pa'i dpal ldan shangs pa'i chos skor gyi 'byung khung yid kyi mun sel.*
11. *Rje btsun kun dga' grol mchog la gsol ba 'debs pa smin grol sgra dbyangs.*
12. Rdo rje tshe dbang, *Dpal ldan shangs pa bka' brgyud kyi chos 'byung.*
13. This translation appears in *The Treasury of Precious Instructions: Essential Teachings of the Eight Practice Lineages of Tibet*, vol. 12, *Shangpa Kagyu, Part Two*, 2023. Used with the kind permission of the Tsadra Foundation.

Tibetan Source

Kun dga' grol mchog. "Mos gus nyag gcig" [Singular devotion]. In *Dpal ldan shangs pa bka' brgyud kyi do ha rdo rje'i tshig rkang and mgur dbyangs phyogs gcig tu bsgrig pa thos pa don ldan byin rlab rgya mtsho* [An ocean of blessings meaningful to hear: Collected vajra lines, dohās, and melodious songs of the glorious Shangpa Kagyu], vol. 12 of *Gdams ngag rin po che'i mdzod* [The treasury of precious instructions], compiled by Jamgön Kongtrul, 521–23. Delhi: Shechen, 1999.

Additional Sources

Gyurme Dorje. Introduction to Gyurme Dorje, *Treasury of Precious Instructions, Volume 18: Jonang,* xiii–xxviii.

———, trans. *The Treasury of Precious Instructions, Volume 18: Jonang: The One Hundred and Eight Teaching Manuals.* Boulder: Shambhala, 2021.

Harding, Sarah, trans. *The Treasury of Precious Instructions,* vols. 11–12, *Shangpa Kagyu, Parts One and Two.* Boulder: Snow Lion, 2022–23.

Jamgön Kongtrul, comp. *Gdams ngag rin po che'i mdzod* [The treasury of precious instructions]. Delhi: Shechen 1999.

———. *Rje btsun kun dga' grol mchog la gsol ba 'debs pa smin grol sgra dbyangs* [Melody of maturing and liberating: Supplication to venerable Kunga Drolchok]. In *Dpal ldan shangs pa bka' brgyud kyi ngo mtshar rin chen brgyud pa'i rnam thar la gsol ba 'debs pa u dum ba ra'i phreng ba* [Garland of udumbara flowers: Supplications to the lives of the amazing jewel lineage of the glorious Shangpa Kagyu], vol. 12 of Jamgön Kongtrul, *Gdams ngag rin po che'i mdzod,* 436–38.

Kalu Rinpoché, comp. *Dpal ldan shangs pa'i chos 'khor gser chos rnam lnga'i rgya gzhung* [Indian source texts of the five golden dharma cycles of the glorious Shangpa]. Sonada, India: Samdrup Darje Ling Monastery, n.d.

Kunga Drolchok. "An Autobiographical Record of the One Hundred and Eight Guidebooks Received." In Gyurme Dorje, *Treasury of Precious Instructions, Volume 18: Jonang,* 131–54.

———, comp. *Jo nang khrid brgya* [The one hundred and eight guidebooks of Jonang]. In Jamgön Kongtrul, *Gdams ngag rin po che'i mdzod,* 18:127–353. Translated by Gyurme Dorje in *Treasury of Precious Instructions, Volume 18: Jonang.*

Rdo rje tshe dbang. *Dpal ldan shangs pa bka 'brgyud kyi chos 'byung* [A history of the glorious Shangpa Kagyu]. Lhasa: Bod ljongs mi dmangs dpe skrun khang, 2014.

Stearns, Cyrus. "Kunga Drolchok." *The Treasury of Lives*. Accessed 15 December 2022. https://treasuryoflives.org/biographies/view/Jetsun-Kunga-Drolchok /4085.

Tāranātha. *Rgyal ba'i bstan pa rin po che spyi'i rnam bzhag las 'phros pa'i dpal ldan shangs pa'i chos skor gyi 'byung khung yid kyi mun sel* [Clearing up the darkness of mind: Sources of the dharma cycle of the glorious Shangpa Kagyu, from the general layout of the victor's precious teachings]. In *Rje-btsun Tā-ra-nā- tha'i gsun 'bum* [Tāranātha's collected works], 17:501–3. Sichuan: 'Dzamtang Dgon, [2000?].

8

The Dawn of Felicity

INTRODUCED AND TRANSLATED
BY JETSUN DELEPLANQUE

TSANG KHENCHEN JAMYANG PALDEN GYATSO (1610–1684) is generally remembered in Bhutanese and Western sources as a scholar who fled from persecution in Tibet following the rise of the Ganden Podrang government and settled in western Bhutan, where he penned the authoritative and much-celebrated biography of Bhutan's founding figure, Shabdrung Ngawang Namgyel (1594–1651).[1] The three untitled short poems translated here are taken from his autobiography, entitled *The Speech That Gradually Opens the Many Doors to the Pāramitās, Dhāraṇīs, and Samādhis*,[2] a long and difficult undated work in manuscript form comprising 458 folios in two volumes and written in highly ornate Tibetan.[3] The first volume describes Tsang Khenchen's activities in Tibet prior to the war of 1642; the second, his life in Bhutan after his exile.

Taken as a whole, Tsang Khenchen's writings reflect a life spent at the pinnacle of seventeenth-century Tibetan scholasticism. His language is complex, and his systematic expositions of Buddhist doctrine draw on an encyclopedic knowledge of Buddhist scriptures. As he states in the introduction to his autobiography, Tsang Khenchen's impetus for writing about his life is didactic in nature, drawing on an astounding wealth of Buddhist concepts in order to explain the phenomena that surrounded him. While his persistent recourse to Buddhist theory and imagery can be at times dizzying, parts of his narrative are also deeply personal and idiosyncratic, indulging his reader in the little details that often make for great storytelling. This tendency is nowhere more apparent than in his poetry, punctuating much of the text, where Tsang Khenchen offers rare insights into his own subjectivity.

The three poems selected represent key moments of transition in Tsang Khenchen's life: his ordination at the age of 13, the death of his root teacher, Khenchen Lungrik Kunga Gyatso (c. 1639), and his crossing into Bhutan after fleeing Tibet (c. 1642). In addition to their exemplification of different poetic styles, the poems address the theme of Buddhist devotion in starkly contrasting ways. From feelings of great felicity and wonder to the heaviness of unbearable grief, Tsang Khenchen masterfully draws his reader into the intimate space of his inner and subjective world. His poetry challenges any normative understandings of Buddhist devotion by bringing to light and celebrating the complexity, fallibility, and humanity of the Buddhist practitioner. Although Tsang Khenchen employs an abundance of figures of speech, his poetry never feels contrived. His use of simple imagery and metaphors make his poems deeply relatable and moving, provoking a complex range of emotions in his reader.

The first poem describes the morning of the fifteenth day of the first month of the year 1622, when Tsang Khenchen was ordained as a novice monk at the age of 13 by his root teacher Khenchen Lungrik Kunga Gyatso and given the name Jamyang Palden Gyatso. The poem is marked by feelings of great felicity and gratitude and makes use of a number of ornamentations, including simile, metonymy, personification, and alliteration. Through a description of the gradual stages of dawn and sunrise, Tsang Khenchen employs various metaphors of light to illustrate and amplify the celebratory feelings he experiences as well as to convey the gravity and consequence of ordination. His choice of sunrise as a metaphor for the dharma and later his lama's compassion captures his intense reverence and awe before the magnitude and irreversibility of the day's events.

The second poem is a supplication prayer (*gsol 'debs*) composed by Tsang Khenchen immediately after the death of his root teacher, Khenchen Lungrik Kunga Gyatso. Tsang Khenchen's autobiography describes in detail the grief that he experienced upon hearing of his master's death and says that he composed this prayer while in retreat after his lama's cremation. The author's intense feelings of grief and sorrow are palpable throughout the poem, and its poignancy is conveyed primarily through rhythm and the use of repetition.

The third and last poem closes the first volume of Tsang Khenchen's autobiography, corresponding to the moment when Tsang Khenchen, accompanied by his brother, crossed into Bhutan from the Tibetan border in 1641/42. Tsang Khenchen had to flee his home monastery in Central Tibet under the cover of night for fear of persecution at the hands of the Mongol armies that were rampaging through Tibet. He describes in detail the carnage that he witnessed on his journey south to the Bhutanese border. In introducing the poem, Tsang Khenchen says that he and his brother crossed a mountain pass, presumably soon after entering Bhutan, and sat at the top to take a rest. With a feeling of "happiness and sadness mixed together" (*dga' skyo 'dres ma'i rnam rtog*) they sang *gur* (*mgur*).

Although the third poem is stylistically less polished than the previous two, its tone is both complex and multilayered. Representing a moment of great uncertainty in his life, when Tsang Khenchen left all that he knew behind and arrived at the Bhutanese border as a refugee, the poem captures transitional feelings of sadness, promise, and finally wonder. The second stanza relates to Tsang Khenchen's concern for his students at his home monastery, whom he had to leave behind. Tsang Khenchen was deeply conflicted about having escaped his monastic seat and abandoned his students. He eventually rationalized his decision by pointing to the fact that owing to his close relationship to the king of Tsang, the fate of his students and the monastery would have been even worse had he stayed behind. The "Malaya-like forest" described by Tsang Khenchen in the poem refers to Bhutan itself; he compares the Bhutanese landscape to the sacred mountain in the Deccan, whose forests of fragrant sandal trees and cool breezes have made it a trope in Sanskrit poetics. The dragon bodhisattva about whose activity he hears is none other than Shabdrung Ngawang Namgyel, Bhutan's founder and hierarch of the Drukpa, or "Dragon," sect of Tibetan Buddhism, who would become Tsang Khenchen's patron in the newly founded state.

Tsang Khenchen's affinity with and mastery of the literary conventions of Sanskrit-influenced poetics (*snyan ngag*), including a careful attention to prosody and the conveyal of multiple and layered meanings, make his poetry especially difficult to translate. Consequently, I am deeply grateful to Nancy Lin and the other members of the Lotsawa Translation Workshop who offered invaluable suggestions and comments on my translation choices. While my English translations below unfortunately fail to capture some of the beautiful subtleties of rhythm and melody of the Tibetan original, including several playful alliterations, they nonetheless strive to maintain some of the multiple and suggestive meanings layering each poem.

Three Untitled Poems
Tsang Khenchen Jamyang Palden Gyatso

Poem One

Then, the various stages of the night passed gradually.
The first door of sunlight illuminated the world,
the smiling light of daybreak which causes lotuses to bloom emerged,
and the especially lucid light of dawn was near.

The melodious vīna voice of the singing rooster
roused me from the bed of worldly ignorance.
Just then the conch of dharma resounded;
hearing it, I awoke with swelling happiness and bliss.

The youthful one sets out for the Going Forth,
the drunken lady of the dark sky runs away and disappears.
With beautiful [saffron] robes the color of morning clouds,
the sun of felicity has arisen within me.

E ma ho!
The night of saṃsāra has now passed
and the day of the noble dharma has dawned.
The lama's sun of compassion has arisen;
today my fortune is blessed.

Born of the lineage of the sun that dispels all darkness, he is yet greater
    than the sun,
comparable to the essence-nectar of the moon, he yet cannot be
    encompassed by the moon.
Owing to the light rays of his compassion which make manifest
    existence and peace,
now I enter the great maṇḍala of the field of liberation.[4]

Poem Two

Seated atop the moon throne of bodhicitta
in the palace of the great bliss cakra at the crown of the head,

chief [deity] of all the maṇḍalas of the oceans of Victors,
emanation body of the lama I implore you,
kind root lama I implore you,
Lungrik Kunga Gyatso I implore you,
I implore you precious lama,
bless me with your immeasurable compassion.

Seated atop the lotus petals of root consonants and vowels
in the palace of the enjoyment cakra at the throat,
the vajra-dharma which is the essence of the Buddhas' speech,
enjoyment body of the lama I implore you,
kind root lama I implore you,
Lungrik Kunga Gyatso I implore you,
I implore you precious lama,
bless me with your immeasurable compassion.

Seated in the mandala of the drop essence of mind's indestructible energy
in the palace of the dharma-cakra at the heart center,
Vajradhāra, the essence of the Buddha's mind,
the dharma body of the lama I implore you,
kind root lama I implore you,
Lungrik Kunga Gyatso I implore you,
I implore you precious lama,
bless me with your immeasurable compassion.

I implore you, may your body bless mine;
I implore you, may your speech bless mine;
I implore you, may your mind bless mine;
I implore you, bless me with your body, speech and mind.

Venerable lord, your body, speech and mind
are inseparable from my body, speech and mind.
Bless me that I may manifest the dharma-body of great bliss
and benefit all beings permeating space.

Even if I become a perfectly enlightened Buddha,
there will never be another master like you.
In all my lives until I reach enlightenment,
may your compassion never leave me.[5]

Poem Three

Just then, my mind was blissful and clear.
My faith painted the Buddha, Sixteen Arhats and attendants
like rainbow-hued clouds in the sky.
I prostrated [before them] and prayed that in their assembly,
the deeds of the Buddha's teaching may flourish and spread.

Although content with any means of livelihood,
unable to forget in my meditation the heartache
of my students' [plight] alone without a teacher,
I implored the dharma protectors and Sixteen Arhats
to protect the teachings, and entered the forest.

While the flowers bloomed in the Malaya-like forest,
I, the [plaintive] peacock, heard the dragon's rolling thunder,
the enlightened activity of a faith-inspiring bodhisattva.
Looking at the clouds, I went there.

Here too the light of the precious teaching,
limitless and victorious in all ways,
is even brighter than the essence of gold.
May it completely pervade everywhere with its auspiciousness.[6]

Notes

1. For more on the life and activities of Tsang Khenchen, see Ardussi, "Gyalse Tenzin Rabgye (1638–1696); Deleplanque, "From Tibet to Bhutan"; and Maki, "Visual Transmission."
2. The full title of Tsang Khenchen's autobiography is *The Autobiography That Follows in the Footsteps and Reveres the Perfect Liberation of all Dharma Holders, Entitled The Speech That Gradually Opens the Many Doors to the Pāramitās, Dhāraṇīs, and Samādhis.*
3. Although the autobiography is undated, its composition can be roughly dated to the mid-1670s, since it was composed before the biography of Shabdrung Ngawang Namgyel. The narrative is unfinished and ends abruptly after Tsang Khenchen's return from his second trip to India. The remaining ten folios of the text are penned by one of Tsang Khenchen's close disciples, presumably Drakpa Gyatso (1646–1719), who recounts the final activities and eventual death of his teacher.
4. 'Jam dbyangs dpal ldan rgya mtsho, *Bstan pa 'dzin pa'i skyes bu thams cad*

kyi rnam par thar pa la gus shing rje su 'jug pa'i rtogs brjod pha rol tu phyin pa
dang gzungs dang ting nge 'dzin gyi sgo mang po rim par phye ba'i gtam, vol. 1,
folio 59b.

5. 'Jam dbyangs dpal ldan rgya mtsho, Bstan pa 'dzin pa'i skyes bu thams cad
kyi rnam par thar pa la gus shing rje su 'jug pa'i rtogs brjod pha rol tu phyin pa
dang gzungs dang ting nge 'dzin gyi sgo mang po rim par phye ba'i gtam, vol. 1,
folios 215a–b.

6. 'Jam dbyangs dpal ldan rgya mtsho, Bstan pa 'dzin pa'i skyes bu thams cad
kyi rnam par thar pa la gus shing rje su 'jug pa'i rtogs brjod pha rol tu phyin pa
dang gzungs dang ting nge 'dzin gyi sgo mang po rim par phye ba'i gtam, vol. 1,
folios 281a–b.

Tibetan Source

'Jam dbyangs dpal ldan rgya mtsho. Bstan pa 'dzin pa'i skyes bu thams cad kyi
rnam par thar pa la gus shing rje su 'jug pa'i rtogs brjod pha rol tu phyin pa dang
gzungs dang ting nge 'dzin gyi sgo mang po rim par phye ba'i gtam [The autobi-
ography that follows in the footsteps and reveres the perfect liberation of all
dharma holders, entitled the Speech that gradually opens the many doors to
the pāramitās, dhāraṇīs, and samādhis: Reproduced from rare manuscripts
from Skyabs khra mtshams brag dgon pa by Kunsang Tobgay]. 2 vols. Thim-
phu, 1975. BDRC: W27482.

Additional Sources

Ardussi, John. "Gyalse Tenzin Rabgye (1638–1696), Artist Ruler of 17th Century
Bhutan." In The Dragon's Gift: The Sacred Arts of Bhutan, edited by Terese
Tse Bartholomew and John Johnston, 88–99. Boston: Serindia, 2008.
Deleplanque, Jetsun. "From Tibet to Bhutan: The Life and Legacy of Tsang
Khenchen Jamyang Palden Gyatso." In Reasons and Lives in Buddhist Tra-
ditions: Tibetan and Buddhist Studies in Honor of Matthew Kapstein, edited
by Dan Arnold, Cecile Ducher, and Pierre-Julien Harter, 149–61. Boston:
Wisdom, 2019.
'Jam dbyangs dpal ldan rgya mtsho. Dpal 'brug pa rin po che ngag dbang rnam
rgyal gyi rnam thar rgyas pa chos kyi sprin chen po'i dbyangs [The song of the
great dharma cloud: The extensive biography of the glorious Drukpa incar-
nate Ngawang Namgyel]. Thimphu: Topden Tsering, 1974.
Maki, Ariana. "A Visual Transmission: Bhutanese Art and Artists from the
17th–19th Centuries." In Mandala of 21st Century Perspectives: Proceedings
of the International Conference on Tradition and Innovation in Vajrayana Bud-
dhism, edited by Dasho Karma Ura, Dorji Penjore, and Chhimi Dem, 102–
21. Thimphu: Centre for Bhutan Studies, 2017.

9

Devotion in the Face of Death

INTRODUCED AND TRANSLATED BY
DOMINIQUE TOWNSEND

WHAT CAN soothe the pain a parent feels when faced with the death of a child? Can words do anything to alleviate such a loss? Surely some words help more than others, but can some constellations of words—such as poems and songs—not merely distract but also help to heal a bereaved parent? Is there any reason to think that poetry or song might be more effective in addressing grief than other forms of literature or communication? Most importantly from a Buddhist perspective, can grief be transformed into awakening, and if so, how? In this chapter, I reflect on these questions through the example of a poem-song, or *gur* (*mgur*), that offers instructions on how to manage the grief of losing one's beloved only child. Terdak Lingpa (1646–1714), who was the visionary founder of Mindrolling Monastery, an expert poet and scholar of Buddhism, and more specifically here, an affectionate brother, wrote the verses for his younger sister Sonam Palzöm. She was a leading figure (*dpon mo*) associated with the Nyingma Ükjalung monastic community, located east of the city of Shigatsé.

Tibetan Buddhist practice provides many ritual opportunities to support and structure the chaos of grief, well beyond the condolence letter. This poem was presumably part of a larger context of ritual activity and personal communication. Terdak Lingpa begins with instructions on the practice of seeing the illusoriness of "reality" and then invites his sister to take up the more esoteric work of recognizing the nature of mind as a way to purify her pain. In literary contexts, Buddhist teachers have often used the imaginary death of a child as a metaphor for suffering more generally. In this instance, the literary trope and Sonam Palzöm's lived experience converge, the metaphor becomes actual, and the hypothetical loss of a child is the immediate reality Terdak Lingpa and his sister face. It is telling that Terdak Lingpa chose *gur* in this critical moment. In this volume's introductory interview, Jetsün Khandro Rinpoché refers to *gur* and related forms of Tibetan poetry as a "balm that soothes the mind," especially the mind of one who pays attention to the world around and notices the pervasive suffering of beings, as Terdak Lingpa and his sister seem to do. It is painful to be aware, and especially painful during experiences of loss, violence, or betrayal. But is Terdak Lingpa's aim here to provide a balm for his sister's suffering, or to snap her out of it? These might appear to be at odds, but through these few melodic verses, Terdak Lingpa encourages his sister to wake up to the reality of impermanence, here terribly exemplified through her loss, and simultaneously soothes her mind through the art of poetry.

The tone is direct and succinct, in keeping with the long-established norms of *gur*. The verses critique the mundane bad habits that shape how we respond to disappointment in general and posit the alternative of recognizing luminous emptiness. This is the nature of the mind according to the Great Perfection view, for which Terdak Lingpa's family lineage was well known. He writes: "Conceptual thought gives rise to pleasure and to pain. / Nothing exists but luminous emptiness—one's mind." Terdak Lingpa opens with standard Buddhist instructions, which might appear to some readers as stark and even cold in the context of his nephew's death. The poem changes direction when addressing the heart of the matter and offers a sharp alternative to sadness. Abruptly, Terdak Lingpa suggests that his sister "crush" her grief. He asks her to work with the particular experiences of the body, speech, and mind to transform that grief into freedom. Rooted in the commitment to the Great Perfection worldview, in this moment of dire need Terdak Lingpa instructs his sister to direct her devotion, cultivated through ongoing dharma practices, to the nature of mind.

But who can tell a grieving parent to "just abandon" the mental misery of mourning? Although it's sound advice in the abstract, *who can say such a thing* to an actual grieving parent? Considering a canonical Buddhist poem in which the loss of a child is invoked as grounds for awakening might help contextualize Terdak Lingpa's verses. The *Therīgāthā*, a collection of Pāli poem-songs attributed to the first female students of the historical Buddha, invokes this terrible scenario when Paṭācārā teaches a group of "five hundred" nuns who are all desperate with the same grief. In those verses Paṭācārā tells the nuns:

He came from there uninvited, he went from here without permission,
he came from somewhere or other, he stayed a bit.

With this, she asks, "He went the way he came, what is there to grieve
about?"
The nuns are spontaneously compelled to agree and they respond:

She pulled out the arrow that was hard for me to see,
the one that I nourished in my heart,
she expelled the grief for a son,
the grief that had overwhelmed me.[1]

The result of the advice, harsh as it seems, is freedom for the bereaved,
wondrously. It seems that these two Buddhist sources, composed in rad-
ically different times and places, agree that the pragmatism of directing
those in mourning to remember impermanence is justified, since this is
a potent moment that can lead to awakening. In their poems to grieving
mothers, both Terdak Lingpa and Paṭācārā bring all their readers (ac-
cording to Buddhism, we have all been mothers to innumerable beings,
after all) face to face with the plain, hard truth that everyone dies, our
cherished children included.

The content here is raw and wrenching. The gravity of the topic might
seem out of keeping with my concerns about literary forms. But to my
mind, the fact that Terdak Lingpa chose this particular meter to address
such painful material offers an opportunity to think about the relation-
ship between form and content in his particular poetic style and in the
composition of *gur* more generally. Although I am not able to reproduce
the meter in English, formal considerations are central to my attempt at
translation. For example, the brevity of the lines and the relative bareness
of the word choice is inseparable from the message the poem conveys, so
it is important to keep the lines short and the language simple. There are
a number of poem-songs addressed to Sonam Palzöm in Terdak Lingpa's
collected letters, and they are all in different meters. This leads me to
wonder whether some meters are better than others at conveying agony
and whether some meters are more effective at sparking new ways of
thinking about old habits and attachments. The original Tibetan poem-
song translated here is composed in eight-syllable lines with a musical
meter that shifts midway through the verses.[2] This shift might be a clue
into the melody, if this was indeed sung as a song. None of this is spec-

ified by the editor of Terdak Lingpa's collected letters, so we are left to contemplate the poem-song's intense call to devote oneself to the nature of mind in the face of devastating loss.

Advice for Sonam Palzöm, a Mother in Grief
Terdak Lingpa Gyurmé Dorjé

Conceptual thought gives rise to pleasure and to pain.
Nothing exists but luminous emptiness—one's mind.

Come what may—transformation comes without action.
Looking toward one's own true nature, it blissfully dawns.

Now that we have won these precious human bodies,
it's crucial to join experience and dharma as one.

Working endlessly, there are so many things to do.
Cast off the distraction of indiscriminate work.

While subduing foes, there are so many to subdue.
Overcome the foes of the afflictive emotions.

Harmonize with kin, although they're easy to resent.
The companions of this life are the cause of *duḥkha*.

Despite hoarding wealth, it's difficult to be content.
Now, resolve to be revolted—this is profound.

As soon as you're deceived by an object of the mind,
rely wholeheartedly on the truthful Three Jewels.

Bereft of your beloved child, your only son,
you must crush your discontented state of mind.

This is the meaning of luminous emptiness.
Rest easy in a state of nongrasping awareness.

In the six realms the bond with one's parents is so deep,
but it's useless to be biased by love and by hate.

Aware of equality and equanimity—
does self-liberation not exist in great bliss?

The true essence of mind is free from mental constraints.
With the everyday appearance of pleasure and pain—

just as the colors of the rainbow don't stain the sky,
don't grasp at the expanse, rest in the state of the sky.

Since castles of earth and stone will all come to ruin,
commit to binding the body in its primordial state.

There is scant meaning to be gleaned from idle speaking.
Instead, recite the pure *yidam* deity's mantra.

Why carry the burden of mental misery?
Through continuous nongrasping, just abandon it.

The activities of indiscriminate distraction—
transform them into the wish for virtuous karma.

The pleasures of this life only last for an instant.
Instead cultivate the pleasure that lasts forever.

The expression of words can confound the intellect—
contemplate what the teacher points out with his finger.

Value the condensed essence, not the many meanings.
Strive for the method that integrates this with your mind.[3]

Notes

1. *Poems of the First Buddhist Women*, 72–75.
2. A version of this letter is in Townsend, *Buddhist Sensibility*, 110–12. Reprinted here with permission.
3. 'Gyur med rdo rje, *Gter bdag gling pa'i zhal gdams dang chab shog*, 85–87.

Tibetan Source

'Gyur med rdo rje. *Gter bdag gling pa'i zhal gdams dang chab shog* [Terdak Lingpa's collected advice and letters]. Dehradun, India: D. G. Khochhen Tulku, 1977. BDRC: W1KG10775.

Additional Sources

Poems of the First Buddhist Women: A Translation of the Therigatha. Translated by Charles Hallisey. Cambridge, MA: Harvard University Press, 2015.

Townsend, Dominique. *A Buddhist Sensibility: Aesthetic Education at Tibet's Mindröling Monastery.* New York: Columbia University Press, 2021.

10

Wandering in the Wilderness

INTRODUCED AND TRANSLATED BY
ALISON MELNICK DYER

MINGYUR PELDRÖN (1699–1769) is known more as a religious teacher in the Nyingma and Kagyu traditions than as a poet. As the daughter of Terdak Lingpa (1646–1714) and Phuntsok Pelzöm, she was born at Mindrolling Monastery and raised to pass on the teachings and practices that her father and his generation had been cultivating for decades. In her youth she took up monastic robes and lived her life as a nun and religious teacher. The teachings she left behind are overwhelmingly instruction manuals, not songs of realization. However, while she is perhaps not known for it, her life story does depict her singing one lament at a pivotal moment in her coming of age. On that one profound occasion, involving intense sadness and fear, she transitions from disciple to teacher, child to adult.

The year was 1717, and the 18-year-old Mingyur Peldrön had left her home at Mindrolling Monastery in the dead of night, sneaking out a back window and running off with a few companions, laden with supplies for their long journey into exile in Sikkim. It was a time of political unrest in Central Tibet, and Mingyur Peldrön's family was prominent in the Nyingma religious community, whose members were at that time persecuted by some supporters of the Geluk tradition. The family had been warned that violence was imminent, and Mingyur Peldrön—as a family member and recipient of the family's religious teachings and empowerments—was seen as a precious future teacher and lineage holder. It was essential that she not be caught by the approaching army, so she fled in the dead of night.

The journey to Sikkim was arduous. Along the way, Mingyur Peldrön received news that Mindrolling had been destroyed. What's more, a brother, her uncle Lochen Dharmaśrī, and other family members had been arrested and executed in Lhasa. It was in this moment of discovery—learning of the murder of her family and the destruction of her home—that she was overcome by grief and broke into song. She sang to her father, who had passed away some years earlier. In her lament, which I have titled "The Canyon of Despair," a phrase taken from a line in the song, she prayed with earnest devotion, calling to him somewhere in the vast expanse for guidance in her time of need.

At the end of the lament, her anguish was dispelled by a reassuring vision of her father in the form of Padmasambhava accompanied by Yeshé Tsogyal, who appeared before her in the sky. This vision lightened her heart, and she was able to continue bravely on her wilderness sojourn, eventually arriving in Sikkim. There she was welcomed as a high teacher from Mindrolling and took up a vocation as a Buddhist lama. As the story goes, from the moment of her song and vision she cultivated disgust for worldly things, a theme that appears throughout her life story. With her internal resolve and renunciation, coupled with her new stature as a teacher, Mingyur Peldrön made a significant life passage as she crossed the Himalayas into new terrain.

Mingyur Peldrön's song is significant for several additional reasons. The first is quite simply that it was sung by an eminent Tibetan woman and so adds to the relatively small record of voices of historical Buddhist women. Second, it does not convey the elevated experience of realization that some "songs of experience" do but rather reflects terror, grief, and the anxieties of the unknown of one going into exile. Consumed by these human emotions and likening her loss to wandering in a frightening wilderness, she sings in anguish, calling out to her father for help. Third, "The Canyon of Despair" does the double work of conveying mundane and spiritual concerns. For her, these are the fear of bodily harm and a longing for release from the suffering of cyclic existence, known as saṃsāra. Mingyur Peldrön vacillates between her concern for her own safety and her concern for the safety of the teachings she carries, grappling along the way with her disgust with human existence. Finally, the song itself plays an important part in her larger life story. It acts as a pivot in her narrative. At the outset, she is a student of the great teachers of Mindrolling, training to assume a role in religious leadership at the monastery. At the end of her lament, she has endured tragedy and finds the resilience to carry on, becoming a mature member of Mindrolling and on her way to becoming a celebrated Buddhist teacher.

The raw emotion expressed in this eighteenth-century song is palpable and carries resonances for anyone who has experienced loss or life in exile, as many Tibetans still do. Rather than a beatific vision of a meditator transcending suffering, Mingyur Peldrön's song conveys the experience of mere mortals witnessing the destruction of the people and places they love best. "The Canyon of Despair" conveys the point that all beings, even privileged and educated women, face suffering and adversity. Moreover, it speaks simultaneously of escape from physical danger and potential release from the suffering of saṃsāra. Both are equally important to her. The song can thus be read as a human experience along the Buddhist path, uttered by a Tibetan woman in a pivotal moment on her way to spiritual realization. The terrifying wilderness represents the world of suffering, and the guidance and reassurance she seeks point to liberation.

Turning to the song itself,[1] if the reader imagines Mingyur Peldrön's situation, the "realization" therein (if there is one) may be recognizing the acute suffering of the human condition, portrayed through her own experience of abject terror. To realize that one is being pursued by murderous soldiers, like a "hunted deer" in her words, is a far cry from what one might imagine as a moment of enlightenment through meditative absorption. The distress is palpable; her mind is wholly focused on her predicament as she supplicates her deceased father with devotion. Yet, in the midst of the terror she finds renunciation and refuge.

The Canyon of Despair
Mingyur Peldrön

Namo Honored Guru!
To you—my only steadfast refuge vast—
With heart so kind atop your lotus throne,
My only father, Dharma King so high,
To you Terdak Lingpa, I pray alone!

Supposedly with compassion supreme
(Yet love without action's but a thought),
Pray you look! I wander here alone,
Mingyur Peldrön, lost and overwrought!

The king of Oḍḍiyāna's treasure fine,
Your "Secret Great Instructions" reigned most high,
Shone brilliant like the sun and moon above.
But now dark clouds obstruct them in the sky.

The living line of masters once grew strong;
Instructions wise, to these they once gave life.
Spring flowers bloomed, and likewise teachings grew.
But now they're choked as autumn's frost spreads rife.

Delightful home! Celestial garden sweet,
I gave it up—cast off like oozing rags—
To wander fearsome forest all alone,
Through the canyon of despair and its dreadful crags.

This worldly form is nothing but a lie!
No "youthful flower"—nothing but fantasy.
I've run from army and saṃsāra's grip
And yet from terror I cannot break free.

True mind—I can't embrace it on my own.
I have become just like the hunted deer
Before Lord Yama—terror's face of death.
Back bowed, I drag the weight of endless fear.

Oh Terdak Lingpa, you I beg alone:
My foes approach! Please tame them—don't you see?
Without your refuge how will I escape?
Look there, now, the army comes for me![2]

Notes

1. In Tibetan, the song has a seven-syllable (2-2-1-2) rhythm. Here it is rendered in metered verse in order to convey the rhythm in a form frequently used in poetry in English. In its original, the poem is unnamed.
2. This song can be found in 'Gyur med 'od gsal, *Rje btsun mi 'gyur dpal gyi sgron ma'i rnam thar dad pa'i gdung sel*, 44b–45b; and 'Gyur med 'od gsal, *Rje btsun mi 'gyur dpal sgron gyi gsung rnam*, 33.

Tibetan Sources

'Gyur med 'od gsal, Khyung po ras pa. *Rje btsun mi 'gyur dpal sgron gyi gsung rnam* [The collected words of Mingyur Peldrön]. Chengdu: Si khron mi rigs dpe skrun khang, 2015. TBRC: W3CN8396.

———. *Rje btsun mi 'gyur dpal gyi sgron ma'i rnam thar dad pa'i gdung sel* [The life of Mingyur Peldrön: A dispeller of distress for the faithful]. Thimphu: National Library of Bhutan, 1984.

Additional Sources

Dalton, Jacob. The *Gathering of Intentions: A History of a Tibetan Tantra*. New York: Columbia University Press, 2016.

Melnick, Alison. "Mingyur Peldrön." The Treasury of Lives. https://treasuryoflives.org/biographies/view/Mingyur-Peldron/9394.

Melnick Dyer, Alison. "Female Authority and Privileged Lives: The Hagiography of Mingyur Peldrön." *Journal of International Association of Buddhist Studies* 41 (2018): 209–34.

———. *The Tibetan Nun Mingyur Peldrön: A Woman of Power and Privilege*. Seattle: University of Washington Press, 2022.

Townsend, Dominique. *A Buddhist Sensibility: Aesthetic Education at Tibet's Mindröling Monastery*. New York: Columbia University Press, 2021.

11

Jigmé Lingpa's Wild Devotion

INTRODUCED AND TRANSLATED BY
WILLA BLYTHE BAKER

IN AN INTIMATE memoir recounting his experiences during the period between his first and second three-year retreats, the popular Nyingma author of the *Longchen Nyingtik* (*Klong chen snying thig*) cycle of teachings, Jigmé Lingpa (1729/30–1798), configures devotion not solely as formal reverence for the human but as a practice of love and yearning for the wilderness, specifically the natural landscape of the Yarlung Valley of Central Tibet. On the one hand, it could be argued that *Turning the Wheel of Diligent Practice in the Forest where Maheśvara Plays* is what it claims to be, a "testament of realization" (*rtogs brjod*) in 74 calligraphed folios, a memoir of meditative experiences and insights.[1] On the other hand, it also unfolds as an adept's travel log, the record of a pilgrimage to the practice dwellings of early Nyingma progenitors Padmasambhava, Yeshé Tsogyal, and their contemporaries—referred to as the "Lotus Born," the "Queen Ḍākinī," and the "ocean of saviors" in the song below—textured with a rich rhetoric of spontaneous sensuality celebrating an atmospheric, vegetative, and sentient wilderness.[2]

The memoir begins in 1759, when Jigmé Lingpa, 30 years old, has just emerged from his first three-year retreat at Pelri Tekchen Ling Monastery, in Chonggye, in south-central Tibet. At first, the fresh graduate teaches a small group of disciples and offers them empowerments, but he is soon overwhelmed with a wave of aversion, lamenting in the second folio, "My home country and monastery are a source of attachment, aversion, and other intolerable faults. I should abandon them like spit in the dust to wander as an itinerant into the depths of the wilderness. From today onwards, I will divest myself of expectations and needs and become a beloved child of this vast world."

Thus the stage is set for a memoir dominated by a fervent devotion not primarily to *persons* but to *place* (*gnas*). The phrase "depths of the wilderness" (*pha gzhis kyi mthil*) could equally be translated more literally as "depths of the ancestral ground." There is a contrast between the first syllable, *pha*, which implies human forebearers, and the second syllable, *zhi* (*gzhis*), which indicates the native or indigenous context in which human forebearers live. The latter term and its cognate (*gzhi*) refer to the simple uncontrived ground of being in meditation manuals of the Dzogchen and Mahāmudrā traditions, establishing a juxtaposition between the complexity of *pha* (as kin) and the simplicity of *zhi* (as ground of being). In further unpacking the juxtaposition, one of my consultants, Kelsang Lhamo of the Buddhist Digital Resource Center, described this compound as meaning "wilderness," connoting the native lands (*gzhis*) nomadically traversed but not settled by forebearers (*pha*). Hence the depths of the wilderness.

Taken as a whole "depths of the wilderness" is the first of Jigmé Lingpa's many references to a wild and sparsely inhabited landscape, one that is forbidding but nevertheless required as the context for the salvific aims of the adept. The passage above marks the cusp of many transformative encounters in this memoir between Jigmé Lingpa and the vast world itself of which he is the prodigal son, especially those places associated both with his spiritual ancestors (*pha*) and with the depth (*mthil*) of that which is wild and unaltered (*gzhi*).

In the first of many songs (*mgur*) embedded in the text between prose passages, Jigmé Lingpa underscores his intentions to eschew the conventions of human company in favor of the wild, harsh beauty of the plateau:

To the natural world,[3] where there are no attachments!
I'll tie the straps of my satchel around my waist
and disappear into the snowless rusty clay ravines,
casting my life into the great unknown.

In this passage, Jigmé Lingpa continues to unfold his rhetoric of the wild with the phrase "natural world" or "natural place" (*gnyug ma'i gnas*). While he means a wilderness here, a place free from the influence of human impact, the term echoes the meditation terminology of his tradition, in which the term *nature* implies something unfabricated, an uncontrived and wakeful quality of being. *Nature* (*gnyug ma*) is primarily joined to nouns as a descriptive (*natural*), as in *natural mind* (*gnyug ma'i sems*), meaning the innate uncontrived seminal consciousness, emerging within the practice of meditation, that is the birthright of every sentient being. Joining the term "natural" with the noun *place*, Jigmé Lingpa begins to situate the wild landscape as a mirror of what the practitioner most diligently seeks.

Having encouraged himself to foray into the natural world and also implicitly toward his own unfabricated nature, Jigmé Lingpa embarks on a fifty-kilometer trek overland with two of his students. After crossing the Tsangpo River at the boat launch of Nyagodru (*Nya mgo gru*), he finds refuge on the mountain above Samyé Monastery, where he wanders slowly around the cave complex of Chimphu, practicing meditation and composing contemplative songs. This brings us to my translation and contribution to this anthology, which is a pair of these songs found in the first half of the memoir, composed as Jigmé Lingpa sits in a cave opening high on the mountainside of Chimphu.

His two songs, titled "Leaping into the Clear Light" and "Appearances as Metaphor," are arranged in the manner of Russian dolls,[4] one song nested within the other, demonstrating Jigmé Lingpa's ability to envelop a didactic religious instruction ("Appearances as Metaphor") in the spontaneous sensuality of the natural world ("Leaping into the Clear Light"). The reader is left with the impression that the mountain vista itself is birthing the practice of Dzogchen, which then in turn mediates the insights of the auxiliary song, "Appearances as Metaphor," at the apparent end of which there is a return to an informal verse structure. This is a conclusion in which the voice of the narrator returns, along with "this mountain that seems to ridicule the sky," the mountain of Chimphu, which is a constant presence in the memoir.

A note on process: In translating the songs, I followed a process of first producing a literal rendition. My second step was to chant the songs aloud repeatedly in Tibetan and English, allowing the rhythm and syntax to inspire space on the page, reconfiguring some stanzas into a less conventional layout. Full disclosure: while translating in that second pass, I stood and moved around the room while holding the folio, chanting until my body started to find a version in English that captured my emotional connection to the material. Getting the *gur* into my body was a critical part of the translation work during the second pass. As a result of this process, the layout in the first song slid into a free-verse format, inspired by a minimally structured versification and creative use of language in the Tibetan. In the second song, I retained the metrical four-line stanza refrain structure to underscore the rhythm and repetitions of the original Tibetan.

These two songs are a study in contrast. "Leaping into the Clear Light" is written unselfconsciously in the first person and takes the mountain vista as its metaphoric base. "Appearances as Metaphor," on the other hand, is written in both the third person and the first person and takes the human as the metaphoric base. The embedding of "Appearances as Metaphor" within "Leaping into the Clear Light" gives the impression that human society is embedded in the wilderness and in the subjective view of Dzogchen, with the wilderness (and Jigmé Lingpa's subjective freedom) as the dominant context. This is underscored by the spatial placement of the human world in a liminal space between sky and earth in "Appearances as Metaphor"[5] and punctuated by the final lines of "Leaping into the Clear Light":

On top of this mountain that seems to ridicule the sky,
by the light rays of the great expanse of wisdom and love
I behave like a demoness indeed!

Jigmé Lingpa seems to situate himself as the liminal interlocutor between the human and nonhuman worlds by signing off as a demoness (gendered female!), part human and part animal, part male and part female, blurring the lines between the human and deep wilderness, between masculine and feminine.

The prose immediately preceding the songs is included in this excerpt because it vividly sets the stage, inviting us to sit on the edge of the cliff with the narrator, our stomachs newly full of barley flour and tea, surrounded by a carpet of wildflowers, shaded by a granite overhang, to "stay awhile."

Stay Awhile
Jigmé Lingpa

Then, while I was in the forest grove of the spinning svastika,[6] an old man with hair whiter than a conch arrived carrying sustenance, which he bestowed. This established an avenue for provisions to continuously arrive thereafter, for which I was grateful.

There, I made a place to stay where flowers sprang up, like a symbol of the innate ḍākinī showing herself. Above, a rock overhang provided a tranquil shelter, and I thought, "This would be a suitable place to stay awhile."

In the distance, a mountain range stretched out on the horizon like regal, white pavilions. While the wind made pilgrimage there, I sang a song of joy about the experience of leaping into the clear light [*'od gsal thod rgal kyi nyams*]:[7]

Leaping into the Clear Light

Father Lotus Born, essence of bliss transcendent,
Queen Ḍākinī, lady of the citadel,
Ocean of Saviors, master and disciples who tend awareness,
the child deep within my heart misses you.

In this seventh month of the Iron Male Dragon year,[8]
the glorious minister of Chimphu stirs
in the throat of the impious vagabond Indra-Maritsye.[9]

Here in this native consciousness,
beyond the unfolding drama of the mind's six senses,
these high snow mountains,
pillars of the sky,
rise.

Sides ringed with slate and clay,
wreathed with crimson vultures soaring,
their base a home for pheasants brooding,
where marmots frolic, pikas burrow.

These virgin slopes, untouched by human travel,[10]
welcome bees, busy in their quest for nectar.

At the apex of this wondrous place,
I dwell within
    a pale tabernacle,

Spontaneous natural cave
        tortoise shell
    stone shape.

A canopy of dark southern clouds erupts above,
a diadem of mist hovers below,
percussed with the haunting caw of crows.

Amid the spontaneous swirling rainbow colors of *tögal*,[11]
light spheres and delicate threads dance,
the timeless three bodies realized,
while atop the crystal cave of sacred Yarlung,
this place ruled by the fire god,[12]
rainbow pavilions of the five colors arc across the sky.

I think, *Surely I've arrived in Oḍḍiyāna.*

These colors, piercing my water bubble eyes,
bestow radical simplicity.

Aimless awareness wanders where it will,
while natural resting overflows abundantly,
punctuated by experiences of infinite bliss,
yet free from the caprice of joy and sorrow.

When my vajra brother said,
"I need three spontaneous homilies
in the lineage of vajra songs,"
the fresh radiance of these reflections gently unfurled
and I sang this song of appearances as metaphor.[13]

Appearances as Metaphor

Ho Ho!
Deep in vast expanse of insubstantial sky above,
crimson vultures bank their wings with confidence, showing off.
So I too soar aimless and free from distraction in this sky
of naturally free expanse of appearances and mind.

Below in verdant gardens with their fecund earth,
the leaves of aromatic shrubs and forests dance.
So I too, in order to proliferate experiences,
train the energy of awareness within the sway of thought.

In between, in the villages of humans of the desire realm,
ravishing goddesses flaunt their clothes and jewelry.
So I too, in the state of the limitless vast expanse,
wear as ornaments these impressions of appearing outer objects.

To the melody of the "Swirling Waves of Kokonor"
dancers clasp the waists of their elegant spouses.
So I too, in order to mix mind with appearances,
reside in the ocean of free resting, but am decisive.

In the courtyards of these great monasteries,
geshés engage in endless debate with refutation and proofs.
So I too rest in a state free from the eight extremes of conceptual
    elaboration,
but forge a path of awareness within the afterglow of saṃsāra and
    nirvāṇa.

On their thrones, dressed in silks, with cushions piled high
great lamas display all kinds of activity.
So I too, in order to adopt the path of interdependence,
sustain the view and meditation that discerns mind from awareness.[14]

Outside a pleasant beautifully arranged estate,
the proprietor cuts bed ropes for the servants.[15]
So I too, in a self-arranged cave,
strongly subdue proliferating objects.

In the snare of many beloved households,
matrons exert themselves in agriculture.
So I too, in the field of authentic behavior,
cultivate the intention of the innate freedom of the paths and levels.

On the turquoise maṇḍala of the highlands,
herders tend their cattle and sheep.
So I too corral these lamb herds of thought
within the enclosure of nonconceptual insight.

On this country's narrow paths and solitary places
numerous bandits try to rob people poor,

So I too let the practice of pursuing the face of appearances
plunder the eight worldly preoccupations.

In these spacious, indeterminate lands
realized yogins fend off the nomads' watchdogs.
So I too, at the portal to the vast expanse of enlightenment,
send the "dog owner" of dualistic clinging on the run.

On the threshold of prosperous households
beloved children play with objects.
So I too, in the hamlet of uncontrived naturalness,
enjoy the amusements of subjective wakeful awareness.

In saṃsāra, various entertainments appear.
In nirvāṇa, there is freedom from good and bad, acceptance and
    rejection.
The entire mind has one basis, but a hundred moods.
It plainly arises as the mirror of ignorance and awareness.

Leaping into the Clear Light (continued)

Those appearances are bound in examples.
Those very examples are joined with meanings.
If those very meanings are commented on with words,
it may irritate the mind of your average person.

But if you take it to heart, this is true speech.
If those with knowledge analyze it, they will understand.

I, this child of good lineage,
cut the subtle threads of hope and fear.
When uplifted and inspired, I take them into a song of life!

I wandered to this unpopulated place,[16] an isolated mountain cave.
My mind free within, I plant the banner of practice,
pursuing the doctrine of primordially pure exhaustion of phenomena.

First, this is awe-inspiring chatter.
Second, this is straight talk.
Third, these are words of the naturally arising enlightened intention.

On top of this mountain that seems to ridicule the sky,
by the light rays of the great expanse of wisdom and love,
I behave like a demoness indeed!

NOTES

1. Kun mkyhen 'jigs med gling pa, *Dbang chen rol pa'i nags khrod du bsgrub pa nan tan gyi 'khor lo la gzhol ba'i rtogs pa brjod pa,* hereafter cited as "Testament."

2. Padmasambhava and Yeshé Tsogyal, who lived around the eighth century CE, are revered throughout the Himalayan region as the mother and father of Tibetan Buddhism. Their images pepper temple walls and are carved in stone on pilgrimage routes, and their stories are told and retold in Tibetan literary culture. For Nyingma lineage practitioners such Jigmé Lingpa, they are particularly important, representing the origins and birth of Buddhist practice, and the promise of intimate relationship to model the transmission of the dharma. They are invoked as the main locus of attention in visualization practice, and inhabit a key role as intermediaries in the salvific transformation of devotees.

3. *gnyug ma'i gnas.*

4. Russian dolls, or *matryoshka* dolls, are a set of painted wooden dolls nested one inside the other, first crafted in nineteenth-century Russia. This is the first time I have run across this phenomenon in Tibetan song (*mgur*) literature.

5. "Appearances as Metaphor" begins by situating the civilized human world between the ethereal Dzogchen world of the sky and the terrestrial world of tangled untamed space. "Deep in vast expanse of insubstantial sky above" progresses to "below in verdant gardens with their fecund earth" and then for the rest of the song continues "in between, in the villages of humans of the desire realm."

6. A left-facing tetragammadion, a visual symbol of infinity in Himalayan religious culture.

7. The phrase "experience of leaping into the clear light" is a reference to the practice of tögal (*thod rgal*), the last of the three advanced stages of Dzogchen practice, in which a practitioner blends the inner subtle body with external appearances (leaps into the clear light), resulting in visions that become the basis for the practitioner's ongoing focus. In the song that follows, the stage of Jigmé Lingpa's tögal visions is set as the mountain's slopes, its animal life, the sounds of the birds, finally culminating with the casting of his gaze out from his cave directly into the sky, replete with clouds, mist, and sunlight.

8. September to October 1760. This date indicates that Jigmé Lingpa's time at Chimphu, prior to entering his second long retreat, extended for at least nine months.

9. "The glorious minister of Chimphu" refers to Padmasambhava, who is implicitly seated in Jigmé Lingpa's throat cakra, impelling him to sing. Indra-Maritsye appears to be an epithet for Jigmé Lingpa.

10. *gzugs can gyi skye bo'i rgyu 'grul med* (lit., "untraversed by embodied beings"). This is another reference to a wilderness untouched by human influence.

11. See note 9 above for the definition of *tögal*.

12. "Fire god" is a poetic reference to the sun. This natural phenomenon, deified as the "ruler" of the mountain, places the nonhuman in control of the space.

13. The word *appearances* (*snang ba*) surfaces often in the memoir in connection to the immediate sensual experiences unfolding on the mountain. The word also refers to a concept critical to Dzogchen, in which *snang ba* refers to all perceivable phenomena, and sometimes to the appearances of *togal*. The task of the meditator is to realize that all appearances are the miraculous display of awareness.

14. Jigmé Lingpa is referring to the Dzogchen practice of *rushen* (*ru shen*, subtle discernment), in which the practitioner conceptually discerns awakened awareness from ordinary mind. Just as lamas engage in activities while seated on their thrones, the meditator engages in the intentional "activity" of conceptual discernment while practicing the view and meditation of Dzogchen.

15. Bed ropes are ropes fashioned out of yak tails or other fibrous materials that are strung across a bedframe for sleeping. In this stanza the proprietor of the house is cutting strands to make beds for his servants, just as the meditator cuts through proliferating objects, a reference to the tendency to grasp at a focal object in Dzogchen meditation (which cultivates spacious attention, free from a focus).

16. *gnas mi med ri sul* (lit., "mountain recess without humans"). The term echoes the earlier references to places that lack human presence, such as *gzugs can gyi skye bo'i rgyu 'grul med* (lit., "untraversed by embodied beings") in the first half of "Leaping into the Clear Light."

Tibetan Source

Kun mkyhen 'jigs med gling pa. *Dbang chen rol pa'i nags khrod du bsgrub pa nan tan gyi 'khor lo la gzhol ba'i rtogs pa brjod pa* [Turning the wheel of diligent practice in the forest where Maheśvara plays]. Scanned at Buddhist Digital Resource Center, 1430 Massachusetts Ave, Cambridge, MA 02138 (unpublished).

12

The Language of Loyalty

INTRODUCED AND TRANSLATED BY RIGA SHAKYA

ĀVYA LITERATURE in both Sanskrit and Tibetan has been
viewed by historians through the framework of history as a
secular and scientific discipline with little room for discus-
sion of literary form. As Hayden White describes in *The
Practical Past*, with the transformation of history into a science in the
nineteenth century literature came to be viewed as the nefarious "other"
of history. These secularized readings are exemplified not only by earlier
European scholars, who considered the ornate style of Tibetan verse an
impediment to the historian's task of mining the text for facts, but also
by later Western, Tibetan, and PRC Marxist scholars (both Chinese and
Tibetan), who sought to reconstruct the historiography of eighteenth-
century Sino-Tibetan relations and instrumentalize their narratives for
nationalist ends. Inherent in these readings is the presupposition that
literary and historical narratives are mutually exclusive.

A common assumption made by readers of a Tibetan narrative that
mixes prose and verse, like the one translated in this chapter, is that the
verse following a prose section is a mere recapitulation of the events de-
scribed in the prose. Verse narratives have therefore been neglected by
historians, who treat them as mere literary gloss. I suggest that by reading
works such as the Tibetan nobleman Doring Tenzin Peljor's (b. 1760)
account of the Gorkha War (1788–92) as simultaneously literary and his-
torical, we may begin to dislodge the conceptual grammar of the colonial
episteme under which the academy operates. The aesthetic experience
of *rasa* (emotional relishes) in this epic verse narrative of a key period in
what we moderns term Sino-Tibetan relations challenges our contempo-
rary understandings of loyalty as inherently national. As his valorization
of a combined Tibetan and Qing victory over foreign invaders shows,
Tenzin Peljor saw no contradiction in his loyalties to multiple courts in

Lhasa and Beijing, as Qing rule was evinced through the overlapping Buddhist ethical, legal, and literary mores of governance. A renewed attention to the role of literary form in our sources might yet serve to enrich our understanding of the past.

The untitled *kāvya* narrative translated here, by Doring Tenzin Peljor, closes his account of his involvement in the Gorkha War in his autobiography, written in the early nineteenth century. Comprising thirty-two verses written in a classical metrical scheme of nine-syllable lines, this acrostic poem (*ka rtsom* or *ka bshad*) goes through the syllables of the Tibetan alphabet twice before cycling through all the consonant syllables with alternating vowel diacritics. Acrostic poems, one of the most challenging forms of verse in Daṇḍin's *Kāvyādarśa*, were historically a favorite of Tibetan literati, who sought to demonstrate their linguistic dexterity and erudition. They remain popular among Tibetan writers today. As part of an epic narrative of a tumultuous period in eighteenth-century Tibetan history, Tenzin Peljor's verse complicates our notions of devotion through the evocation of entangled loyalties to both the Ganden Podrang state and the Qing court.

The study of poetics and the five lesser sciences was instrumental to the religio-political institutions of the newly established Ganden Podrang state and the emergence of a class of literati-statesmen during the eighteenth century. During the Tibetan-Qing interface in the eighteenth century, *kāvya* was the de facto language of *belles lettres* in the Tibetan cultural sphere, with expertise in poetics becoming a marker of high culture among both religious and lay elites. Yet more than being just a status marker, *kāvya* furnished Tibetan elites with a rich conceptual grammar for configuring relationships among gods, humans, and disparate polities. The Indic literary aesthetics of *kāvya* began to inform the bureaucratic, legal, and ethical realms of the centralized government of the Dalai Lamas.

Born to the Tibetan minister and interim regent Gönpo Ngödrup Rabten (1721–1792) (better known as Doring Paṇḍita for his achievements in the five fields of worldly knowledge, the *rikné nga*), Tenzin Peljor received a thorough training in literary aesthetics from Lama Chözongpa (Bla ma chos rdzong), a teacher from the Mindrolling Monastery, the foremost center of lay elite education in Central Tibet. By 1783, Tenzin Peljor had risen to the office of *kalön*, or cabinet minister. The Gorkha War was a conflict between the Ganden Podrang, supported by the Qing empire, and the Gorkha kingdom ruler Rana Bahadur Shah

(1757–1797). The conflict arose from a trade dispute over the quality of silver coins that had been minted in Nepal for the Tibetan government since the time of the Malla kings. According to Ganden Podrang sources, the tenth Shamarpa, Mipam Chödrup Gyatso (1742–1793), leveraged his influence at the Gorkha court to instigate the conflict over unrealized claims on the inheritance of the estate of his stepbrother, the sixth Paṇchen Lama, Lobsang Palden Yeshe (1738–1780). Tenzin Peljor served as a guide (sne shan) for Qing troops and later, in 1789, as the Tibetan representative at treaty negotiations. Conflict would break out again in 1791, and during peace talks in Nyalam Gorkha troops captured Tenzin Peljor along with his fellow minister Yuthok Tashi Dondrub. After spending most of 1791 in captivity in Kathmandu, they were eventually freed by a combined Tibetan and Qing force led by the Manchu general Fu'kanggan in 1792.

Much is lost when Tibetan verse is translated into English. Among other failures, my translation does not capture the rhythmic meter of the original piece. Nor have I done justice to the nimbleness of Tenzin Peljor's diction, which articulates a complex account of the war in the constrained form of the alphabetic acrostic while maintaining integrity of prosody. I have endeavored to represent the frequent use of kennings (mngon brjod), common in kāvya, such as "land of the snows," "Viṣṇu's city," "women of the Ganges," with particular attention to numerous appellations and epithets used to address the Qing emperor—ranging from "the great king of Beijing" to "compassionate emperor" to "heavenly mandated emperor"—which demonstrate the elasticity of poetic form in capturing new forms of political relations. Following this, and reflecting the multilingual, cosmopolitan landscape of eighteenth-century Tibet, we see the use of non-Tibetan words—which I have left untranslated—such as taiji, which denotes a hereditary title, and batur, or "hero," both of which come from the Mongolian.

Doring Tenzin Peljor is known by many Tibetan scholars as a masterful literary stylist and poet. I have therefore attempted to capture some of the many different rasas, or emotional relishes, that are evoked in his verse. These include amazement, the heroic, the fearful, grief, parental affection, the violent, and devotion. Tenzin Peljor takes us from epic scenes of battle (war elephants and bloodthirsty soldiers) to the intimate (the death of his "uncle" Pasang Tsering) and the devotional (faith and respect for the Dalai Lama and the Qing emperor). The evocation of such a diverse range of emotional states in a succinct war narrative recalls scenes

of martial prowess, tragedy, and eroticism in Sanskrit classics such as the
Rāmāyaṇa and the *Mahābhārata* and shows a deep and expansive under-
standing of *kāvya* aesthetics.

Kāvya Narrative of the Gorkha War
Doring Tenzin Peljor

Gorkha soldiers clad in muslin robes,
sacked the lands of upper Tsang,
the wealth of the incomparable Tashilunpo
was plundered in a flash of conceit.

The battlefield resounded with cries of the wounded,
this unforeseen enemy was unfamiliar with the land
and soon exhausted all tea, chang, and provisions—
like fish who wandered onto a sandy bank, they turned homeward.

The six-armed protector of the tathāgatas
transformed into a pair of ordinary crows
and entreated them to follow a secret shortcut,
leading them to safety without suffering casualties.

Like sheep following the path of an endless knot,
the enemy marched vigilantly from Tsang to Ü
with their banners waving in the wind;
later in four directions they escaped to the border.

Arriving at Jayul in the holy land of Tsari,
their party was afflicted by great heat and
their march slowed as if they were the beautiful
women of the Ganges afflicted by miscarriage.

By the benevolence of the doctrine holder of the yellow hats,
we were blessed with a reincarnation wondrous as brocade embroidery,
I, who was born of the Gazhi lineage, experienced
wondrous dream prophecies that only confirmed our certainty.[1]

When the regency of the land encircled by snow mountains
fell to Kyabgön Tatsak Rinpoché,
the meat-eating, blood-drinking Chinese, Mongolian, and Gyalrong
soldiers arrived in Tibet at the behest of the lord Emperor.

Though not well versed in worldly affairs,
my late uncle was devoted to the dharma of emptiness,
his name was marvellous *taiji* Pasang Tsering
and he passed to the other realm while traveling.

Before the imperial ministers who were like support pillars,
my father, the crown of the snow lands,
was consoled by the peerless heavenly mandated Emperor
when I was captured by the enemy.

From prudently conserved stores of grain,
the compassionate Emperor bestowed a portion to
supplement the *tsampa* of the troops at Jayul
that measured forty thousand *bo*.[2]

"You were once minister by appointment of the Dalai Lama,
Paṇḍita, versed in ways of figurative language;
serve us once more," the decree came,
and even in his old age he was pure in his exertions.

Mingyur Sönam—my young son,
may you exceed your father and enjoy imperial protection
as changeless as a multi-storied pavilion that pacifies
the evil thoughts and harsh words of the unworthy.

Though I lived on a mountain peak like a grass-eating goat,
an urgent turquoise decree[3] was sent to me from
Tengyeling where they suffered as in the hot hells—
I was a vixen who had fallen into an important plot.

The Shamarpa's instigations brought forth our ruin,
deprived of food and drink our bodies began to deteriorate,
yet by meeting adversity as our friend, we were
not frightened but instead practiced mind training.

Goats, water buffalo, hog deer, mountain pigs, and
elephants among other animals were slaughtered in great numbers,
cuts of meat and cups of blood were offered to foreign gods.
We passed three worlds in a single step to arrive at Viṣṇu's city.

Sweeter than the scent of sandalwood
from the vast and pure land of Naran,
Ema! The stūpa erected by the poultry-woman[4] is immense!
Aho! I have arrived at the site of Jharung Khashor!

The Gorkha soldiers who speak the tongue of Kisa
have returned home like the cuckoo flying to Mön,
displaying Gesar-like feats of bravery they
offer their wondrous spoils to the Shamar.

Evil thoughts and deeds flowed like water down a slope
and out of the terrible ripening of black karma;
statues made of the rarest gold and silver
were torn apart like mere commodities to make jewelry.

Possessing intention as white as Mount Kailash,
endowed with the knowledge of Thönmi Sambhota,
my great father was master of these two wisdoms,
and when he passed into dharmadhātu,

the great king of Beijing made appropriate funerary offerings.
Extensive rites were carried out in the upper and lower regions,
grief that came from an intense longing
afflicted all those I saw.

The soldiers of China and the troops of the Land of Snows
were sent by commands from Tengyeling to the land of Nepal to
capture the Shamarpa who was distracted by his beloved companions
and the sensations of taste.[5]

Many of my companions had already crossed to the next realm,
I myself was but an ordinary person who
heard the roaring cries of battle and
cleared my mind in preparation for transference.

Like a wild animal I lived off grass and water,
and so we were freed like a herd of liberated lambs
from the stūpa that housed ancient relics.
This ordinary person achieved such a fortunate fate.

He he! I laughed realizing it was not a dream.
Though this Olo was afflicted with dreams of sin and defilement,
by the compassion of the Lama, embodiment of Heruka,
I was close to the stūpa blessed by Padmasambhava.[6]

From Kisa, glorious Chinese and Tibetan troops
with weapons gripped in clenched fists,
set off like Gesar's army to subdue the demons—
leaving the Gorkha king ministers bewildered.

Despite their numerous war councils,
just as the flood burst the dam,
their resistance, no matter how passionate,
gave in to suffering as they sounded the retreat.

Fine steeds and battle elephants brought
forth the worthless Gorkha king,
we must leave this place now, the sooner the better—
he cried like a maid and broke into the whining of a fox.

The soldiers of the heavenly mandated king of Beijing
encircled the upper and the lower valley
as resolutely as the gnarly roots of an oak tree—
revealing the Shamarpa as nothing but a sow-headed tantrika.

As powerless as a mouse in a flooded nest
leaving this mortal realm,
the king of foxes departed for the next life
crying out in the face of adversity.

Unable to settle on the path of peace or war,
the two enemies could not reconcile.
Eya! The triumphant cries were sounded, and
imperial officials submitted reports from the chaotic battlefield.

Like a rabbit carried away in the talons of an eagle,
or a sheep in the jaws of the wolf, the Gorkha host
fled to the furthest edges faced with the terrible power
of Solong Batur's victorious Gyalrong troops.[7]

He he! They boomed with laughter as they charged,
as if swallowing the enemy with a single gulp.
Ema! The feats of the wondrous emperor's soldiers,
fill this Olo's heart with pure devotion.

NOTES

1. The Gazhi (Ga'bzhi) family is better known by the name Doring (Rdo ring),
    after their manor house in Lhasa.
2. Tsampa, roasted barley, is a staple of the Tibetan diet. The term 'bo refers to
    a unit of measurement for grain.
3. Most likely the decree was on Tibetan paper and bound in turquoise silk
    wrapping; alternatively, it may have been a rare instance of a decree on silk,
    which had precedence during the reign of the Fifth Dalai Lama. The latter
    were, however, usually on yellow satin weave.
4. Samvarī, the poultry woman, is said to have established the Boudhanath
    Stūpa. Often referred to simply as a *bya rdzi* in Tibetan sources, her name is
    given in a terma revealed by Ngakchang Shakya Zangpo.
5. The Tengyeling Monastery, one of the three regency seats of Lhasa, was
    founded in 1762 by the sixth Demo, Ngawang Jampel Delek Gyatso, who
    was regent to the Eighth Dalai Lama. Although the Eighth Tatsak Rinpoché
    Yeshe Lobsang Tenpai Gönpo held the regency during the Gorkha War, he
    was only granted the regency seat of Kundeling Monastery in 1794, and thus
    wartime communications were conducted from Tengyeling.
6. *O lo* is an affectionate form of address in the Tsang region for a younger
    brother, boy, or young man.
7. This likely refers to soldiers of the Chuchen King of Gyalrong (chu chen
    rgyal po, d. 1776), who had been drafted into military service to the Qing
    following their defeat during the Second Jinchuan Campaign (1771–76). Re-
    ferred to as "Suo nuo mu" in Qing sources, the Chuchen King himself was
    executed by Lingchi in June 1776. I thank Palden Gyal for this reference.

TIBETAN SOURCE

Rdo ring bstan 'dzin dpal 'byor. *Rdo ring paṇḍi ta'i rnam thar* [The life of Dor-
ing Pandita]. Chengdu: Si khron mi rigs dpe skrun khang, 1987.

Additional Sources

Atwood, Christopher. "Worshiping Grace: The Language of Loyalty in Qing Mongolia." *Late Imperial China* 21.2 (2000): 86–139.

Bronner, Yigal. *Extreme Poetry: The South Asian Movement of Simultaneous Narration.* New York: Columbia University Press, 2010.

Brophy, David John. "The Junghar Mongol Legacy and the Language of Loyalty in Qing Xinjiang." *Harvard Journal of Asiatic Studies* 73.2 (2013): 231–58.

Erhard, Franz Xaver. "Genealogy, Autobiography, Memoir: The Secular Life Narrative of Doring Tenzin Penjor." In "*The Selfless Ego II: Conjuring Tibetan Lives,*" edited by F. X. Erhard and L. Galli, special issue, *Life Writing* 17.3 (2020): 327–45.

Shakya, Riga Tsegyal. "Entangled Objects: Gift, Reciprocity and the Making of the Imperial Subject in 18th Century Tibet." *Revue d'Etudes Tibétaines* 58 (April 2021): 139–64.

Sperling, Elliot. "Awe and Submission: A Tibetan Aristocrat at the Court of Qianlong." *International History Review* 20.2 (1998): 325–35.

White, Hayden. *The Practical Past.* Evanston, IL: Northwestern University Press, 2014.

13

Songs of the View

INTRODUCED AND TRANSLATED BY RACHEL H. PANG

S HABKAR TSOKDRUK RANGDRÖL (1781–1851) is one of the most celebrated composers of songs of spiritual realization, or *gur* (*mgur*), in the history of Tibetan Buddhism. He is considered to be an emanation of the eleventh-century poet-saint Milarepa. "Shabkar" means "white feet" in Tibetan. Shabkar is also known as "The Singer of Tibet," an epithet given to him by the resident deity of the sacred mountain Amnyé Machen in Amdo Province. The oral tradition of Shabkar's songs is still preserved by the *ngakpa* community of the Rebkong valley. The *ngakpa,* sometimes translated into English as "tantrists," are nonmonastic religious specialists who are often married; they can be easily identified by the long dreadlocks twisted around their heads. With just under twelve hundred entries, Shabkar's *Collected Songs* is the largest collection of songs of spiritual realization currently extant in Tibetan literature. His autobiography contains some six hundred songs that are not found in the *Collected Songs.*

Born into a religious family in the Rebkong valley of Amdo Province, on the northeastern edge of the Tibetan plateau, Shabkar trained from an early age with the local *ngakpa* community of Zhopong village. At the age of 20, he renounced worldly life and received ordination from the Geluk master Arik Geshé. Shabkar then went to train under a Nyingma master, Chögyel Ngakyi Wangpo. After mastering the Dzogchen practices, Shabkar embarked on a pilgrimage across the Tibetan plateau lasting nearly two decades. During his travels, he received empowerments, transmissions, and spiritual instructions from a variety of sectarian lineages, spent time in meditative retreat, and taught a devoted group of disciples.

Shabkar believed that he belonged to an illustrious lineage of Buddhist singers, beginning with Saraha and including Tibetan figures such as the twenty-five great siddhas (lit., "accomplished ones") of Chimphu at

Samyé, Milarepa, Longchenpa, and Kalden Gyatso, among others. In the introduction to his *Collected Songs*, Shabkar describes composing them "with an utterly pure altruistic intention of encouraging others in the dharma." The majority of his songs were sung while in meditative retreat at holy sites such as Tsonying Island, Mount Kailash, and Amnyé Machen. The audience included himself, other retreatants, and his disciples, as well as animals, deities, and nature. Shabkar's songs are often playful and humorous, especially when he is giving advice to himself and others. The songs that he sings in solitude often demonstrate his humility, as they remind him to remain true to the Buddhist teachings.

Shabkar's songs cover a great variety of topics, including letters of greeting, spiritual advice, expressions of meditative realization, praises of nature, admonishment against eating meat, and so forth. His songs are also composed in a variety of meters, ranging from three to fifteen syllables per line, with the majority comprising lines of six to nine syllables. The three songs translated here are taken from the small number (approximately 1%) of his songs that contain lines of four or five syllables. These songs are of particular interest not only because of the rarity of the meter but also because a high proportion of them are "songs of the view," aimed at directly conveying Shabkar's enlightenment experience to listeners.

In the first song, Shabkar describes his experience of enlightenment upon seeing a rainbow at Mount Tsari. In the second and third songs, composed in retreat at Tsonying Island in Qinghai Lake, he offers himself spiritual advice. In terms of enhancing our understanding of the range of emotions that exist within Buddhist devotional contexts, these songs give us a glimpse into the mental state of an awakened Buddhist master, as well as how one might try to articulate a spiritual experience that is said to be ineffable. One can also detect Shabkar's profound feeling of reverence and awe toward the awakened state itself. This helps us to appreciate the different shades of Buddhist devotion: devotion is not necessarily directed to an anthropomorphic form but can be directed toward a state of mind as well.

The theme of devotion permeates these poems in both explicit and implicit ways. In terms of explicit references, the second and third poems, for example, begin with homages to the guru in Sanskrit language: "Namo Guru." Paying homage to spiritual teachers at the beginning of a song—*guru* in Sanskrit, *lama* in Tibetan—is a standard feature of the *gur* genre. The second song also specifies the spiritual teacher, or lama, as the object of one's reliance on the spiritual path. The third song asks for the lama's blessing from the very beginning. Together, these explicit references make clear that the lama is an essential guide on the spiritual path to awakening. Still, devotion figures in these poems in implicit ways as well. For instance, the aesthetic pleasure generated by these profound, pithy, exquisite songs of the view may serve to enhance the audience's level of devotion to Buddhism and to yogic adepts like Shabkar. Shabkar's virtuosic ability to pack deep Buddhist insights into three, four, or five syllables per line makes the experience of reading these poems both delightful and awe-inspiring; it is difficult not to feel devotion toward awakening and Shabkar himself upon reading them.

While the language of these songs may seem simple on the surface, the meaning contained within them is profound. It has been a challenge to render them into English in a way that does true justice to their beauty, simplicity, and profundity in classical Tibetan peppered with colloquialisms. Not only is the spiritual experience conveyed within these songs difficult to put into words but the language is stripped down to its basics. There are very few grammatical particles. Hence, the literary form that gives these poems a disarming pithiness also contributes to a great degree of interpretative ambiguity for the translator. Working collaboratively with Lama Jabb and the other members of my translation group at the Lotsawa Translation Workshop, as well as the venerable Lama Tashi Döndrup, I have tried my best to preserve the songs' meaning and simple elegance, while adding as few English insertions as possible. Finally, the original Tibetan songs do not have titles. For the purposes of this edited volume, I have given each one a title based on a representative line that best captures the particular song's essential message.

The Five-Colored Rainbow
Shabkar Tsokdruk Rangdröl

the five-colored rainbow,
and the sky, empty and luminous,
are within the vast expanse

in terms of emptiness,
they dwell as one taste,

but in terms of appearance,
they arise as many—

a marvelous spectacle!

seeing this itself,
it is certain that cause, effect, and interdependence
are infallible—
that, I understand

the phenomena of saṃsāra and nirvāṇa,
and the mind itself, empty and luminous,
are within the vast expanse

in terms of emptiness,
they dwell as one taste,
but in terms of appearance,
they arise as many—

a marvelous spectacle!

seeing this itself,
all obstacles—eternalism, nihilism and so forth—
are liberated without remainder
in the expanse of the dharmadhātu

all spiritual instructions—
such as those that dispel obstacles and enhance practice—
just take a rest
for awhile

give this song to people
who appreciate good melodies;
they will say, "it's beautiful"
and make it widely renowned

*One day, having seen a rainbow arise, the renunciant Tsokdruk Rangdröl
said this at the solitary place of Tsari.*[1]

"Think I need this?" Keep this in mind!
Shabkar Tsokdruk Rangdröl

Namo Guru
Tsokdruk Rangdröl:

> need something to rely on
> rely on the lama
>
> need something to abandon
> abandon bad friends
>
> need something to renounce
> renounce this life
>
> need something to take
> take retreat provisions
>
> need somewhere to go
> go to a solitary place
>
> need somewhere to stay
> stay on the mat
>
> need something vast
> take a vast view
>
> need something narrow
> apply narrow conduct
>
> need something great
> adopt great qualities
>
> need something small
> have small negative emotions
>
> need something to accomplish
> accomplish for one's own benefit

need something to do
do for the sake of others

If you think "I need this,"
Keep this in mind—ya!²

A Beneficial Song
Shabkar Tsokdruk Rangdröl

Namo Guru Bhya
Lama, grant your blessings!
hey, Tsokdruk Rangdröl,
sing a beneficial song!

know all that appears and exists as mind;
realize the mind itself as empty.
realization is not one-sided:
this is the ultimate view.

foster non-distraction;
dwell in a state that is uncontrived.
to hold something in mind without being fixated on it:
this is the ultimate meditation.

incorporate the disagreeable as part of the path;
sever attachment to that which is agreeable.
to not adopt, reject, negate, or affirm:
this is the ultimate conduct.

know that whatever appears is not ultimately real;
there's no good or bad, abandoning or adopting.
to let things arise naturally without a care:
this is the ultimate form of removing obstacles.

appearances hazy,
delusions unsteady,
when clinging subsides:
these are the ultimate signs of proficiency.

karma, afflictions, and ignorance cleared away,
the dharmakāya is realized naturally.
the rūpakāya acts for the benefit of others:
this is the ultimate fruit.

I, the singer, having also sung
this song, am off to a solitary place.
may this song benefit
the minds of whoever hears it![3]

Notes

1. Zhabs dkar tshogs drug rang grol, "Lnga ldan gyi 'ja' tshon."
2. Zhabs dkar tshogs drug rang grol, "Na mo gu ru."
3. Zhabs dkar tshogs drug rang grol, "Na mo gu ru bhya."

Tibetan Sources

Zhabs dkar tshogs drug rang grol. "Lnga ldan gyi 'ja' tshon" [The five-colored
   rainbow]. In *Bya btang tshogs drug rang grol gyis phyogs med ri khrod 'grims
   pa'i tshe rang gzhan chos la bskul phyir glu dbyangs dga' ston 'gyed pa rnams kyi
   bar cha* [Feast of melodious songs [by] the renunciant Tsokdruk Rangdröl to
   encourage self and others in the dharma while wandering without direction
   through the mountains, middle volume], vol. 4 of *Zhabs dkar tshogs drug
   rang grol kyi bka' 'bum* [The collected works of Shabkar Tsokdruk Rangdröl],
   594–95. 14 vols. New Delhi: Shechen, 2003.
———. "Na mo gu ru" ["Think I need this?" Keep this in mind!]. In *Bya btang
   tshogs drug rang grol gyis phyogs med ri khrod 'grims pa'i tshe rang gzhan chos
   la bskul phyir glu dbyangs dga' ston 'gyed pa rnams kyi stod cha* [Feast of me-
   lodious songs [by] the renunciant Tsokdruk Rangdröl to encourage self and
   others in the dharma while wandering without direction through the moun-
   tains, initial volume], vol. 3 of *Zhabs dkar tshogs drug rang grol kyi bka' 'bum*
   [The collected works of Shabkar Tsokdruk Rangdröl], 382–83. 14 vols. New
   Delhi: Shechen, 2003.
———. "Na mo gu ru bhya" [A beneficial song]. In *Bya btang tshogs drug rang
   grol gyis phyogs med ri khrod 'grims pa'i tshe rang gzhan chos la bskul phyir
   glu dbyangs dga' ston 'gyed pa rnams kyi stod cha* [Feast of melodious songs
   [by] the renunciant Tsokdruk Rangdröl to encourage self and others in the
   dharma while wandering without direction through the mountains, initial
   volume], vol. 3 of *Zhabs dkar tshogs drug rang grol kyi bka' 'bum* [The collected

works of Shabkar Tsokdruk Rangdröl], 383. 14 vols. New Delhi: Shechen, 2003.

ADDITIONAL SOURCES

Chang, Garma C. C., trans. *The Hundred Thousand Songs of Milarepa.* New York: Oriental Studies Foundation, 1962.

Dowman, Keith. *The Flight of the Garuda: The Dzogchen Tradition of Tibetan Buddhism.* Boston: Wisdom, 1994.

Jackson, Roger R. "'Poetry' in Tibet: Glu, mGur, sNyan ngag and 'Songs of Experience.'" In *Tibetan Literature: Studies in Genre,* edited by José Ignacio Cabezón and Roger R. Jackson, 368–92. Ithaca, NY: Snow Lion, 1996.

Pang, Rachel. "Songs against Meat by Shabkar." In *The Faults of Meat: Tibetan Buddhist Writings on Vegetarianism,* edited by Geoffrey Barstow, 211–21. Boston: Wisdom, 2019.

Shabkar Tsokdruk Rangdröl. *The Life of Shabkar: The Autobiography of a Tibetan Yogin.* Edited by Constance Wilkinson and Michal Abrams. Translated by Matthieu Ricard, Jakob Leschly, Erik Schmidt, Marilyn Silverstone, and Lodrö Palmo. Ithaca, NY: Snow Lion, 2001.

———. *Rainbows Appear: Tibetan Poems of Shabkar.* Edited by Matthieu Ricard. Boston: Shambhala, 2002.

Sujata, Victoria. *Journey to Distant Groves: Profound Songs of the Tibetan Siddha Kalden Gyatso.* Kathmandu: Vajra Books, 2019.

———. *Songs of Shabkar: The Path of the Tibetan Yogi Inspired by Nature.* Cazadero, CA: Dharma, 2012.

14

The Emissary of Renunciation

INTRODUCED AND TRANSLATED BY ORIANE LAVOLÉ

REMORSE AND weariness with the trappings of saṃsāra form the emotional fodder for the yearning for the exalted state of the guru. By juxtaposing the pitfalls of misguided dharma practice and the methods of the path to liberation in the song translated in this chapter, Jamyang Khyentsé Wangpo (1820–1892), an eminent Buddhist master and scholar from Degé, Eastern Tibet (Khams), highlights the gap that may be felt between ordinary practitioners and their enlightened gurus—a distance that creates longing akin to yearning for an absent lover. Nevertheless, although the practitioner successively lays bare all their imperfections verse by verse in this song, the repeated reminder of a connection with the guru kindles hope. The heartfelt confession of faults serves to enact the practitioner's surrender to the guru, a surrender that is born from renunciation and results in the devotion that will finally reunite them with the ultimate guru: the nature of mind. In this way, Khyentsé Wangpo's underlying tantric perspective is elicited by the affect of guru devotion that runs throughout this call for renunciation, written in the form of a guru supplication. Thus, in a style reminiscent of the famous genre of "calling the lama from afar" (*bla ma rgyang 'bod*) supplications, Khyentsé Wangpo's song serves both as a confession of the practitioner's faults and as a prayer to the guru for support in overcoming those faults.

"The Emissary of Renunciation: A Spontaneous Vajra Song of Recollection of the Glorious Guru and Universal Lord" (*Khyab bdag dpal ldan bla ma rjes su dran pa'i rdo rje'i thol glu nges 'byung gi pho nya zhes bya ba*) is extracted from Khyentsé Wangpo's collected poetic writings. At an early age, Khyentsé Wangpo was recognized as a reincarnation of the Sakya master Tartsé Khenchen Jampa Namkha Chimé, and he later also came to be seen as the mind incarnation of the famous Nyingma treasure revealer Jigmé Lingpa (1729/30–1798).[1] Khyentsé Wangpo was a prolific scholar who notably contributed to the ecumenical collections of scripture known as the *Five Treasuries* (*Mdzod lnga*), which were put together by his close associate Jamgön Kongtrül Lodrö Tayé (1813–1899). Khyentsé Wangpo was also a prophesied treasure revealer and worked closely with another revealer, Chokgyur Dechen Lingpa (1829–1870), to reveal and decode many of the teachings contained within the *Chokling Tersar* (*Mchog gling gter gsar*), or *New Treasures of Chokgyur Lingpa*. In this way, though originally educated in the Sakya tradition, Khyentsé Wangpo embodied the ecumenical ideal of *rimé*, or nonsectarianism,[2] collaborating so closely with the Kagyu master Jamgön Kongtrül and the Nyingma master Chokgyur Lingpa that the three were known under one epithet as the Khyen-Kong-Chok triumvirate. Khyentsé Wangpo's activities and writings were thus in large part an expression of a nonsectarian ideal they saw as underlying all of Tibetan Buddhism, which embraces all practices—from the Foundational Vehicles of the Listeners and Solitary Realizers,[3] through the Mahāyāna Great Vehicle, up to the Tantric Vehicle of Vajrayāna—as progressive stages of one comprehensive path.[4]

The short song included below is drawn from a collection of mystical songs and poetry entitled *Feast for the Ears of the Fortunate: A Garland of Spontaneous Vajra Songs* (*Gang shar rdo rje'i glu phreng skal bzang rna ba'i dga' ston*). This collection includes a variety of texts that Khyentsé Wangpo composed throughout his lifetime in many different genres, from practice texts and supplications to songs of realization. There is little information about the compilation of this anthology, which carries no colophon, although many of the individual entries have one. The very absence of a colophon for the collection might be an indicator that it was compiled by Khyentsé Wangpo himself, since it is likely that anyone else would have included editorial information marking the importance of the creation of such a collection. Likewise, though some of the texts in the collection are dated, not all of them are, and "The Emissary of Renunciation" belongs to the latter category. The song's own colophon indicates that it was composed in Lion Sky Fortress (Sengé Namkha Dzong), a sacred site in Khyentsé Wangpo's home province of Degé.

"The Emissary of Renunciation: A Spontaneous Vajra Song of Recollection of the Glorious Guru and Universal Lord" is a compelling example of Khyentsé Wangpo's skill in articulating all stages of practice of the successive vehicles as part of a coherent Tibetan Buddhist tradition that gradually guides the practitioner toward the ultimate view of the

highest vehicle. The title of the piece itself announces a skillful juxta-
position of the seemingly basic theme of renunciation to the markedly
tantric sentiment of guru devotion. The author then sets the tone for
the song by opening with devotional verses of homage replete with tech-
nical language and references that relate to the highest teachings in the
Nyingma tradition, namely, the vehicles of Anuyoga and Atiyoga, which
is also referred to as the "Great Perfection," or Dzogchen. Following this
esoteric homage, Khyentsé Wangpo introduces the main subject matter
by expressing the fundamental Buddhist yearning for renunciation, first
from the approach of the Foundational Vehicle, then from that of the
Great Vehicle, and finally from that of the tantric practices of develop-
ment and completion, culminating once again in the Great Perfection. By
both opening and closing his piece with the highest view in the Tibetan
tradition, Khyentsé Wangpo intimates that he has never deviated from it,
even throughout his exhortations to more basic levels of practice.

These complex dynamics of meaning and sentiment are elicited
throughout the song by the author's use of evocative imagery and lan-
guage. Khyentsé Wangpo expresses his yearning for liberation in a tone
that is alternately harsh and inspirational, gradually pushing readers
away from their lower views and alluring them to an increasingly ele-
vated one. His use of poetic language and devices triggers a wide range of
emotions that both form part of renunciation and build up to the emo-
tional release of devotion: the practitioner's surrender to their guru in the
face of difficulties. One notable example of this progression is Khyentsé
Wangpo's use of the image of playful deer in the beginning and at the
end of the text. In the first verse following the homage, the author uses
the image of the deer scathingly, as an analogy for the futility of people's
actions in these degenerate times. Later in the text, the same young deer
are referred to in a more affectionate tone, as he describes himself as their
"weary friend," expressing a detachment from the world that no longer
seems to be motivated by disgust. In this way, the author smoothly guides
the reader toward a vaster and gentler understanding of renunciation
characteristic of the higher tantric teachings of Tibetan Buddhism.

Although rhetorically positioning himself as the disciple calling out
to his guru, throughout his song Khyentsé Wangpo in fact delivers an
important teaching by pointing out the common pitfalls of dharma prac-
tice that impede the path. He does so by modeling a practitioner's deep
recognition of self-deception at every step of the way, a self-examination
that is essential to traversing the path swiftly and completely. To this end,

Khyentsé Wangpo successively warns against unvirtuous friends; attachment to loved ones; the display of altruism motivated by selfish aims; and the reification of generation and completion stage experiences. These pitfalls can be associated with, respectively, the worldly path of virtuous humans; the path of renunciation of the Foundational Vehicle; the bodhicitta path of the Mahāyāna; and the tantric path of the Vajrayāna. Khyentsé Wangpo may thus be delivering his ultimate teaching by way of the very persona he expresses in song: that of a skilled and learned tantric guru who nevertheless continues to take guru devotion as the path toward fully surrendering his own ego.

The translation presented here aims to mirror the force of the original language employed as well as its evocative eloquence in order to arouse a similar array of sensations and emotions in the reader. It attempts to render the Tibetan original's dense and complex ideas into clear and precise English verse, hoping to leave space for the delicate simplicity and openness of Khyentsé Wangpo's style to shine through his words of heartfelt exhortation. In order to retain some of the meter and rhythm of the original, which is written in verse with eleven-syllable lines, the English version is in lines of equal length (fourteen syllables), arranged whenever possible into four-line verses as customary in Tibetan. The use of repetition and refrain is likewise retained in the English, in the hope that it may give a taste of the rhythmic flavor of the original song. Finally, the translation generally follows the line order of the original, with the intention to preserve the progression of the author's own train of speech.

The Emissary of Renunciation: A Spontaneous Vajra Song
of Recollection of the Glorious Guru and Universal Lord
Jamyang Khyentsé Wangpo

Aho!
In the lucid hollow of self-arisen wakefulness,
innately free of constructs, negation, and affirmation,
all things, bound and freed, dissolve—glorious guru, to you
I bow down within self-liberated, natural resting.

Dancer of the essence drop of empty-bliss unity
manifest as a youth adorned with union's marks and signs,

everlasting Heruka—glorious guru, to you
I bow down within the non-conceptual *prāṇa*-mind.

Devourer of the three realms, the Vajra Queen's fire tongue,
A-HAṂ union ignites in the five *cakra* citadels.[5]
With this blazing and dripping meditative equipoise,
you clear the skies of all clouds—glorious guru, to you
I bow down within innately arisen melting bliss.[6]

Aho!
That I may see defiled behavior, like the brush deer's play,
as endless profusion, mere flashes of joy, and renounce
all schemes for ruining myself and deceiving others,
please bless me, glorious guru and universal lord.

Friends and family who disbelieve words of benefit,
foolish people who take pleasure in violence and sex—
that I may renounce them all, this den of poisonous snakes,
please bless me, glorious guru and universal lord.

The field of conventional knowledge is as vast as space;
bare, supreme awareness-emptiness is deep as the sea.
Hence, scholar-practitioners are rarer than daytime stars,
so there's no point in pursuing provisions and renown!

Among secluded bodhi trees—renunciates' mansions,
dwellings of the old sages, the master meditators—
that I may go as a weary friend to young deer at play,
applying myself to practice entirely, please bless me!

Bonds with friends and enemies change quicker than summer clouds,
as fickle and uncertain as a dancer's supple hands—
seeing this, that I may go from the household and renounce,
and thereby actualize true discipline, please bless me!

Though lacking all intention to benefit anyone,
to display altruism for the sake of my own aims—
that by this inclination I may always be repulsed,
mastering instead sincere bodhicitta, please bless me!

Solidified generation and completion, tethered
by clinging to beliefs and concepts, cause only torment—
that I may see this and strive whole-heartedly to arrive
at the natural state, aware-empty wisdom, please bless me!

Seeing that tonight, Death's own emissary may strike,
and by tomorrow, I may well be but a lifeless corpse—
that I may know all efforts to be delusions, pointless,
and take quick hold of the truly meaningful, please bless me!

And through this, that I may see the true face of perfection,
absolute truth, this unsettled mind's intrinsic nature,
in which all comes to dissolve; and that in this central space
void of adoption and rejection, leaving and reaching,
I may instantly perfect the paths and grounds, please bless me!

These words of spontaneous inspiration have burst forth
from the Lord of All Families, Guardian of the Circle,
when urged by the emissary of fiercest devotion
while in the vajra palace of luminous natural state.

*The venerable vidyādhara[7] who belongs to the ranks of those who please
Padma[8] uttered this in one breath in the vicinity of the site of supreme sid-
dhas[9] known as Lion Sky Fortress.*

NOTES

1. In the Tibetan system of recognition of reincarnations, certain masters are
   said to have had several simultaneous reincarnations, which are often clas-
   sified in terms of the five characteristics of buddhas—body, speech, mind,
   quality, and activity.
2. Gene Smith coined the phrase "rimé movement" to describe the nonsectarian
   activities spearheaded by the Khyen-Kong-Chok triumvirate. *Among Tibetan
   Texts*, 237–50. However, *rimé* functioned more as a shared sensibility among
   a circle of luminaries focused on textual and lineage preservation than as a
   movement per se. See Gayley and Schapiro, *Gathering of Brilliant Moons*, 18.
3. The Listeners (Skt: śrāvaka, Tib: *nyan thos*) and Solitary Realizers (Skt:
   pratyekabuddha, Tib: *rang sangs rgyas*) are the two foundational vehicles rec-
   ognized in the Tibetan tradition as constituting the Hinayāna. It is impor-
   tant to note, however, that Hinayāna, meaning "Lesser Vehicle," does not

correspond to any Buddhist group's self-identification but instead is a derogatory term used by followers of the self-appointed "Great Vehicle," the Mahāyāna, to distance themselves from nonadherents to their teachings.

4. For a detailed account of Khyentsé Wangpo's life story, see Jamgön Kongtrul, *Life of Jamyang Khyentsé Wangpo.*

5. *'khor nga'i grong khyer* (the citadel of the five cakras).

6. *Aham* refers to the Great Self (*bdag nyid chen po*), which is sometimes used as an epithet of the ultimate nature. The syllables *A* and *Ham* individually stand in for the white and red pure essences of the body, and their union symbolizes the union of skillful means and knowledge. When they are united through the practice of blazing and dripping, the innate wisdom of great bliss manifests. This is related to *tummo*, or inner heat practice. See Jigme Lingpa, Patrul Rinpoche, and Geshe Mahapandita, *Deity, Mantra, and Wisdom,* 192.

7. The term *vidyādhara* (*rig 'dzin*) can be translated as "knowledge holder." According to Jigme Lingpa, Patrul Rinpoche, and Geshe Mahapandita, "In this term, 'knowledge' refers to deity, mantra, and the wisdom of great bliss. One who 'holds' these three, then, with profound and skillful means is a 'knowledge holder.'" *Deity, Mantra, and Wisdom,* 189.

8. *Padma* refers to Padmasambhava, Guru Rinpoché, the Indian master who brought tantric Buddhism to Tibet in the eighth century and is regarded by many Tibetans as the second Buddha.

9. A *siddha* (*sgrub pa*) is an accomplished tantric practitioner.

TIBETAN SOURCE

Mkhyen brtse'i dbang po. "Khyab bdag dpal ldan bla ma rjes su dran pa'i rdo rje'i thol glu nges 'byung gi pho nya zhes bya ba" [The emissary of renunciation: A spontaneous vajra song of recollection of the glorious guru and universal lord]. In *Gang shar rdo rje'i glu phreng skal bzang rna ba'i dga' ston* [Feast for the ears of the fortunate: A garland of spontaneous vajra songs], vol. 22 of *Mkhyen brtse'i dbang po gsung 'bum* [The collected works of Khyentsé Wangpo], 341–43. 24 vols. Gangtok: Gonpo Tseten, 1977–80.

ADDITIONAL SOURCES

Gayley, Holly, and Joshua Schapiro, eds. *A Gathering of Brilliant Moons: Practice Advice from the Rimé Masters of Tibet.* Boston: Wisdom, 2017.

Jamgön Kongtrul. *The Life of Jamyang Khyentsé Wangpo.* Translated by Matthew Akester. New Delhi: Shechen, 2012.

Jigme Lingpa, Patrul Rinpoche, and Geshe Mahapandita. *Deity, Mantra, and*

Wisdom: Development Stage Meditation in Tibetan Buddhist Tantra. Translated by the Dharmachakra Translation Committee. Ithaca, NY: Snow Lion, 2007.

Smith, Ellis Gene. *Among Tibetan Texts: History and Literature of the Himalayan Plateau.* Boston: Wisdom, 2001.

15

Delighting the Bard-Saints

INTRODUCED AND TRANSLATED BY MIGUEL SAWAYA

THE GREAT Jamyang Khyentsé Wangpo (1820–1892), one of the most important figures of nineteenth-century Tibetan Buddhism, was around 20 when he made the first of two journeys from his native Eastern Tibet to Central Tibet for religious pilgrimage and additional studies.[1] In the course of one of his journeys, he composed a short devotional song titled "A Platform to Delight the Bard-Saints." Judging by the colophon, it seems likely that this song dedicated to Padmapāṇi, an important form of the great bodhisattva Avalokiteśvara, gave voice to a devotional impulse associated with a visit to sacred sites in Lhasa, especially the famous Rasa Trülnang Temple, which is today known as the Jokhang. The song is notable for its balance between formal compositional technique and emotive, evocative content.

In addition to its literary qualities, the song is compelling for the insight it provides into Khyentsé Wangpo himself, a seminal figure whose influence, direct or indirect, can be discerned in many facets and sites of Tibetan Buddhism today. With this song, we are able to glimpse the concerns, motivations, and proclivities of Khyentsé Wangpo as a young man, a spiritual master during his formative years of intensive training. It provides an intimate portrayal of the perennial challenges and potential aberrations associated with spiritual pursuits and the key role that devotion and prayer play in Tibetan religion. For instance, we have reason to believe that the verses of lament are heartfelt and representative of matters troubling the young Khyentsé Wangpo: he wrote elsewhere of the dearth of religious figures with a broad, unbiased appreciation for the rich spectrum of Buddhism represented in Tibet's many traditions. Khyentsé Wangpo acted on such concerns; he was, in fact, a primary figure in the nonsectarian movement in Eastern Tibet in the nineteenth century that promoted the appreciation and preservation of this religious diversity.

Jamyang Khyentsé Wangpo was born in the village of Dilgo in Degé, Kham. At the age of 12 he was identified as a *tulku*, or reincarnate lama, of the Sakya tradition, and at 21 he was ordained at a major Nyingma monastery, Mindrolling, in the Lhoka region of Central Tibet. He studied with many important teachers in both Eastern and Central Tibet, and he was particularly strong in Sanskrit, grammar, and poetics. Khyentsé Wangpo was a polymath, renowned as a scholar, mentor, and inspiration to his contemporaries, diplomat and counselor to politicians and generals, contemplative adept, and eminent *tertön* (revealer of concealed spiritual treasures and teachings). He collaborated closely and formed lasting relationships with the Kagyu luminary Jamgön Kongtrul Lodrö Thayé (1813–1899) and with the renowned *tertön* of the Nyingma tradition, Chokgyur Lingpa (1829–1870). It is particularly as part of this trio that he is considered an important figure in the nineteenth-century ecumenical movement of Eastern Tibet.

Khyentsé Wangpo's song, which is included in his twenty-four-volume collected works, is divided into four sections: praise, lamentation, the actual supplication, and a song-internal colophon. The first verse is a general praise of Padmapāṇi's fundamental essence and its manifestation, presenting the beloved bodhisattva as the embodiment of the great compassion of all the victorious buddhas, as well as that of the advanced bodhisattvas who are frequently referred to as the buddhas' heirs or offspring. The five verses that follow extol, respectively, the bodhisattva's sublime body, speech, mind, qualities, and activity. Following the opening panegyric, we find seven verses of lamentation. First is a general lament regarding the current state of affairs, with mention of the basic unsatisfactoriness, or *duḥkha*, that characterizes all ordinary, conditioned existence. The eighth verse bemoans intelligence that has gone off track, especially in terms of dharma practitioners of some learning who are pridefully interested in fame and reputation. The next three verses lament degradation associated with, respectively, the foundational forms of Buddhism that emphasize ethical discipline; the Mahāyāna and its ideal practitioner, the altruistic bodhisattva; and the Vajrayāna, or tantric Buddhism, and its ideal practitioner, the tantric master, or *vidyādhara*. The last two verses of this section bemoan mistaken approaches to study and reflection, as well as meditation gone awry. Having thus praised the mighty bodhisattva and then described the many troubles in the world, the author is poised to ask for help. Indeed, the following two verses are the actual supplication to Padmapāṇi, while the final verse is a colophon internal to the song.

Khyentsé Wangpo's literary training is evident in this piece, which makes generous use of refrains and repetition. The rhetorical power of repetition is common to both Tibetan and English, and so I have sought to highlight such repetition in my translation. Most of the verses contain metaphorical imagery, whose figurative richness I have also aimed to convey. There is a metrical precision and distinct cadence to the Tibetan, every line made up of nine syllables with a weak or unaccented antepenultimate syllable. Although I have not attempted to produce verses in meter, I have paid attention to the length of lines in English, with an eye (and an ear) to linear balance. In fact, these elements—metaphoric, rhythmic, linear, musical—contributed significantly to my initial interest in this piece.

The song is a classical, well-organized expression of a range of emotions: the inspiration, awe, and devotion within songs of praise; the heart-heaviness, dejection, and even despair associated with lamentation; and the fervor and spiritual longing of exhortation, when the aspirant calls upon divinity to act for the sake of goodness in the world. Overall, "A Platform to Delight the Bard-Saints," subtitled "A Supplication to the Supreme Ārya, Padmapāṇi; A Spontaneous Vajra Song Invoking His Commitment," is a study in the balance between emotiveness and formal precision, exemplifying the devotional impulse as a refined affect. It gives voice to the modes and stages by which this impulse is felt in the human psyche and expressed in literature.

A Platform to Delight the Bard-Saints
Jamyang Khyentsé Wangpo

Amazing! Appearing as the embodiment of the wisdom
and limitless compassion of all the victors and their heirs,
you bring all wandering beings to the state of liberation.
To you, most exalted Padmapāṇi, I bow down.

Youthfulness of the new moon free from clouds,
embraced by the dazzling beauty of marks most exquisite,

you deliver sentient beings to the repose of liberation.
To you, most exalted Padmapāṇi, I bow down.

Blending the strains of the lute, delightful in sixty ways,
with the nectar of dharma, both lexical and lived,
you bestow sounds of sustenance upon the ears of fortunate ones.
To you, most exalted Padmapāṇi, I bow down.

Your mind is the sonorous play of emptiness and compassion.
Accompanied by the radiance of sublime knowledge, twofold but
    indivisible,
it obliterates the thick darkness of existence and quiescence.
To you, most exalted Padmapāṇi, I bow down.

The immediate and final desires of embodied beings
are fulfilled by merely hearing your name.
You are a wish-granting jewel of inexhaustible qualities.
To you, most exalted Padmapāṇi, I bow down.

All the realms of infinite sentient beings, without exception,
are held in the gaze of your unswerving love,
and you delight in the massive task of liberating them.
To you, most exalted Padmapāṇi, I bow down.

Alack! Alas! In this degenerate age all these beings
are enmeshed in *duḥkha*, so hard to bear,
while the sun of the Buddha's teachings sinks
behind the western peaks—how sad indeed!

The embodiment of the one unfailing, constant refuge is
the victors and their progeny. Yet they cast away these guides
and their intelligence submits to haughty impulses within.
To be thus stricken by evil forces—how sad indeed!

In the immediate, they pretend to cherish,
as their own life, minor regulations and observances.
Thus, in the final account, they wantonly engage in non-virtue.
This façade of ethics—how sad indeed!

Telling tall tales of altruism and helping beings,
they inwardly pursue their own interests,
competitive when it comes to power and prestige.
The empty renown of such "bodhisattvas"—how sad indeed!

They receive empowerments, transmissions, and pith instructions from
    the guru,
the presiding master who is the root of spiritual accomplishment,
but then they utterly dispense with faith and sacred commitments.
This debasing of the vidyādharas—how sad indeed!

Although they study and reflect on many texts,
they become proud and increasingly haughty,
considering the different parts of the victor's teachings to be contradictory.
This abandoning of the dharma is a heavy sin—how sad indeed!

Although they pursue meditative concentration in solitude,
they leave tantra, scripture, and instruction far behind
and wear themselves out with delusional meditation.
This pointless exhaustion of a human life—how sad indeed!

In brief, whatever I think of bears the marks of degeneration
and so is a cause for depression.
Thus, lord, with all my heart I urge you to action:
the time is ripe for a miracle of love!

Consider the engraved contour of your pledge—
to delight solely in eternal altruism—
and deliver us to the grandeur of an unfading spring of lucid joy,
a nourishing feast for the teachings and beings of the Snowy Land.

At the hub of the four parts of Central Tibet,
just below the second Potala palace,
in the midst of the willow grove,
this was written by an inept, penniless yogin.

*On the slopes of the Palace's Red Hill, near the great Rasa Trülnang Temple
(the Vajrāsana of snowy Tibet), on an auspicious day of the Vaiśākha month,
what came to mind was expressed in song.*

Note

1. For biographical information regarding Jamyang Khyentsé Wangpo, I have relied primarily on Akester, *Life of Jamyang Khyentsé Wangpo*. Readers may consult that text for further details.

Tibetan Source

Mkhyen brtse'i dbang po. *'Phags mchog phyag na padmo la gsol ba 'debs pa thugs dam bskul ba'i rdo rje'i thol glu drang srong dgyes pa'i 'bab stegs* [A platform to delight the bard-saints: A supplication to the Supreme Ārya, Padmapāṇi; a spontaneous vajra song invoking his commitment]. In *'Jam dbyangs mkhyen brtse'i dbang po bka' 'bum* [The collected works of Jamyang Khyentsé Wangpo], 22:377–80. 24 vols. Gangtok: Gonpo Tseten, 1977–80. TBRC W21807.

Additional Sources

Akester, Matthew. *The Life of Jamyang Khyentsé Wangpo*. New Delhi: Shechen, 2012.

Thondup, Tulku. *Masters of Meditation and Miracles*. Boston: Shambhala, 1996.

16

Nechung's Dream

INTRODUCED AND TRANSLATED BY NATASHA L. MIKLES

NECHUNG'S SONG translated here—which I have titled "The Dream on Which I Dare Not Think"—is found in the final episode of the Gesar epic *The Great Perfection of Hell* (*Dmyal gling rdzogs pa chen po*).[1] It relates the final chapter of Gesar's life—describing his elevation to Dzogchen teacher, his descent to hell to debate the nature of tantric violence with King Yama while saving his mother, and the deaths of himself and his whole court of heroes. A living bardic tradition across the Himalayan plateau, the Gesar epic relates the story of King Gesar as he builds an idyllic kingdom and defends Buddhist practice from the destructive effects of surrounding demon-kings. Like other renditions of the Gesar epic, this episode alternates between prose and song. This particular song comes at the moment when the kingdom of Ling is celebrating Gesar's safe return from hell. His young cousin Nechung (alt. Ne'u Chung) approaches with a prophetic dream that sets the stage for the end of Gesar's compassionate activities in the world and the eventual destruction of Ling.

From the standpoint of textual history, this particular episode is unique for its status as both a treasure text and a published episode with a named author, rather than an oral text revealed by visionary bards. The purported author of *The Great Perfection of Hell*, Chökyi Wangchuk (Chos kyi dbang phyug), is himself a character in the story, charged by Gesar's compatriot Denma with writing down the final deeds of the warrior-king. The text was revealed from the Red Water Lake of Golok (Dmar chu rdzing bu) by Lingtsang *tertön* Draktsel Dorjé (Gling tshang gter ston Drag rtsal rdo rje). While no date is given for the text's revelation, its stylistic similarity to Longchen Nyingtik materials makes it likely a product of the late nineteenth or early twentieth century. Similarly mysterious, there is little historical record or reference of the *tertön* outside this text, though one other Gesar episode, *The Taming of A Yan* (*A yan 'dul ba'i rtogs brjod*), was recovered from the region by a Dorjé Wang Draktsel (Rdo rje dbang drag rtsal) and may be a product of the same *tertön*. Only one block print was made of *The Great Perfection of Hell*, at Wara Monastery in Chamdo under the sponsorship of Damchö Tenpa (Dam chos bstan pa). While no publishing date is specified, it must have been prior to Damchö Tenpa's death in 1946, putting the likely date of publication in the early twentieth century; possibly it was a preliminary publishing exercise to gather the necessary craftsmen for producing the Wara canon. After the Tibetan diaspora, *The Great Perfection of Hell* was republished several times, often from handwritten manuscripts based on the Wara original. This particular rendition is from the 1979 Bhutanese edition, though I utilized the original Wara Monastery blockprint to correct or interpret the text in select places.

Nechung's prophecy marks the transition into the climactic end not only of *The Great Perfection of Hell* but of the entire Gesar epic itself. Up to that point, the epic follows the feats of the warrior-king Gesar as he defends his kingdom of Ling from surrounding demonic forces. Among his divine court of heroes, he is often interpreted as an emanation of a bodhisattva and Buddhist protector. Gesar's violence and warfare, therefore, are generally understood within tantric frameworks as necessary to defeat forces antithetical to the Buddhist teachings. At the end of the epic, after all the battles have been fought and won, Nechung's song uses terrifying imagery to foretell the destruction of Ling, the death of Gesar and his band of warriors, and the end of Gesar's idyllic Buddhist kingdom. In effect, it foretells a mini-apocalypse. This song, therefore, is very different from other Gesar literature, which focuses on the experiences of warfare and battle or alternatively on Buddhist realization and practice.

To convey the emotional range found in "The Dream on Which I Dare Not Think," my translation seeks to replicate two specific moods that are inherent to the text—horror and lament. As for the horror, this song is the first step in the eventual death and decline of King Gesar, his warriors, and the Buddhist kingdom he has created. Although Nechung claims not to know the meaning of the dream, the verbs of trepidation and anxiety surrounding her initial audience with King Gesar reveal that she has some idea that the meaning is not good. King Gesar has just returned from hell, and this song is sung at what is meant to be a joyous feast celebrating his return. Despite this celebration, however, both the reader and the song's epic characters come to understand that Nechung's vision represents their coming demise and the approaching end of Ling. In the translation, I sought to capture this sense of horrifying revelation arising from the realization that the world of heroes is coming to an end in the middle of what is otherwise supposed to be a happy event.

As for lament, this song takes place in two simultaneous timelines—within the text as part of the narrative but also as a song heard, read, and digested by a contemporary reading or listening audience for whom Gesar often has enduring spiritual and cultural significance. Contemporary readers and listeners of the epic may experience a deep sorrow and nostalgia that the kingdom of Gesar has disappeared, particularly within the context of their own cultural losses under Chinese rule. For many Tibetans living in Kham and Amdo, Gesar plays a central role in their regional identity as a symbol of Tibetan strength; his demise represents the loss not only of a great Tibetan king but also of an immense source of Buddhist teaching. For readers in English, I have tried to inspire the sorrow and bitter remorse that many Tibetans feel when reading of the dying heroes and the end of Gesar's glorious empire.

At the same time, I partially domesticate the text so that it is recognizable in English as an epic ballad, similar to the resonance of the Gesar epic in Tibetan. To accomplish this, the translation relies heavily on replicating the style of other English "folk" literature through use of the iambic tetrameter, as well as the playful inversion of subject, object, and verb. This song represents, therefore, the first translation of Gesar literature in English that puts the epic nature of the narrative at its center and attempts to explicitly pair it with the structure and tone of English epic literature. Utilizing the structure and vocabulary of English folk poetics for the Tibetan song also further contributes to the translation's sense of melancholy and preternatural disturbance, as such songs in English often detail the glory and downfall of a lost prior age. As epic literature also necessarily involves significant world-building through alluding to people and places already familiar to most readers, I have included notes detailing Gesar's familial connections as mentioned in the translation. If a place in the song is named that is identifiable today, I have included its name in both phoneticized English and, in the notes, Wylie transliteration.

Regardless of stylistic framing, the song—in both English and Tibetan—is raw with emotion, specifically devotion to King Gesar and the Buddhist mission he represents. Using fantastic and extraordinary imagery, the song explores the horror of losing a living source of Buddhist teachings, as well as the extreme sorrow that Gesar and his compatriots feel at their approaching deaths, along with those who will be left behind. These emotions highlight the reciprocal nature of devotion. The feeling of devotion as expressed in Tibetan contexts is based, at least in part, on the desire to be physically close to one's teacher so that they may guide the student and care for their spiritual development. Death threatens that closeness, representing a catastrophic loss of guidance and affection. For this reason, students deeply dread the death of their spiritual teacher. The expressions of lament and horror found in this song highlight the devotion not only on behalf of those surrounding King Gesar to their warrior-king but also of Gesar to the people of his kingdom and the future welfare of Buddhists in Tibet. "The Dream on Which I Dare Not Think," therefore, represents a unique window into the contours of devotion in Tibetan epic poetry.

The Dream on Which I Dare Not Think
Revealed by Draktsel Dorjé

Oh, Noble Prince of Earth Divine,
while on the path of sleep last night,
a brilliant vision early came,
though through the night's three terms I slept.

On Mother Tārā fixed my mind
in heart's true center shining bright,
and with her essence I did mix
that undivided we became.

My sleeping mind became unbound,
appeared a dream in ways like this.
Unsure of meaning—fair or foul.
Its secrets, those I dare not think.
I humbly offer, precious king.

A great garuḍa stretched its wings
on golden roof of Tiger Peak.[2]

In right and left garuḍa's eyes,
emerged the shining sun and moon.
These portents all I dreamt and more.

The creature's neck was iron blade,
erupting sparks and tongues of flame.
From great garuḍa's five-hued wings,
a dazzling rainbow spread o'er land.
These portents all I dreamt and more.

From twelve wide feathers of its tail,
the wisdom spread like lava flows.
The great garuḍa cried "Dring Drong!"
While hawk ascends to rocky pass.
These portents all I dreamt and more.

That soaring hawk, above the world,
did sandal tree contort to ground.
Then sudden vagrant winds appeared
and sandal tree did fall to plain.
These portents all I dreamt and more.

In empty sky o'er falcon fort,
the sunlight dimmed and darkness reigned.
All earthly bedrock quaked and shook,
while greatly did the tumult blaze.
These portents all I dreamt and more.

The iron bird, garuḍa's form,
exhaled a tongue of spreading flame.
A peacock bore the flare below,[3]
and put the sandal tree to blaze.
These portents all I dreamt and more.

Though burnt, from top a rainbow came,
and pierced the five directions free.
One rainbow pierced the deepest hell,
and tortured realms were blessed with light.
These portents all I dreamt and more.

The fivefold buddha families bright—
like jewels did shine in Chipön's[4] halls.
The Temple Long of Falcon Fort
was ornamented by their light.
These portents all I dreamt and more.

Clear light into my vision burst:

And in the space o'er Castle Tea—
Senglön's home, your sire dear—
a horn appeared with shell-white dove,
delightful there for all to see.
These portents all I dreamt and more.

The shell-white bird encircled Ling.
Then flew to heavenly land beyond.
The great garuḍa made pursuit,
and joined the bird in land divine.
These portents all I dreamt and more.

Clear light into my vision burst:

A horse of hue bright red then ran
a circle round Trothung's[5] great fort—
the Raven's Heart—he neighed three times,
and fort destroyed from top to ground.
These portents all I dreamt and more.

Though horse had left with neighs so loud
the fort still stood by one great mast.
From massive window light did fall,
all creatures felt abundant bliss.
These portents all I dreamt and more.

Far raven flew with Vajra small,
and down he shot to land of hell.
For bird like that—garuḍa great—
a pot he layered rich with gold.
These portents all I dreamt and more.

Clear light into my vision burst:

And rays of sun on High Ma[6] fell.
By melting snow, the lion sank
and lamas ten and three of Ling
appraised the length of turquoise mane.
These portents all I dreamt and more.

The lion's bones in cloth were tied
and shining crystal came their house.
While these mementos relics made,
a conch's crescendo lay on bed.
These portents all I dreamt and more.

Clear light into my vision burst:

And Golden Water of Upper Ma[7]
turned bare and dry as withered leaf.
While shining bird to sky did fly,
the bed retained its feathers gold.
These portents all I dreamt and more.

From golden fowl, a rainbow shone,
those born below were graced by gold.
And golden conch on golden lake
encircled lakes of Ling so vast.
These portents all I dreamt and more.

Clear light into my vision burst:

Within your palace—Tiger's Peak—
dismay in great protector's shrine.
The prophesier's lance fell down,
and silken pennant burst in flames.
These portents all I dreamt and more.

Destroyed protector's soul in three,
the stone, the wheel, the statue tall,
then white- and red-hued tongues of flame

across the realms of hell ignite.
These portents all I dreamt and more.

Ambrosia drowned the flames so white
and scorch'd hells filled with nectar sweet.
Then sun down shined through flames of red
and icy hells did melt with heat.
These portents all I dreamt and more.

Clear light into my vision burst:

A wind tore through divine feast halls
the crystal, treasure vases broke.
A burning sign apparent made,
the "Hriḥ" did float into the west.
These portents all I dreamt and more.

Clear light into my vision burst:

A tide of blood drown'd Achen north.[8]
A swan was blacken'd by the mire.
Garuḍa's claws held tight the swan,
and flew towards southern setting sun.
These portents all I dreamt and more.

Clear light into my vision burst:

A rainbow shrouded Gyatsa's[9] son,
and planet dark eclipsed the moon.
Deluge of water rushed the black,
but once more sun to sky did rise.
These portents all I dreamt and more.

Clear light into my vision burst:

Your sire's home, its turquoise lake,
the sun's harsh rays did all deplete.
Though cuckoo climbed high to sky,
his feathers on the bed remain.
These portents all I dreamt and more.

Clear light into my vision burst:

The corner beam of Trothung's Fort
was shattered into mulch and dust.
The temple crumbled to the ground,
though flowers rose upon the bed.
These portents all I dreamt and more.

NOTES

1. This episode is a revelation by Draktsel Dorjé, attributed to Chökyi Wang-chuk. The song translated here is a selection (pp. 253–57) from the much larger song, which appears on pp. 252–60 of *Gling rje ge sar gyi rnam thar las dmyal gling rdzogs pa chen po thos pa rang grol ngan song chos kyi bskul glu zhes bya ba.*
2. Tib: Bsam grub stag rtse. This is the name of Gesar's palace, which some Tibetans believe to be near Drigu ('Dri stod) county in contemporary Yushu, while others place it in the Rma Valley. In most other Gesar literature, the name of Gesar's palace is Seng phrug stag rdzong (Lion Cub Tiger Fortress) or Seng 'brug stag rtse (Lion Dragon Tiger Peak). The Wara original of the text, however, has Bsam grub stag rtse, which this 1979 Bhutanese edition retains. To work around the ambiguity, I have elected to refer here to the castle simply as "Tiger Peak" (Stag rtse).
3. My thanks to Catherine Hartmann for her help with this particular line.
4. Gesar's beloved uncle, leader of the younger lineage of Ling.
5. Gesar's jealous uncle, who repeatedly attempts to betray and ensnare him. However, he is also an emanation of Hayagrīva and ultimately works to extend Gesar's compassionate action by acting as his human adversary.
6. Matö (Rma stod), a county in present-day Golok.
7. Matö Sertsho (Rma stod gser mtsho), a lake in Matö county.
8. An epithet for the evil kingdom of Hor, whose three kings kidnapped Gesar's wife Drugmo earlier in the epic, causing a great battle between Hor and Ling. While the kings were destroyed, the evil minister Atro Ngomnak remained in Hor spreading evil lies.
9. Dralha Tsegyel, Gesar's nephew via his elder half-brother Gyatsa. He is here named metonymically by reference to the Mercury Castle, where Gyatsa's family resides.

Tibetan Source

Chos kyi dbang phyug. *Gling rje ge sar gyi rnam thar las dmyal gling rdzogs pa chen po thos pa rang grol ngan song chos kyi bskul glu zhes bya ba* [From the life of King Gesar: *The Great Perfection of Hell*, the rousing song of dharma that liberates one from bad rebirths]. Thimpu: Druk Sherig, 1981.

Additional Sources

Kornman, Robin, Sangye Khandro, and Lama Chönam, trans. *The Epic of Gesar of Ling: Gesar's Magical Birth, Early Years, and Coronation as King*. Boston: Shambala, 2012.

Mikles, Natasha L. "Buddhicizing the Warrior-King Gesar in the *Dmyal gling rdzogs pa chen po*." *Revue d'Etudes Tibétaines* 37 (2016): 231–46.

———. "The Power of Genres and the Project of Secularization: Publishing the Gesar Epic in Contemporary China." *Culture and Religion* 20.3 (2019): 322–50.

Thurston, Timothy. "The Tibetan Gesar Epic beyond Its Bards: An Ecosystem of Genres on the Roof of the World." *Journal of American Folklore* 132.524 (2019): 115–36.

17

A Fantasy Tale of Two Birds

INTRODUCED AND TRANSLATED BY
CHRISTINA LEE MONSON

T HIS FOUR-PAGE poem, a sweet tale of two birds, begins thir-
teen pages of short writings by the extraordinary Tibetan
Buddhist female teacher Sera Khandro (Se ra mkha' 'gro,
1892–1940) grouped together under the broader title "Vajra
Laughter: Connecting Signs with Meaning." The poem can also be
found in her *Profound Secret Treasury of the Ḍākinī's Pure Visions*.[1] The
other pieces in this short collection span a range of topics, presented in
both verse and prose, and include other prophetic visions, prayers, and
a teaching on the meaning of "secret companion" and "wish-fulfilling
jewel." These writings are classified as "pure vision" (*dag snang*), a method
of transmission found throughout the Nyingma tradition of Tibetan
Buddhism and common nomenclature among the lineages of *tertöns*, or
"treasure revealers," with whom Sera Khandro spent most of her life in
the wilds of Golok in Eastern Tibet.[2] In the narrative poem translated
here, Sera Khandro invites the reader into her mystical life through a
drama that unfolds within the display of the natural world. Spiritual les-
sons of love's transcendental power are transmitted through the rhythms
of the changing seasons and migrating birds in a landscape infused with
symbolic meaning and rich emotion.

The story features two birds, Golden and Turquoise, enraptured by
the blissful enjoyment of a beautiful environment and intimate compan-
ionship. Despite such perfect circumstances, both birds are keenly aware
of the dangers of becoming so carried away by pleasure and comfort that
spiritual practice falls by the wayside. Golden opens their dialogue by re-
flecting on the importance of being prepared to die and invites Turquoise
to join him in a mutual promise to practice the dharma. What follows is
a reflection on the benefits of retreat practice through a short introduc-

tion to the classical Buddhist typology of view, meditation, conduct, and result. Terms of endearment are interspersed throughout the dialogue, which is presented in eight-syllable verse and set off from the prose narration that lays out the context for the conversation. The exchange is replete with profound dharma instruction presented amid a spectrum of emotions ranging from intimate tenderness to the despair and heartbreak of separation.

At the core of this pure vision is love. This is not surprising. Two of the seven volumes of Sera Khandro's collected works chronicle her life—and the love of her life, her lama and treasure-revealing partner, Drimé Özer (Dri med 'od zer, 1881–1924).[3] Upon her first glimpse of him from the window of her parental home at the tender age of 15, Sera Khandro's heart was captured.[4] With deep intuition, she recognized him as the one who would catalyze the blossoming of her own realization and associated discovery of treasure teachings. This was exactly what came to be after her daring decision to leave all she knew in her hometown of Lhasa and follow her destiny with him to the nomadic areas of Eastern Tibet.

Sera Khandro's relationship with Drimé Özer and their mutual love and devotion are defining features of her life and principal themes that run throughout her writing.[5] Excerpts from a prayer to Sera Khandro (referred to below as Dewé Dorjé) authored by Drimé Özer, a rare remnant of his original writing contained within her collected works, laud her as follows:

You're magnificent as a precious jewel,
with inexhaustible noble qualities,
but accept that others see you as less.

Originally, you're truly and completely enlightened,
but you behave in ways your disciples can comprehend.

Great yoginī Dewé Dorjé, we are relying on you,
as our only hope now and in the future!

If you don't listen to this, my written appeal,
I as your spiritual hero am ready to go together indivisibly with you
to the isle of Khachöd, for you are my only hope now and in the future![6]
How could it be otherwise?

From now until I reach the heart of awakening,
may I never be separated from you, Great Bliss Dewé Dorjé.[7]

In the verse of homage that begins Sera Khandro's biography of Drimé
Özer, composed in her thirty-fourth year, she writes,

You are the actual embodiment of the omniscience, love, and wisdom
of all triumphant buddhas in infinite pure lands,
great treasure-revealing master, Pema Ledrel,
before whom I forever bow
with unwavering devotion in body, speech, and mind.
Please, transfer your wisdom blessings into my heart,
and compassionately hold me
inseparable from you throughout all my lifetimes![8]

Inseparability throughout space and time defined the connection be-
tween Sera Khandro and Drimé Özer. Predicted for each other by mul-
tiple human and nonhuman messengers, they dedicated themselves to a
love that was both beyond the complexities of their respective relation-
ships with other partners and stymied by them. The relationship's devo-
tional flavor empowered them to embrace it as transcendent compared
with ordinary worldly attachment. In its essence, their love for each other
was intertwined with their love for the dharma, which infused it with
meaning. Sera Khandro's tale of Golden and Turquoise offers a window
into her meaning-making processes for living within the fullness of the
human emotional experience, which encompasses both fear of loss and
also hope for eternal connection.

We can imagine that the vision of Golden and Turquoise springs from
Sera Khandro's need to process the poignancy and power of her rela-
tionship with Drimé Özer. His voice may be heard in Golden, and her
own in Turquoise.[9] A flock of birds arriving at her retreat at Tsari trig-
gers the vision, tinged with longing, memory, and fantasy, which invites
a catharsis of emotion held deep in her heart. The conversation between
Golden and Turquoise is a tender reflection on loving and leaving, on
matters of the world, and on spiritual practice. The intimate and trusting
tone between the two birds can be seen in the use of "agreeable to the
mind" or "congenial" (*yid mthun*) three times in Golden's opening verse.
The choices I made in the translation of this piece required insight into

the nature of the relationship between Golden and Turquoise. A sense of their being "best spiritual friends" comes through in the back-and-forth dialogue that ensues. Love felt for one's closest companion on the spiritual path weaves together Golden and Turquoise's determination to overcome all attachment through practicing the dharma with the very real pain of their forthcoming separation. Their birdsong language gives meaning to the truth of impermanence by seeking the inseparability that lies beyond it.

Another translation challenge I confronted in this poem was how to transmit bird sounds. In the tale, Turquoise communicates through the syllable *ki* in Tibetan. It is repeated throughout Turquoise's speech to indicate agreement with Golden's advice, delight at receiving Golden's teachings, and heartbreak upon their parting. We can envision Sera Khandro during her session break, spaciously present, open, and awe-filled, letting bird sounds lead her into the language of her heart's joy, wonder, and pain. One way to read the Tibetan *ki ki* refrains is as the bird equivalents of the statements that follow, such as "It is right!" and "It is good!" Surely, English-language speakers can understand *ki* precisely as the sound of a bird's chirp, and so the translation leaves *ki* rather than impose a domesticating translation through English words like *chirp* and *tweet*. Thus, the Tibetan terms summon the reader closer into Sera Khandro's sensory experience and lived world during her session breaks, listening to the euphony of birdsong and the emotions it evoked.

One of the meanings Sera Khandro distills is that the sounds of birds point out the relative nature of all things of the world: impermanence. Gathering is sure to end with parting. Another possible meaning relates to the ultimate, introduced by Golden in the final instructions given to Turquoise: "Unborn, unceasing, and unchanging, it's self-knowing awareness, Samantabhadra, the one taste of the non-dual nature of all things of saṃsāra and nirvāṇa." The recognition of awareness brings the "vajra laughter" (*rdo rje'i gad mo*) evoked in the collection title. This refers to the unchanging fundamental nature of reality and its unceasing expressiveness as anything and everything that appears, such as birds, love, and good-byes. Getting the joke requires a shift in perspective from one based on dualistic habitual thinking to one that is vast, open, and uncontrived. As Golden tells Turquoise, it is this awareness that is to be sustained by them rather than sorrow. Within such recognition, all expressions become awareness manifesting itself, and the entirety of phenomenal experience, including love and sorrow, is encountered as teacher and teaching—as meaningful signs pointing to truth.

At various junctures of their time together, Sera Khandro and Drimé Özer seal their love with a mutual commitment to stay in the world and support each other as long as possible, through upholding their treasure lineages and realizing the true nature of reality, the goal of the Buddhist path.[10] With this agreement, both tacit and explicit, they uplift their love beyond both themselves and ordinary passion into the domain of the sacred. Such love channeled toward a higher aim becomes sanctified and infused with determination to achieve its transcendent aim. However, even the most noble of loves must end at last. For Sera Khandro, striving for realization with the one she loves slightly sweetens the bitterness of impermanence with the possibility of an unchanging unity, found at last in the secret of her own heart.

A Tale of Two Birds
Sera Khandro Dewé Dorjé

It was during my session break on the twenty-fifth of the lunar month, a fine day in the sacred pleasure grove called Dragon Plain in Tsari, when a flock of birds came swirling around. Among them, two were exceptional: Golden and Turquoise. Both were peaceful and open-minded. Constant and steady friends, they had faith in the dharma and yearned to spiritually awaken for the benefit of others. As they were harmoniously discussing spiritual matters, Golden said:

> Hello there dear, blessed blue Turquoise!
> When you pay attention to the dharma and understand its teachings,
> you won't be confused about what to do and what not to do.
> Flocks of birds singing in harmony abound,
> but not for a second do they think about spiritual practice.
> Utterly distracted, they watch life's appearances flash by,
> and when death suddenly arrives, being ill-prepared,
> they are destined for unfortunate states.
> Hurry now! Let us strive to practice the sacred dharma!
> O Fortunate Beloved, let us hold this commitment close in our hearts.
> Do you understand, my dear divine friend?

When you practice in isolated and solitary abodes,
uncontrived realization dawns from within.
Once the power of practice blazes automatically,
you will realize the view, the single taste of saṃsāra and nirvāṇa.
Then, when meditation reveals the natural expression of your innate
  nature,
conduct is free and easy, the self-liberation of whatever occurs.
Baseless and without origin, this transcendent state is utterly open,
while appearances of the path are spontaneously present, varied, and
  unblocked.
The result is a sky-like state of non-conceptuality.
Samantabhadra's exalted state of wisdom intent is none other
than this: self-existent wakefulness. That itself is it!
Dearest—have you understood it in this way?

Turquoise replied:

Ki ki! It is right!
Ki ki! It is good!
True! Your pleasing heart advice is true.
We must cut attachment to saṃsāra, which has no essence,
and go practice dharma.
Some gather enjoyments for living this life,
but various negative deeds ruin it and the lives to follow.
When the Lord of Death arrives, such means are useless.
How pleasing are grassy meadows of this pleasure grove where we
  have alighted
and how happy and dear is our friendly flock.
But these won't help us when it's time to roam the *bardo.*
We enjoy the pure taste of ambrosial rains,
but they won't cool the hot torment of the intermediate states.
We must think well about what this means
and then follow the path of dharma.

You, enriched with the gold of excellent fortune,
are a sublime master with sage instructions.
Ki ki! When they reach my ears,
your teachings—that all things of saṃsāra and nirvāṇa
are illusory manifestations, that the uncontrived natural state

is beyond attachment, and that empty-appearances are self-liberated
within luminous awareness, the transcendent state of Samantabhadra
with its six special features—are most profound![11]

All phenomena subsumed by dualistic perception are non-dual.
They are one taste in their self-liberation, the Great Madhyamaka,
the ultimate expanse of emptiness beyond the eight elaborations.[12]
The great self-radiance of unchanging wisdom
is the yoga of Mahāmudrā, where realization and liberation are
    simultaneous.
Primordial purity is self-arisen, unborn, and transparent,
and wisdom's manifestation is the fundamental nature of the Great
    Perfection,
where whatever appears is naturally freed within an all-pervasive
    expanse.
Beloved, resolve this, and I too shall abide in that state.

Turquoise then rested in a blissful and empty meditation. She actualized
the truth of ultimate reality, inexpressible and inconceivable, and then
achieved the realization of a fourth-level awareness holder.[13] Later, she
attracted disciples in four ways and benefitted them through vast enno-
bling deeds.[14]

In late autumn, when birds must return home, Golden prepared to
go to India, and Turquoise to Bhutan. Before departing, they once again
exchanged intimate advice.

Ki ki! Divine Friend!
Ki ki! Sublime Partner!
I, Turquoise, here before you,
am a little blue bird without any protection
whose time has come to fly away.
Now we have no choice but to part,
and my sorrow is unbearable.
In recalling your profound and sublime teachings,
I am chilled by the dark winds of separation's intense pain
and by the scattering of our carefree and loving flock.
Yet I shan't regret, for such is the nature of all that gathers.
Pure Golden, though I have no wish to leave you,
this very experience defines saṃsāra as that which is compounded.

We must leave, never to see or hear from each other again.
Kyé hud, kyé hud! Dearest Golden,
keep in heart our promise to recall the noble teachings,
so that at death we will be sure not to hold any regret.
Travelers are we, congregated here in the market,
and upon us are the last days of autumn, the time for farewells.
Let us focus on the precious teachings of the dharma,
and effortlessly perfect our practice
to realize the indivisibility of empty-awareness,
the dharmakāya, self-awareness.
Upon this, the royal throne of Samantabhadra,
an ever pure and unimpeded state,
may we and all others be freed!

Turquoise spoke and sat sobbing, *Ki ki ki ki.* Golden replied:

Here in this excellent place, the Dragon Plain of Tsari,
our flock has delighted and relaxed
in lovely grassy meadows and deepened our meditation.
Safe from all harm, we birds have stayed together.
In this divine and sacred pleasure garden
we came to meet, my blue Turquoise.
Gathering and parting are the nature of saṃsāra,
so triumphant buddhas from the past have validly taught.
Since nothing at all is permanent or stable,
don't exhaust yourself in sorrow, darling!
All things of the world and beyond are illusory manifestations,
unobstructed empty clarity, like reflections in a mirror.
They appear and vanish simultaneously, like water and waves.
Dualistic mind's natural purity is an uncontrived and fresh state
endowed with twofold purity beyond thought and expression.[15]
Unborn, unceasing, and unchanging,
it's self-knowing awareness, Samantabhadra,
the one taste of the non-dual nature of all things of saṃsāra and
   nirvāṇa.
Perfected within the primordially pure expanse, free from any basis,
it's experienced as great exaltation, the indivisibility of space and
   wisdom.
Sustain this, the state of naturally liberated primordial wisdom!

Having finished speaking, Golden rested in the realization of this wisdom. After sharing in their sorrow, the other birds returned to their own places. Golden went to India and Turquoise went to Bhutan, where the forest hermitage of Serthang Pangri transformed into the pure land of Turquoise Space-Activity. All the birds with fortunate connections eventually arrived there too.

This is a fantasy tale written by a lazy and misperceiving mendicant. May it be virtuous and auspicious!

Notes

1. Sera Khandro's revealed treasures contain two major collections: the *Ḍākinīs' Heart Essence* (*Mkha' 'gro thugs thig*) and the *Secret Treasury of the Dharmatā Ḍākinīs* (*Chos nyid mkha' 'gro'i gsang mdzod*). Her collected writings include both practices and experiential accounts that arise from "pure vision" (*dag snang*).

2. Cycles of teachings with the signifier "pure vision" are found in the collections of other *tertöns* (*gter ston*) who significantly influenced Sera Khandro, such as the visionary Dudjom Lingpa (Bdud 'joms gling pa, 1835–1904), the father of Sera Khandro's lama and consort, Drimé Özer. Several of Dudjom Lingpa's twenty-one volumes of treasure revelations and writings contain practices and teachings from "pure vision" transmissions.

3. Arriving in Eastern Tibet in 1907, Sera Khandro never met Dudjom Lingpa in person. Nevertheless, her connection to his lineage through her partnership with Drimé Özer is a defining feature of her life. Throughout her own life story and that of Drimé Özer, she emphasizes her commitment to preserving and spreading the two treasure lineages of father and son, Dudjom Lingpa and Drimé Özer.

4. In her long autobiography Sera Khandro describes the first moment she lays eyes on Drimé Özer, "Among [the pilgrims] was one with long dreadlocks. As soon as I saw him, my entire perception changed. I thought, 'He truly is the one called the Omniscient Longchenpa,' and my eyes filled with tears. With goosebumps all over my body, I clasped my palms together and said, 'Through your great compassion, may I never separate from your side throughout all my lifetimes.'" See Se ra mkha' 'gro, "Dbus bza' mkha' 'gro'i rang rnam skal ldan dad pa'i mchod sdong," 93–94.

5. For an exploration of Sera Khandro's writings and the role of love in them, see Jacoby, *Love and Liberation*.

6. Khachöd (*mkha' spyod*) is the buddhafield associated with Sera Khandro's personal practice deity, Vajravārāhi, and references those dwelling in the

celestial realms ("enjoyers of space," or *ḍākinīs*). Sera Khandro spoke often of being ready to go there.

7. From Se ra mkha''gro, *Chab shog sogs skor zhig bzhugs*, 3:343.
8. See Se ra mkha''gro, *Sera mkha' 'gro bde chen bde ba'i rdo rje'i gsung 'bum*, 7:2–3.
9. Sera Khandro tells us in her short autobiography, "The Excellent Path of Devotion," 285, regarding Drimé Özer: "Moreover, out of his kindness, my Lord of Refuge, the Wish-Fulfilling Jewel actually had regarded a miserable dog like me as a 'lion with a turquoise mane.'"
10. Sera Khandro and Drimé Özer become aware of their prophesized destiny as treasure-revealing partners through numerous signs, visions, and predictions. These bring to light the nature of their timeless connection spanning many lifetimes. Nonetheless, the various challenges of an actual life together and the intensity of Sera Khandro's own struggle to find a place of safety and belonging for herself and her children lead her repeatedly to question the benefit of her remaining in the world. Recounting an emotional exchange prompted by Drimé Özer's discovering some writing by Sera Khandro on practices for death as well as some advice for him, Sera Khandro writes, "Drimé Özer said, 'What is the meaning of this teaching on the practice of combining and transferring with the five elements at the moment of death? Whichever way I examine your behavior, your body and such, there is something I doubt. Does this mean that you are going to cast your two children and especially me from your heart and not stay here any longer? Who will focus our minds and lead our hearts? As you know, I in particular have no refuge or place of hope other than you, who are both my partner and my lama. I will be devastated if you give up on me.' He sat heavy-hearted. I couldn't bear it. I told him everything that had caused my thinking in the past without hiding anything and gave my promise not to think that way going forward." "Dbus bza' mkha''gro'i rang rnam skal ldan dad pa'i mchod sdong," 365–66.
11. Samantabhadra (Kun tu bzang po) is the name of the primordial buddha. The six special features describe Samantabhadra's mode of enlightenment: (1) exalted from the ground, (2) self-appearing to himself, (3) discerning, (4) liberated upon that discernment, (5) abiding within the nature, (6) unmoving from that state. For more information see Thondup, *Practice of Dzogchen*, 59.
12. "The antinomies of production and cessation, eternality and annihilation, sameness and difference, and coming and going, which constitute the eight deluded views of sentient beings." Buswell and Lopez, *Princeton Dictionary of Buddhism*, 835.
13. A fourth-level awareness holder is one who has attained the qualities of a "spontaneously accomplished vidyādhara" (*lhun grub rig 'dzin*), where the

full extent of what must be abandoned and what must be realized on the
Vajrayāna path is reached. See Jigmé Lingpa and Kangyur Rinpoché, *Trea-
sury of Precious Qualities.*

14. The four methods for gathering disciples are explained to be: being gener-
ous, speaking nicely, behaving in a meaningful way, and being consistent in
word and deed.

15. "Twofold purity" describes that which has been purified of both conceptual
and emotional obscurations.

Tibetan Sources

Se ra mkha''gro. *Chab shog sogs skor zhig bzhugs* [Collected letters]. In *Dbus bza'
mkha' 'gro gsung 'bum* [Collected works of Üza Khandro], vol. 3. Sichuan: Si
khron mi rigs dpe skrun khang, 2009.

———. "Dag snang 'kha''gro'i gsang mdzod zab mo las brda don 'brel ba rdo
rje'i gad mo bzhugs so" [Vajra laughter: Connecting signs with meaning, from
the *ḍākinī's* profound secret treasury of pure visions]. In *Dbus bza' mkha' 'gro
gsung 'bum* [Collected works of Üza Khandro], 3:362–66. Sichuan: Si khron
mi rigs dpe skrun khang, 2009.

———. "Dbus bza' mkha''gro'i rang rnam skal ldan dad pa'i mchod sdong" [A
shrine for faithful and fortunate disciples: The autobiography of the *ḍākinī*
from Central Tibet]. Vol. 1 of *Dbus bza' mkha' 'gro gsung 'bum* [Collected
works of Üza Khandro]. Sichuan: Si khron mi rigs dpe skrun khang, 2009.

———. *Se ra mkha' 'gro bde chen bde ba'i rdo rje' gsung 'bum* [The collected
works of Sera Khandro Dechen Dewé Dorjé]. Vol. 15 of *Gangs can skyes ma'i
dpe tshogs* [A collection of printed works of Tibetan women]. Sichuan: Si
khron bod yig dpe rnying bsdu sgrig khang, 2015.

———. "Skyab rje thams cad mkkyen pa grub pa'i dbang phyug zab gter rgya
mtsho'i mnga bdag rin po che padma 'gro 'dul gsang sngags gling pa'i rnam
par thar pa snying gi mun sel dad pa'i shing rta ratna'i chun 'phyang utpa la'i
phreng ba bzhugs so" [An utpala garland of blooming flowers to ornament
the ears and a chariot of devotion to enlighten the heart: The story of the lib-
eration of Pema Dodrul Sangngak Lingpa, the omniscient refuge lord, mas-
ter of accomplished ones, and precious keeper of infinite profound treasures].
In *Se ra mkha''gro, Se ra mkha' 'gro bde chen bde ba'i rdo rje'i gsung 'bum.*

Additional Sources

Buswell, Robert, Jr., and Donald Lopez. *The Princeton Dictionary of Buddhism.*
Princeton, NJ: Princeton University Press, 2014.

Jacoby, Sarah. *Love and Liberation: Autobiographical Writings of the Tibetan Buddhist Visionary Sera Khandro*. New York: Columbia University Press, 2014.

Jigme Lingpa and Kangyur Rinpoche (Longchen Yeshé Dorjé). *The Treasury of Precious Qualities: Book Two, Vajrayana and the Great Perfection*. Boulder, CO: Shambhala, 2020.

Khandro, Sera. "The Excellent Path of Devotion: An Abridged Story of a Mendicant's Experiences in Response to Questions from Vajra Kin." In *Refining Our Perception of Reality*, translated by Ngawang Zangpo. Boston: Snow Lion, 2013.

Thondup, Tulku. *The Practice of Dzogchen: Longchen Rabjam's Writings on the Great Perfection*. Boston: Snow Lion, 2014.

18

Love, Death, and Devotion between *Yab* and *Yum*

INTRODUCED AND TRANSLATED BY SARAH H. JACOBY

C AN TRUE love defy death, as it does in fairy tales?[1] Or are love and death attracted to each other like moths to a flame? Perhaps Denis de Rougemont was right when he famously stated, "Romance only comes into existence where love is fatal, frowned upon and doomed by life itself."[2] European love stories such as that of Tristan and Iseult or Romeo and Juliet depict this darker view in which passionate love and death dance hand in hand. Much Tibetan Buddhist writing also shares in this vision of passionate love as lethal. For instance, Dza Patrül Rinpoché's *Holy Dharma Advice: A Drama in the Lotus Garden* narrates the love story between two frolicking honeybees enamored of each other until one is smothered to death.[3] Invoking motifs drawn from the Sanskrit aesthetic of eroticism, *śṛṅgārarasa*—including honey, bees, blooming flowers, and rain clouds—Patrül Rinpoché repurposes them as illustrations of how "losing one's mind" (*yid shor ba*), the literal Tibetan etymology for falling in love, distracts lovers into an oblivion devoid of dharma in which they forget the truth of impermanence.

Surely Prince Charming's vitalizing kiss is a world away from the austerities of Buddhist renunciation and the rigors of spiritual practice. But is there no space for loving devotion toward one's guru, a Buddhist version of *bhakti* in which the disciple's fervent desire to merge her mind with that of the guru shares in the vocabulary of passionate love? No, Patrül Rinpoché's honeybee love story would seem to insist, and Western scholarship reiterates, there is no *bhakti* devotion in Buddhism.[4] Lest we misunderstand, in his famous beginner's guide to Nyingma Tibetan Buddhist practice, *Words of My Perfect Teacher*, Patrül Rinpoché clarifies what type of longing disciples should harbor when performing *guruyoga* and visualizing themselves as Vajrayoginī "gazing longingly at the heart of her teacher." This is not the longing of a lover yearning for her beloved, for here "longingly (*rings pa'i tshul gyis*)" means "expressing a sense of impatience to be with the teacher, this being the only source of joy."[5]

But doesn't Patrül Rinpoché's effort to pin down what type of longing Vajrayoginī should feel for Guru Rinpoché suggest the possibility that devotional longing and passionate longing could share discursive and affective space? Is the surplus of intense emotion disciples feel for their gurus, which forms the heart blood of Tibetan Buddhist biography, always expressed through metaphors other than lover and beloved, such as the love a child feels for her parent? Is devotion (*dad pa; mos pa; mos gus*) always an upward-bound gaze, an expression of feeling from an inferior toward his superior in knowledge, age, or rank? Can devotion be mutual, a powerful bond of *samaya* between guru and disciple, *yab* and *yum*, or would that push its scope into territory closer to the infatuation of passionate love?

Coursing through the passage I translate here, somewhere in that common ground between love and devotion, a death-defying power emerges, one that shares more with fairy tales than with stories of star-crossed lovers. The year is 1922, and the site is Nyimalung, or Sun Valley, not far from Dartsang, Serta, the former seat of the renowned Dudjom Lingpa and current residence of some of his descendants. The scion of the Dudjom line, Drimé Özer, referred to in the following translation as "the Master" or "Wish-fulfilling Jewel," is giving empowerments for his treasure teachings to a crowd. One day, after completing the teachings, he climbs off his throne and heads straight away to the tent where one of his consorts sleeps. She comes from faraway Lhasa, hence her nickname Üza Khandro, or Ḍākinī Lady from Central Tibet. She is not the mother of his children and in fact has just extricated herself from a discordant decade-long marriage with a religious hierarch from Benak Monastery in the Mar Valley of Golok. Drimé Özer makes a beeline to her bedside because he intuits that she is leaving him. And he is not wrong: death comes to beckon her sensuously, not as some ghoulish Grim Reaper but as a sumptuous rainbow display of *ḍākinīs* (Tib: *khandros*) and offering goddesses, each joyfully welcoming her to the Palace of Great Bliss with offering substances pleasing to the senses.

As this crystalline technicolor radiance intensifies, Üza Khandro's coarse physical body grows colder and more lifeless. Drimé Özer begs her to revive, using standard devotional phrasing that a disciple would use toward his guru. Heartsick, he bemoans that losing her would mean losing his reference point, his source of refuge, the object of hope upon whom he can rely—it would mean losing his lama. But he is the son of Dudjom Lingpa, and she is a visionary and female consort eleven years his junior, with no local religious pedigree! If she were lamenting his loss in words like these (which she does when he dies only two years later), we would not raise our eyebrows. But in the reverse, a senior male *tulku* supplicating a young female outsider to Serta/Golok territory, these are heavy words, laden with a respect and devotion that is startling in its direction and intensity.

Like Prince Charming's kiss, Drimé Özer's teardrop pierces through her magnificent *ḍākinī* vision, resuscitating her earthly body. Üza Khandro will have to wait longer to return to the castle in the sky with her *ḍākinī* sisters. First, she will have to grieve Drimé Özer's loss, then she will become Sera Khandro after Sotrül (Natsok Rangdröl) takes her in at his monastery in Serta named Sera Tekchen Chönkhor Ling. As she processes her losses and saṃsāra's adversities, she will reveal her own treasures and write the story of her life. From it, a century later, we will learn that not only did Sera Khandro feel deep loving devotion for Drimé Özer but he felt the same for her.

Unlike Patrül Rinpoché's *Drama in the Lotus Garden*, the love story penned by Sera Khandro between herself and Drimé Özer was at once a story of guru devotion and a mutual sacred biography of love between *yab* and *yum*. She presented that relation as one characterized not by hierarchy, misogyny, and manipulation but by inspiration and sustenance. Earthly life was certainly no fairy tale—her *ḍākinī* interlocutors name the enmity and hostility others in her midst directed toward her, including the antagonism of other female consorts. These challenges serve to further highlight the moments when saṃsāra's woes give way to rainbow-colored buddhafields, and love prevails over death.

A Teardrop of Devotion
Sera Khandro Dewé Dorjé

Early in the third month of that year [1922], the Master Drimé Özer gave empowerments and reading transmissions to nearly three hundred people. At that time, I wrote down a set of instructions on combining and transferring the five elements and a final testament for the Master about how to carry out his present and future deeds. I hid them by my pillow in a chest for sacred objects and kept them secret from him. One day, he abruptly left the reading transmission and came to my place just as dusk was falling.

"Why have you come straight here without having dinner?" I asked.

The Master replied, "A suspicion arose, so I came. I wonder what you have in this chest for sacred objects?" As soon as he said this, suddenly he jumped up and grabbed the small chest.

Even though this made me uncomfortable, he didn't seem to notice.

He opened the chest. When he saw the texts, he asked, "What are these?"

"These aren't important," I responded. "Earlier I thought that if I had the opportunity to go to Sotok (Bswo thog), I would need something like these, so I wrote them."

The Master replied,

If you intended this as advice for me while you were there, why have you written about combining and transferring the five elements at the time of death? Examining your conduct, your body, and so forth, I don't believe you. What is the meaning of your casting both your son and daughter and especially me from your heart and not remaining in this life? Upon whom can we place our trust and affection? In particular, you know that aside from you, there is no one who is my source of refuge and hope upon whom I rely as both my consort and my lama— you casting me from your heart is such misery!

He was devastated.

Unable to bear this, I told him what had caused me to think this way earlier without keeping anything secret, and I pledged that from now on, I wouldn't do this. I said, "This time, my life force is not exhausted, but my mental force is near its end, so please be careful. Since we have a profound connection through aspirations over many lifetimes, it is certain that benefit will arise."

Then, that month on the night of the 27th, *khandros* arrived to escort me. The *ḍākkis*[6] said,

E ma!
Joyous blissful *yoginī*,
supreme messenger of the *khandros* of the three lands,

though you came here for the sake of beings,
you experience all sorts of miseries—
enmity from dharma siblings and consorts,
hostility from the corrupt community,
and the degeneration of the times.
Please consider this method of actually traveling, like magic,
to the Palace of Great Bliss
on the authentic excellent path of sky expanse,
the innately radiant and outwardly luminous five-colored lights
of originally pure naturally radiant primordial wisdom:

I am Zhinzé Karmo (White Beauty),
the messenger *ḍākkima* of the vajra family.
Bringing your body on the eastern path,
the white silk path of mirror-like primordial wisdom,
I am the emissary of the vajra *khandro*.

I am Sermo Dondrup (Golden Accomplished One),
the messenger of the jewel family *khandroma*.
Bringing your mind southward
on the yellow silk path of equanimous primordial wisdom,
I am the emissary of the jewel *khandro*.

Marmo Zhinzema (Red Beauty),
messenger of the lotus family *khandroma*,
brings your mind westward
on the red silk path of discriminating primordial wisdom.
I am the emissary of the lotus *khandro*.

I am Zhindzé Jangmo (Green Beauty),
messenger of the karma family *khandroma*.
Bringing your mind northward on the
green silk path of all-accomplishing primordial wisdom,
I am the emissary of the karma *khandro*.

Zhindzé Tingsel (Brilliant Blue Beauty),
messenger of the buddha family *khandroma*,
brings your mind on the blue silk path
of ultimate reality primordial wisdom

to the naturally manifesting buddhafield.
I am the emissary of the buddha *khandro*.

Depart on the silk path
traversed by the *vidyādharas*
and come to the land of *khandros*,
where you can enjoy inconceivable happiness and bliss,
abundant pleasures of joyous heroines
and bliss-emptiness of co-emergent bodhisattvas.

More deeds that benefit yourself and others await you in the
    buddhafield,
so even after the *khandro* citadels[7] in your channel centers *rtsa gnas*
dissolve into light, transform your contaminated elements
into the ultimate sphere of awareness-emptiness.

Having purified vital essence into the boundless space of ultimate
    reality
and the movement of wind *rlung* into primordial wisdom,
and blend them inseparably with life-supporting wind.

Come now, *ḍākkima* of the expanse,
to the secret palace of clear light.
Dance over here, swaying,
adorned with jewels of spontaneous presence,
with ribbons of silk fluttering in the wind,
hair bobbing about in a topknot,
and the rest cascading down.

This magical scene,
filled with wondrous rainbow light,
billowing clouds of heroes and heroines,
and reverberating melodious music
is naturally arising spontaneous presence—*e ma ho!*

As soon as she said this, rainbow light pervaded everywhere. Within
it, the white vajra lady of form held a crystal mirror, the red vajra lady
of sound held a golden stringed instrument, and the green vajra lady
of smell held an incense burner with the six medicinal substances. The

bright red vajra lady of taste held a resplendent food offering. The deep blue vajra lady of touch held a divine brocade garment. The white vajra lady of phenomena held a "source of phenomena" triangle.

The white flower lady held a garland of red lotuses. The yellow incense lady held an incense pot. The bright red lamp lady held a lantern. The green perfume lady held a conch shell. The bright blue food lady held something delicious. The green music lady held cymbals. The red vajra drummer lady held a magical small drum. The bright blue vajra *vīṇā* lady held a melodious *vīṇā*. The yellow vajra flute lady held a six-toned flute. The green vajra clay drum lady held a loud clay drum.

Interspersed among these were the group of beautiful vajra ladies, the group of dancing vajra ladies, the eighteen skeleton heroes, the four siblings who are lords of the charnel grounds, as well as other sons and daughters of divinities. All carried abundant offering objects such as parasols and victory banners made of various precious substances, pendants, yak-tail fans with bejeweled handles, tassels, streamers, and magical hanging banners. Their dancing bodies swayed while their melodious Brahma-voices sang *GURU SIDDHI, HA RI NI SA*, and more. With earnest hearts and gestures, they welcomed me.

When this appeared, the four elements dissolved from the outside in, and it felt like my body had emptied out. My mind was the same as outer space—discriminating insight was naturally purified, allowing me to see saṃsāra and nirvāṇa vividly. When it became difficult for me to distinguish what I was seeing, everyone in the inner circle headed by the Master and Sotrül wept and wailed. Other members of the religious encampment community also felt uncomfortable. As when a hawk destroys a bird's nest, there was a commotion. In particular, the Master was devastated. He placed my head in his lap with his hands and said,

> Dear one, if you cast me from your heart and depart for the buddha-field, I too will definitely not delay in concentrating on joining you. Let alone maintaining and propagating my Treasure Dharma and so forth, I won't leave even a trace of it! You are the object of my hope and trust in this and future lifetimes. You are the great chariot that traverses the quick path. My consort, jewel of my heart, may I be inseparable from you in all my lifetimes!

In devastation, a single teardrop of his fell into my ear. It felt as if it hit my heart. Even though my external breath was about to stop, I seemed to regain a bit of consciousness. Again, the Master touched his face to my ear and said over and over,

> Dear one, don't forget me. Concentrate on *A NRĪ HŪNG* in your heart center and your consciousness will become clear.

After this, I remembered the words of the Wish-fulfilling Jewel, and when I focused on him, the entire vision I'd just had receded further and further into the distance and then disappeared. My perception of all the coarse material things of this world seemed clear at times and unclear at others. Even my illusory body was like a frozen rock. Like a person abruptly awakened from sleep, I forgot the whole previous vision. Disoriented, my eyes could see a little bit, so I looked around. The entire house was filled with butter lamps. Sotrül and Tupzang were trying to warm my legs by the fire. With my head still on his lap, the Master performed rituals that stabilized my body maṇḍala's sense faculties and summoned my longevity. Even so, I was unable to say anything, as if I had become mute. At daybreak, when all the other doctors and ritualists thought that I was dying, due to the great blessing power of my secret consort Wish-fulfilling Jewel, and due to my negative karma not having completely ripened, he gradually resuscitated me from the brink of losing my external breath. The whole group of disciples gathered there, especially the Master and Sotrül, were extremely joyous and rejoiced as if the living had reunited with the dead.

NOTES

1. I would like to acknowledge the Tibetan translation class at Northwestern University in which Dhondup T. Rekjong, Joshua Brallier, and I read this passage together in the midst of the deep isolation of the pandemic in the spring of 2020, which was a life-sustaining experience of a different sort than the one of which Sera Khandro wrote. I'd also like to thank Lama Jabb and Loppön Jigme Rinpoche for reading parts of this with me and answering my many questions—their kindness has made this a better translation.
2. De Rougemont, *Love in the Western World*, 15.
3. For the Tibetan, see Dpal sprul rin po che, *Gtam padma'i tshal gyi zlos gar*; and for an English translation, see Thondup, *Enlightened Living*.
4. Beyer, "Notes on the Vision Quest," 339–40.
5. Dpal sprul rin po che O rgyan 'jigs med chos kyi dbang po, *Rdzogs pa chen po*

klong chen snying thig gi sngon 'gro'i khrid yig kun bzang bla ma'i zhal lung, fol.
240r, lines 4–5; Patrul Rinpoché, *Words of My Perfect Teacher,* 313.

6. *Dākki* (and *dākkima*) are diminutives of *dākinī*, which in Tibetan is *khan-droma* (*mkha' 'gro ma*) or *khandro* (*mkha' 'gro*) for short, referring to a class of female divinities whose etymology means "sky-goer." Sera Khandro varies her usage of all these different terms, as reflected in this translation.

7. For "*khandro* citadels," I am reading the manuscript spelling, "mkha' 'gro'i grong," not the printed edition, which reads "mkha' 'gro'i grogs."

Tibetan Source

Dbus bza' mkha' 'gro. "Dbus mo bde ba'i rdo rje'i rnam par thar pa nges 'byung 'dren pa'i shing rta skal ldan dad pa'i mchod sdong" [The autobiography of the Central Tibetan woman Dewé Dorjé: A chariot leading to renunciation and a reliquary of faith for fortunate ones]. In *Dbus bza' mkha' 'gro'i gsung 'bum* [Collected works of Üza Khandro], 1:364–71. Chengdu: Si khron mi rigs dpe skrun khang, 2009.

Additional Sources

Beyer, Stephan. "Notes on the Vision Quest in Early Mahayana," In *Prajñāpāramitā and Related Systems: Studies in Honor of Edward Conze.* Berkeley: University of California Press, 1977.

De Rougemont, Denis. *Love in the Western World.* New York: Pantheon, 1956.

Dpal sprul rin po che. *Gtam padma'i tshal gyi zlos gar* [Drama in the lotus garden]. Chengdu: Si khron mi rigs dpe skrun khang, 1986.

Dpal sprul rin po che O rgyan 'jigs med chos kyi dbang po. *Rdzogs pa chen po klong chen snying thig gi sngon 'gro'i khrid yig kun bzang bla ma'i zhal lung* [The words of my perfect teacher: Explanatory manual on the preliminary practices of the heart essence of the vast expanse, the Great Perfection]. Delhi: Konchhog Lhadrepa, n.d.

Jacoby, Sarah H. *Love and Liberation: Autobiographical Writings of the Tibetan Buddhist Visionary Sera Khandro.* New York: Columbia University Press, 2014.

Patrul Rinpoche. *The Words of My Perfect Teacher.* San Francisco: HarperCollins, 1994.

Thondup, Tulku, trans. *Enlightened Living: Teachings of Tibetan Buddhist Masters.* Boston: Shambhala, 1990.

19

Inspiration for Spiritual Practice

INTRODUCED AND TRANSLATED BY CHIME LAMA

The meritorious scent that delights mother beings and *ḍākinīs* will certainly dispel the stench of the five degenerations in an instant!

—Khenpo Gangshar

KHENPO GANGSHAR WANGPO (b. 1925) lived during the height of 1950s turbulence in Tibet leading up to the Cultural Revolution. He was a learned scholar and meditation master of Eastern Tibet and a disciple of Shechen Kongtrul Rinpoché (1901–1960). Khenpo Gangshar received training at Shechen Monastery in Kham, one of the six principal monasteries of the Nyingma tradition. He would later become a senior professor there and at the Kagyu Surmang Monastery, as well as an influential tutor to many masters, including Chögyam Trungpa (1940–1987), Tulku Urgyen (1920–1996), and Thrangu Rinpoché (1933–2023). He is renowned for his pithy and profound dharma teachings and for the meditation instructions that he gave to monastics and laity alike. He freely shared esoteric Mahāmudrā and Dzogchen teachings with those he met, pointing out to them the nature of their own minds. He remained in Tibet to teach students following the Chinese invasion and occupation; the details concerning his death remain unclear.

"Songs to Inspire Spiritual Practice" (*Nyams len la skul 'ded kyi mgur ma*) is drawn from Khenpo Gangshar's collected works.[1] It is composed of two distinct *gur*, or songs, that are pedagogic in nature. The first song features persuasive language, through which the author emphasizes the importance of mind training and virtuous action. The second song assumes a more foreboding tone, cautioning disciples who, like timid deer, are approaching a dangerous pasture. In fact, Khenpo Gangshar wrote the following prophecy of the impending events of the Chinese invasion of Tibet:

> Within the first month, *Zing zing zing!*
> Within the second, *U ru ru!*
> Within the third month, *Sha ra ra!*
> Within the fourth month, *Tra ra ra!*
> Within the fifth month, wails of *Sha ra ra!*
> Within the sixth, the Chinese shout *So!* will ring out.
> Within the seventh, they'll control the realm of Tibet.
> If on the cusp of the fifth, sixth, and seventh,
> you do not go to a hidden land, delaying,
> there is no doubt you will be made Chinese.[2]

Through these two songs, Khenpo Gangshar urges his students to remember the guru and persevere in their practice, assuring them that such dangerous times are precisely when a practitioner needs to remember the guru the most. In that sense, one can understand these songs to have been written during wartime, which explains the sense of dread and urgency that pervades them.

Repeatedly throughout the songs, Khenpo Gangshar exhorts the reader to recall the guru. The guru can be understood as the anchor to which wandering practitioners can fasten themselves in times of need. When stirred by disruptive thoughts, recall the guru, he advises. "When sad, befriend sadness; when suffering, befriend suffering," just as the guru does. Khenpo Gangshar explains that emulating the guru's way of life can serve as a cure-all medicine that frees one from suffering. Entrusting one's well-being to the guru can be understood as devoting oneself to the guru. Khenpo Gangshar not only advises this; he asserts that he himself has done this. Devoting oneself to the guru unlocks the blessings of the dharma and provides all that is needed for the practitioner's temporary and ultimate well-being. The guru and the dharma are not described as two separate things. Rather, the guru can be understood as the embodiment of the dharma, and by recalling the guru with devotion, one accesses the dharma and its many blessings. Thus, he encourages us to drink the nectar of the dharma "endlessly, day and night."

These songs are particularly relevant to beginning practitioners. Far from falling into the category of specific and advanced visualization instruction, they are practical reminders of how to apply one's dharma training in daily life. At the time of composition, they were meant to be applied in a real-world setting, and a chaotic one at that. The earliest instructions we encounter advise us to recognize and admit our own selfish tendencies and to praise the goodness of others. One can easily envision that these instructions, if applied within our own communities, would have a calming and strengthening effect upon our minds and relationships. Khenpo Gangshar commands us to have unfaltering integrity and to watch out for the negativities that would degrade us. In other words, we are to respect our highest nature. Doing so will certainly bear fruit. He assures us:

> If you always keep these teachings in mind,
> you will be liberated by this path whether you are lay or ordained.
> You will be liberated by this path whether you are male or female.
> There is no one who has not been liberated by this path.[3]

According to Khenpo Gangshar, there is no doubt that if one maintains the guru's teachings, one will be successful. At the end of the first song, he discloses that these instructions are identical to his own personal practice, which is "what the holy guru has granted."

In translating these songs, I grappled with meter. In the Tibetan text, every line in the first song contains exactly eight syllables, and in the second song, eleven. I was unable to preserve this pattern within my translation since Tibetan language can convey much more in a few syllables than English can. However, I attempted to reflect the line breaks as much as possible, and in particular the number of lines within a given verse. Certain phrases and verbal constructions were particularly confusing, and I would like to thank Bardor Rinpoché, Mingyur Rinpoché, and Lama Yeshe Gyamtso for their help. Lastly, I would like to thank my Lotsawa Translation Workshop leader, Jules Levinson, for his support and encouragement.

Songs to Inspire Spiritual Practice
Khenpo Gangshar Wangpo

Song One

The pith instruction of the Practice Lineage
is to discipline your mind continuously.
If you don't tame your mind internally,
it is difficult to secure the welfare of others externally.

Therefore, repeatedly examine your mind.
If stirred by desirable objects,
recall the advice of the father guru time and again.

The practice that pleases the exalted Buddha
is to publicly proclaim your self-serving duplicity
and to raise the virtues of friends and others to the sky.

I kept the cause of present and future happiness,
supreme bodhicitta, within my heart.
I nurtured the natural state, the supreme crown of remembrances,
the intention of the innate Great Perfection.

Whomever you befriend, do not resent them,
and wherever you go you will be free of weariness.
Whatever you do, strive to benefit others.

Cherish the great Vajrayāna *samaya*[4]
as you cherish your round eyes.
Now, honestly protect it like it's your life.

Although there are many enumerations of *samaya*,
they are all included in the two great tenets:

Thoroughly overcoming the causes of confusion is the *samaya* of view.
Engaging in the great work of love and compassion is the *samaya* of conduct.
If these two meet, the dual purpose of self and other is achieved.

Having obtained the hard-earned body with its freedoms and riches,
do not allow your mind to fall under the influence of afflictive emotions.
By means of mindfulness, introspection, and heedfulness
use this human body for what is essential.

Train in the practice of Mahāmudrā.
Contemplate death and impermanence over and over.
Analyze cause and effect as finely as mustard seeds.
Breed discontent for the six realms of existence.
Dry this great ocean of samsaric suffering!

Supplicate the undeceiving refuge,
the Three Jewels, with sincerity.
Pierce again and again with the arrow of love and compassion
mother sentient beings roaming in saṃsāra.

Take up the friend, the helpful accumulation of merit.
When the foe, the wicked eight worldly dharmas surface,
arise in the form of glorious Vajrasattva.

Whatever the activities of the blessed guru may be,
now with certainty and great confidence
set yourself ablaze with the force of uncontrived devotion.
Hold whatever the guru has accomplished in reverence
and sustain the father guru's essence of self-awareness.

If you always keep these teachings in mind,
you will be liberated by this path whether you are lay or ordained.
You will be liberated by this path whether you are male or female.
There is no one who has not been liberated by this path.

My own practice is like this.
This is what the holy guru has granted.
Since the quintessence of all dharma, sūtras, and tantras,
is none other than the key points of these words,

I will act in accordance with them throughout all my lives,
and hold them in my heart
always and without fail.

Friends, you should act in accordance with this teaching as well
and practice from the bottom of your hearts.

Song Two

Oh! Listen, herd of most fortunate disciples:
when the timid deer walk to grass and water,
who else is the evil hunter that boasts and whirls his arrow of mischief
but the very embodiment of the five degenerations?

When the helpless deer are entrapped in that fearful pasture,
the only way to endure it is by vividly recollecting
their kind and carefree guru, who treated them so affectionately.

Those maidens you occasionally fancied
have left their old homes and disappeared without a trace.

Don't crave the thrill of recollecting them for even a moment.
For when the razor meets your naked youthful flesh
in the binding dungeon prison of karma's courtyard,
where have your conditional and fickle-minded friends gone?

Therefore, now that you have within your hands
the one you have always been with but never seen,
just this mind itself—a jewel that cannot be bought by all the things
in the trichiliocosm world system—do not devalue and discard it.
For even if you sought it for ten thousand eons, it would still be unattainable.

Why not adopt the effortless manner of the sublime father guru?
When sad, befriend sadness; when suffering, befriend suffering;
and when happy, befriend happiness.
Whenever needed, it is ceaselessly before you.
Why not endeavor in such an exceptional dharma?

The innermost essence of the wish-granting gem, the angelic dharma,
is to spread the white wings of benevolence and compassion
through the crevice made by Mahāmudrā that cuts attachment to selfish
    desire.

When there is the slightest danger of dreadful winds arising,
why slacken method and wisdom's magical wings?

If you have been encircling delusive loops of endless distraction,
it is now time to do something meaningful.
Don't follow after the senseless noise of empty fame
nor think of accomplishing meaningless work.

Cease the pointless activities of this life, like bubbles in water.
Trifling self-interest is as hollow as a plantain tree.
Why not delight in upholding the worthy doctrine?

The essence of the teachings, the supreme vehicle of effortless clear light,
is the nectar path of profound instructions of the Sakya, Geluk, Kagyu,
     and Nyingma.
Drink it endlessly day and night. Why ever be satiated?

The path of the arduous vehicle increases hardship.
It is like child's play; do not become attached to it.
Yet, it is improper to have the slightest antipathy
toward the teachings of conventional symbols, like the earlier vehicles.[5]

By means of differentiating supreme correct causality,
separate the provisional and definitive meanings
according to the inclinations of disciples.

The preceding words are whatever came to mind
from the perspective of Gangshar, who rests in primordial simplicity.
These few lines of heartfelt advice given instantly upon recollection
I offer to the ears of my dharma siblings.

I, the beggar monk, have lost my thoughts to compassion.
I vow to engage in the practice of benefitting others forevermore.
The meritorious scent that delights mother beings and *ḍākinīs*
will certainly dispel the stench of the five degenerations in an instant!
Ha ha!

This advice was given in the turbulent earth dog and pig years (1958–59) and
concerns continuously upholding spiritual practice.

NOTES

1. Gang shar dbang po, "Nyams len la skul 'ded kyi mgur ma."
2. Thrangu Rinpoché, *Vivid Awareness*, 3.
3. Gang shar dbang po, "Nyams len la skul 'ded kyi mgur ma," 33.
4. *Samaya* is the sacred bond between guru and disciple. See Kongtrul, *Timeless Treasures*.
5. This refers to the Theravāda school, or "Way of the Elders," in Buddhism.

TIBETAN SOURCE

Gang shar dbang po, Mkhan po. "Nyams len la skul 'ded kyi mgur ma" [Songs to inspire spiritual practice]. In *Mkhan chen rdo rje 'dzin pa kun bzang gang shar rang grol dbang po'i gsung 'bum thar pa'i lam ston* [The collected works, which show the path to liberation of Great Khenpo Vajradhara Kunzang Gangshar Rangdrol Wangpo], 29–38. Kathmandu: Dharma Kosha, 2008.

ADDITIONAL SOURCES

Kongtrul, The Third Jamgon. *Timeless Treasures: Teachings of the Third Jamgon Kongtrul Rinpoche*. Kathmandu: Rigpe Dorje Institute, 2012.

Thrangu Rinpoche. *Vivid Awareness: The Mind Instructions of Khenpo Gangshar*. Boulder, CO: Shambhala, 2011.

20

The Non-Song

INTRODUCED AND TRANSLATED BY LOWELL COOK

KHANGSAR TENPÉ WANGCHUK (1938–2014) was a contemporary Dzogchen master and treasure revealer from the Golok region of Tibet. He was born into the nomadic community of Akyong Khangsar on 1 January 1938, upon a confluence of "four tigers." That is to say, he was born at dawn, the time of the tiger, on a tiger day of the tiger month during the earth-tiger year. Amid these and other auspicious signs, the young child was recognized as the reincarnation of Payak Onpo Rigdzin Dorjé, an emanation of Yudra Nyingpo. Like the majority of monks who lived through the tumultuous Cultural Revolution, Khangsar Rinpoché was unable to receive a proper education in traditional grammar and poetics. Despite this, his writings in general are known for their freshness and ability to inspire, his commentaries for their profundity and depth, and his poetry for its use of the "ornamentation" typical of Indian *kāvya* poetry. This effortless yet impeccable writing style is attributed to his ability to allow realization to spontaneously burst forth from the expanse of timeless awareness.

Khangsar Rinpoché's collected works, published in 2005, comprise five volumes in book format and eight volumes in traditional *pecha* format. His writings include numerous commentaries on seminal works such as the *Thirty-Seven Bodhisattva Practices, The King of Aspirations, Treasury of Dharmadhātu, Three Words That Strike the Vital Point, Beacon of Certainty, Wisdom Guru,* and *Mañjuśrī Great Perfection,* among others. In addition, his writings contain a plethora of original compositions, including songs and poetry, pith instructions, revealed treasures, ritual texts, and other miscellaneous writings.

The song of realization below is found in the first volume of Khangsar Rinpoché's collected works, in a chapter entitled "The Luminous

Expanse: Songs of the View and Great Perfection." As its title would suggest, "The Non-Song" describes a non-dual form of devotion in which the subject-object duality no longer applies. Hence, no elaborate offerings need to be arranged for a guru out there, and no words of praise need to be uttered by a student over here. Rather, as Khangsar Rinpoché shows us in his song, the ultimate expression of devotion is simply to rest in the recognition that from the very beginning, the guru's wisdom mind and one's ordinary mind have never once been separate. And yet, this is not a detached or nihilistic form of devotion, since emptiness and compassion rest together in union. In stanzas 9 and 10, Khangsar Rinpoché's heart aches for all the beings in saṃsāra who remain unaware of the nature of their minds. The great treasury of awakening sits right in front us, yet we fail to see it—what a "gloomy tragedy" indeed. As profound realization and non-dual compassion flow from the expanse of Khangsar Rinpoché's wisdom mind onto the page, the reader is invited to feel the same devoted yearning not only to recognize this state of innate wakefulness for themselves but to help others to do the same.

This song is a reminder that genuine devotion does not entail artificially going through a set of prescribed motions in hopes of grand realization. Rather, devotion is the boundless and wakeful expression of our very nature, free and uncontrived. For Khangsar Rinpoché to guide us in a teaching such as this—his "profound heart of hearts"—is the highest form of kindness. He offers these instructions in the form of a song to his readers, "with love the likes of a mother for her child," the perfect expression of bodhicitta. The song's colophon states that Khangsar Rinpoché wrote this song spontaneously for a personal student while he was in prison near the Tsaidam salt marshes of Qinghai. The fact that his concerns lie not with his lack of personal freedom in the confines of the physical prison but rather with freeing his student from the "cage of pleasurable and painful perceptions" speaks volumes about this master's devotion to awakening.

Readers of the original Tibetan will notice that each line of the song begins with the same syllable. This is a classical poetic form known as "matching initial letters" (thog ma'i zung ldan). In this song, that initial syllable is the Tibetan ma, which almost always acts as a negation. These negations highlight the text's content, the inconceivable and unfabricated nature of the Great Perfection. Needless to say, this poetic form was challenging to reproduce in English. Many translators might have acknowledged it in a footnote and otherwise completely avoided re-creating it in English. However, given that it is such an indispensable element of the song, I attempted to re-create this pattern and experimented with different approaches throughout the sixteen stanzas. Often, I translated the syllable *ma* in the form of English prefixes such as *un-*, *in-*, *im-*, or *non-*. To reflect that the song is written in a classical style, I capitalized the first letter of each line. In other places, I translated it with a negating word, such as *never, without,* or *don't.* I favored placing these words at the beginning of the line as per the original Tibetan, but I also experimented with placing them at the end of the line, as in stanzas 4 and 15, or in the middle, as in stanza 8.

In an attempt to reflect *The Non-Song's* profound voice and ultimate perspective, I often translated verbs as subclauses instead of main verbs to add to the sense of openness. To re-create the song's unelaborate simplicity, I tended to translate into the passive voice. While this does not make for so-called strong English, it does help to diminish the dualistic sense of an agent or doer that tends to come with the active voice. I intentionally minimized Sanskrit and diacritics, opting to translate into English as much as possible so that the naturalness and familiarity of the translation's language would reflect the free and natural state of mind described in the song. Punctuation was also intentionally omitted as a nod toward the naked, natural state.

As is the case with the higher teachings of the Great Perfection, there is a strong sense of secrecy. This is clear in the final stanza as well as in the seal to *samaya* at the conclusion of the song. The conclusion of the text is marked with "Samaya. Seal. Seal. Seal." This formula is typical of treasure literature and suggests that this song was not composed in an ordinary sense, but rather revealed. While texts of this nature are generally restricted to the initiated, Tulku Sonam Dorjé, a direct student of Khangsar Rinpoché's and senior lama at his monastery, said it was permissible for me to translate this song and publish it in this volume. Readers are encouraged to read this song with an open and respectful frame of mind. I would like to extend my humble gratitude to Tulku Sonam Dorjé for providing me with Khangsar Rinpoché's collected works, the inspiration to translate this song, and the reading transmission to do so. May it be of benefit!

The Non-Song on the View of the Great Perfection
Khangsar Tenpé Wangchuk

Uncontrived is the primordially pure dharma body, unborn
Unimpeded is the enjoyment body of bliss-emptiness, non-dual
Uncertain is the way the emanation body manifests, miraculously
Undeluded are these three bodies, completely present in you

The Great Guru's sacred commitments, the quintessence of realization
     ever stainless,
The heart blood of mother sky-dancers, their assemblies always boundless,
And the treasury of instructions on natural liberation beyond meditation
     forever limitless—
With these you rule the primordial throne in a state entirely effortless

Without being caged in the trap of ignorance, subject-object duality,
Without being abandoned, the five poisons dawn as the five wisdoms
Without delusion, the dharma body's natural face manifests
Without practicing, the ultimate result is spontaneously present

When resting in the four modes of letting be, uncontrived,
The timeless natural state dawns spontaneously and unassisted
This luminous state—clarity and emptiness non-dual and unimpeded—
Is inseparable from all the buddha's awakened minds uncountable

Without delusion, refuge is sought in the awareness of the three bodies
Without realization, the supreme motivation is born free from confusion
Without exception, the obstructing enemies, subject-object ignorance, are
     dispelled into the expanse
Without refinement, empty saṃsāra and nirvāṇa are the protection circle

Never generated, self-originating awareness is invoked
Never fading, it resides immutably throughout the three times
Never distracted, the natural face is met with homage
Never arranged, offerings of sense pleasures are the ornament of awareness

Never praised, it is beyond being praised by the three spheres unreal
Never known, deluded ignorance is confessed into primordially pure space
Never fabricated, rejoicing is offered to clarity and emptiness non-dual
Never exhorted, the vast dharma wheel of infinite spaciousness turns

Dedicate to the state where inexhaustible phenomena are exhausted
Aspire to the space where impure obscurations are naturally pure
May primordial awakening dawn, impossible not to be awake
This is the ultimate ritual, immune to elaborations, free from constructs

Unawakened in the thick darkness of unaware ignorance
Uninhibited in the cage of pleasurable and painful perceptions
Uncertain about the dharma body, the natural state of awareness
Unceasingly wandering through saṃsāra, what a gloomy tragedy

Immemorially pure is the face of the unborn dharma body
Imperceptible when obscured by the latent conditions in the all-ground
Impurity and delusion proliferate like ripples on a lake
Imaginary samsaric beings, our dear mothers, so worthy of compassion

Unattached to the delusions of the eight worldly concerns
Uncommitted and free like a hawk escaping its cage
Unimpededly wandering through mountainous solitude
Unconceived but spontaneously present, bliss erupts forth

Without deviating from the intent of the Sole Mother, Perfection of
    Wisdom
Without arising or ceasing, all is as the stainless sky
Without fluctuation within the ever lucid natural state
Without distraction just simply resting, we are now liberated

Don't distort—a mind that distorts is but confused thoughts
Don't analyze—a mind that analyzes is just conceptual thoughts
Don't sustain—the natural state unmaintained is brilliantly luminous
Don't restrict—whatever arises is perfect as awareness's ornament

Never unmingled, the wisdom and ordinary minds mingle as one
Never unarisen, arising and liberation simultaneously occur

Never utterly empty, appearances and emptiness rest in union
Never unequal, all is of the vajra taste of equality

Into the primordially pure ground disperse confusion and impurity
May all wandering beings be liberated with impartiality
Into the spacious sky of the great mother, the queen of basic space imbued
With the seven branches of union, embracing all that there is immeasurably

This non-song, my profound heart of hearts
Is revealed in writing to you, my student
With love the likes of a mother for her child
Share it not! Keep it hidden from improper recipients

Samaya. Seal. Seal. Seal.

At the repeated requests of a personal student, this was spontaneously written by Padyak Wöntrul Tenpé Wangchuk in the Kahé prison near the Tsaidam basin.

Tibetan Source

Khang sar bstan pa'i dbang phyug. "Rdzogs chen lta ba'i ma mgur" [The non-song on the view of the Great Perfection]. In *Lta mgur dang rdzogs pa chen po'i skor 'od gsal klong yangs las* [The luminous expanse: Songs of the view and Great Perfection]. Hong Kong: Tian Ma, 2008.

Additional Sources

Chökyi Nyima. *Sadness, Love, Openness: The Buddhist Path of Joy.* Boulder, CO: Shambhala, 2018.

Klong-chen-pa Dri-med-'od-zer, Bstan-pa'i-dbań-phyug and Padmakara Translation Group. *The Precious Treasury of the Fundamental Nature.* New York: Shambhala. 2022.

Padmasambhava, et al. *Perfect Clarity: A Tibetan Buddhist Anthology of Mahamudra and Dzogchen.* Compiled by Marcia Schmidt. Hong Kong: Rangjung Yeshe, 2013.

Schmidt, Marcia B., ed. *The Dzogchen Primer: Embracing the Spiritual Path According to the Great Perfection.* Boston: Shambhala, 2002.

21

The Lament of an Old Man

INTRODUCED AND TRANSLATED BY PALDEN GYAL

> Initially, when I made strong aspirations in front of Bodhisattva Mañjuśrī at Mount Wutai in China, my highest aspiration was to guide all sentient beings across the world to the path that brings liberation. My middling aspiration was to lead as many people in this nation as possible to the path to liberation, and the lowest was to at least to bring the majority of people in the snow land of Tibet onto the path of liberation.
>
> —Khenpo Jigmé Phuntsok

"MELANCHOLIC SONG of an Old Man" (*Skyo glu rgan po'i gdung yus*) is a song of spiritual experience, or *gur* (*mgur*),[1] sung spontaneously by the great Tibetan yogin Jigmé Phuntsok, widely known as Khenpo Jigmé Phuntsok (Mkhan chen 'jigs med phun tshogs, 1933–2004), from Golok (Mgo log) in Eastern Tibet. He was recognized as the reincarnation of Lerab Lingpa (Las rab gling pa, 1856–1926), a Dzogchen master and treasure revealer (*gter ston*) from Kham. In the midst of the Cultural Revolution upheaval, Jigmé Phuntsok withdrew to the mountains of Serta to lead a contemplative life of spiritual practice with fewer than a dozen followers.[2] In a time of systematic annihilation of sacred Buddhist sites and monastic institutions as relics and representations of feudal thought, this act of seclusion was as much an act of resistance against repression of religion as it was a renunciation of the world.

The small group of hermits led by Khenpo Jigmé Phuntsok began to attract Tibetan Buddhist practitioners and scholars from across the plateau and beyond, and in the next few decades the hermitage was transformed into one of the largest of all Tibetan monastic institutions. What began a few decades ago as a temporary "encampment" (*sgar*) of a few hermits in a remote valley of Serta (Gser rta, alt. Gser thar) has today bloomed into a flourishing monastic university of more than ten thousand monks, nuns, and lay students from all over Tibet, China, and Southeast and East Asia.[3] The transformation was brought about by the moral charisma and ecumenical spiritual atmosphere envisioned and actualized by Jigmé Phuntsok during a period of relative political stability that saw a spiritual revival in the post–Mao era in China. As this *gur* indicates, Jigmé Phuntsok was a tireless and devout pilgrim who adopted the itinerant lifestyle of a wandering ascetic and traveled to many Buddhist countries and sacred pilgrimage sites, including Bodh Gaya in India, Paro Taktsang in Bhutan, and Wutai Shan in China.[4] His austerity and humble comportment recall St. Francis of Assisi, minus the mendicant nature of the Franciscan movement. Similarly, Jigmé Phuntsok was perturbed by the state of his tradition and inspired by a sense of urgency to revive and preserve religious traditions without sectarian bias—in Jigmé Phuntsok's case, Buddhism in Tibet was reeling after decades of devastation under Mao Zedong and needed resuscitation. Inarguably, except for the Tenth Panchen Lama, no other religious leader on the plateau achieved the level of spiritual influence and authority among the general Tibetan population in post-1950s Eastern Tibet.

In his comprehensive study of classical Tibetan poetry, Döndrup Gyal (Don grub rgyal) classifies *gur*, or "songs of spiritual experience" (*nyams mgur*), into seven major types, and Khenchen Jigmé Phuntsok's "Melancholic Song of an Old Man" fits into at least three of those types, types that (1) inspire the practice of dharma, (2) give instructions on how to practice, and (3) advise the uprooting of evil.[5] His classification shows the difficulty of classifying songs of spiritual experience into fixed categories, because a *gur* can contain several of these elements and approaches. Similarly, the modern understanding of *gur* as primarily a religious genre in contrast to folk song, or *lu* (*glu*), and ornate poetry (*snyan ngag*) as chiefly "secular" or "literary" is also not entirely reliable and stable, for there is much overlap between *glu*, ornate poetry, and *gur*.[6] By studying Dunhuang documents and classical Tibetan literature, Döndrup Gyal argues that *gur* and *lu* were used interchangeably and meant the same thing before the later diffusion of dharma in Tibet (*bstan pa phyi dar*); it was after this period that *gur* gradually came to be associated with songs of spiritual experience, while *lu* maintained its "secular," or folk, sense. Ornate poetry, on the other hand, took on a highly restrictive and elite literary character in both form and content, particularly following the transmission of Sanskrit poetic traditions (13th century) through works like Daṇḍin's *Kāvyādarśa* and others.[7] However, not only did *kāvyic* ornate poetry influence and inspire the *gur* and *lu* genres but these genres affected the evolution of *kāvyic* poetry and, as Lama Jabb contends, modern Tibetan literature as well.[8]

"Melancholic Song of an Old Man" was composed on the spur of the moment when Khenpo Jigmé Phuntsok was about to leave for a pilgrimage in China.[9] Like many of his other *gur*, it was composed extemporaneously in the form of song and committed to ink by one of his attendants on the spot.[10] One of the essential features of *gur* is the practice of spontaneous composition. In "Melancholic Song of an Old Man," the quality of spontaneity is also reflected in its thematic fragmentation, or a certain sense of unpredictability in the flow of the song. As I will explain, the thematic leaps and cursory treatment of seemingly inconsequential matters demonstrate the song's natural and extemporaneous composition. As one reads the poem, this thematic "disorder" also reveals a certain degree of originality and ingenuity on the part of the author.

With regard to language and style, this song represents what Döndrup Gyal and Ju Kalsang consider a *gur* that embodies influences and aspects of *lu*, *gur*, and ornate poetry. As in most *gur* and *lu*, the language is fairly simple, and the number of lines in each verse varies. For instance, unlike most of the verses, which have the standard four lines, the second and the twelfth verses of this song have seven lines each. This variation in the length of verses is a common characteristic of *gur*.[11] Despite the occasional insertion of doctrinal terms and concepts, such as the Three Trainings (*bslab pa gsum*) or the Four Kāyas (*sku bzhi*), the language in general is quite simple and accessible. That said, it also contains some fairly unusual expressions, such as "striking the nose with a sickle of ashes" (*thal skya'i zor sna phog*), which I interpret from the context as "to criticize" or "to throw ashes at." My sense is that it is either an archaic expression from classical Tibetan literature or a phrase from the local patois. Additionally, the second verse reads like a classic example of ornate poetry in the *kāvyic* tradition. The use of Indic kennings (*mngon brjod*) like foot-drinker (*rkang 'thung*) for "tree" and *rainy-season summoner* (*char ldan dus ston 'gugs byed*) for "cuckoo" clearly indicates the influence of *kāvyic* poetry, which occupies a significant position in Tibetan literature since the thirteenth century. The juxtaposition of animal themes, such as that of cuckoos to crows, is another common aspect of *kāvyic* literature.

"Melancholic Song of an Old Man" begins with the indispensable verse paying homage to the author's root guru, the deity Bodhisattva Mañjuśrī, and by seeking refuge from the dread of existential melancholy, or *kyoshe* (*skyo shas*), a deep sense of dejection and disillusionment with the world. The second verse, a beautifully crafted seven-line verse embellished with rich metaphor and imagery, addresses the importance of prudence or skillful means. The third focuses on the mother-child relationship, whereby the mother stands for tradition, passing down advice and "stories of the old days," not to be rejected by the impudent child. Verses 4 to 6 deal specifically with socio-moral issues, lamenting the moral decadence of the age and invoking the values and wisdom of the past as a remedy. Verses 7 through 10 return to the mother-child relationship by suggesting the violence involved in rejecting one's culture and tradition. The last three verses revolve around the author's spiritual commitment, disillusionment with the world, and resolve to practice dharma for the liberation of all sentient beings. The first half of the eleventh verse narrates the death of an unnamed "lama" in a "foreign land," which seems to be the reason for his departure for a pilgrimage to China, possibly to Wutai Shan. These two lines disclose the real reason behind Jigmé Phuntsok's pilgrimage to China. It was to "help" or "lift" (*'degs*) a certain lama whom the Lord of Death had visited, possibly by conducting the necessary rituals. The last verse, like the very first, follows the usual convention of summoning courage and conviction in oneself to toil toward the higher goal of teaching the dharma for the benefit of all sentient beings, a resolution Jigmé Phuntsok vows before Bodhisattva Mañjuśrī, whose omnipresent care and compassion will guide him.

Despite its apparent thematic disconnectedness, the chief subject matter of "Melancholic Song of an Old Man" is socio-moral decay. Perhaps it is unusual for a song of spiritual experience to dwell primarily on social concerns, but this should not be surprising because Khenpo Jigmé Phuntsok spent a large portion of his life communicating Buddhist teachings to the general public and commenting on socio-moral values. This is a legacy his successors continue to carry on today through various public engagement initiatives even while Larung Gar has become a reputable center of higher learning. Is a song a *gur* if it is chiefly concerned with "secular" or societal issues? This might seem a relevant question because part of the conceptual distinction between *gur* and *lu* or *kavyic* poetry is based upon an apparent division of subject matter. As indicated above, *gur* came to be generally associated with religious experience or matters of spiritual concern, while *lu* and ornate poetry are supposed to be about "secular," or non religious, affairs. Although it primarily addresses socio-moral concerns, Jigmé Phuntsok's song can still be considered a *gur* because the author sees and treats the social realities as objects of his spiritual endeavor. It is a song of spiritual experience prompted by the deplorable state of affairs in the society, inspiring resolve and commitment to dharma practice for the sake of all sentient beings. For the dharma practitioner and author in this context, there is no clear limit to what counts as "spiritual" or "secular" as long as it concerns the phenomenal world. This song demonstrates the instability of the above mentioned literary categories and defies easy typification even as a *gur*.

"Melancholic Song of an Old Man" expresses a sense of moral decadence in the society, where proper moral order and values of the past such as filial piety have declined, and a personal angst born of the author's incapacity to remedy the situation. Jigmé Phuntsok laments that children disregard parents' advice as "pointless stories of the past," merchants don't care about the consequences of their deeds as they travel from place to place for another profitable enterprise, and proper expressions of gratitude for giving and taking are reversed when the manners of leaders and followers are merged. And he is both perplexed and pained by his inability to act against the power of the "superiors" and for the aspirations of the "inferiors" and the weak in society. His focus on the mother-son relationship seems personal at times, but I interpret it as only metaphorical. Jigmé Phuntsok is deeply troubled by the ungrateful demeanor of children toward their mothers, whose love and affection for them is unfathomable. He even paints a graphic scenario of the physical injury and suffering a mother would endure for her children (verse 8). For him, a mother's unconditional love and care for her children can represent the nurturance of culture and tradition while also epitomizing a bodhisattva's compassionate disposition toward all sentient beings, a conviction to which he announces he will devote his whole life, as long as space endures. He also employs the parental metaphor in his frequent reference to Mañjuśrī as his "only father" (verses 9 and 12). Through these metaphors, Khenpo emphasizes how the work of preserving Tibetan culture and tradition serves as a critical remedy for the current societal moral crisis. In a nutshell, Khenpo's lament over moral decadence evokes a longing for Tibetans to awaken to the importance of reorienting their lives in line with dharmic values.

The Melancholic Song of an Old Man
Khenpo Jigmé Phuntsok

I

In the wretched plain of this dreadful city of saṃsāra
I wander, without any refuge, on the endless path of error.
May the precious teacher, Mañjuśrī, the embodiment of wisdom,
bestow upon me the relief by which melancholy is self-liberated.[12]

2

In the proudly youthful grove of emerald-green trees,
the pleasing voice of cuckoos heralds the rainy season.
A wonderful landscape fitting and friendly to all
yet without proper regard to timeliness.
If cuckoos sing incessantly for too long
their singing could be mistaken for the annoying caws of crows
and they will be embarrassed when ashes are thrown at them.[13]

3

When children, who are lovingly cared for,
turn a deaf ear to their mother's advice and
disregards her speech as pointless stories of the old days,
what is delightful in such carefree indifference?

4

When the manners of leaders and followers are merged
and proper expressions of gratitude for giving and taking reversed,
recall to mind the tales of earlier generations
as you will certainly find there a measure of discernment.

5

The clever merchant who came from the southwest
carried out a few transactions of valuables over the summer.
As it is customary for merchants to journey through foreign lands,
he should reflect upon departure on the consequences of his deeds.

6

Pressed by the commands of superiors and pained by the aspirations of
    inferiors,
when your path is obscured by uncertainty and confusion,
although you can't always bring yourself to have a warm conversation,
does the escort with ill will accord with the enlightened mind?

7

You are nursed by your mother with a lifetime of care and benefit,
yet a wish to repay her gratitude is as fictional as a lotus in the sky.
Think back on the times you scowled at her (and ask yourself):
what is holding me back from forsaking this attitude?

8

When the old mother is kicked off a cliff as she approaches its edge
and her organs are spread on the sandy earth,
Don't you think the old mother, left only with an ounce of life,
would still touch her head to her child's foot?[14]

9

There is no wrongdoing by children their mother fails to tolerate.
Let children forswear their heartless hatred toward their mother,
for they shall live happily in this life and beyond
by joining the entourage of the only father, Mañjuśrī.

10

Now, displeased by this sorcerous device, the crooked and illusory body,
despite my desire for the natural radiance of pure wisdom in the celestial
    realm
and the path of liberation adorned by the five colors,
I despair to realize that I haven't earned such karmic merit.

11

If it were not for the sake of the lama a the foreign land
whom the envoy of the Lord of Death suddenly visited,
I would have left behind my attendants and hidden myself at home,
for there arises in me a desire to observe my mind with little worry.

12

In brief, from now till as long as the sky abides,
benevolent teacher, I shall promise to toil without respite
for the great benefit of Buddhadharma and all sentient beings.
Through seeing, hearing, touching, and remembering,
and with my only father Mañjuśrī Kumāra's compassion,
I shall seek the vast knowledge of the Three Trainings
and aspire to attain the supreme empowerment of the Four Kāyas.[15]

Notes

1. Drawing on Dhondup Gyal's analysis of *mgur* and its characteristics, Roger R. Jackson maintains that *mgur* is a subgenre of *glu* (song), which increasingly came to refer to "religious songs with an experiential component" after the later diffusion (*phyi dar*) of the dharma. However, the classification of *mgur* as primarily a religious genre dates chiefly from the time of Milarepa. See Jackson, "'Poetry' in Tibet."

2. For a brief biography of Khenpo Jigmé Phuntsok, see Terrone, "Khenpo Jigmé Puntsok."

3. For Larung Gar and its history, see Gayley, *Voices from Larung Gar.*

4. During Khenpo Jigmé Phuntsok's travel to India, he met with and gave initiations to the current Dalai Lama in Dharamsala. The Dalai Lama later composed a song of devotion in memory of Khenpo Jigmé Phuntsok entitled "Verses of Aspiration for the Fulfillment of the Enlightened Vision of Khenchen Jigmé Phuntsok, the Reincarnation of Tertön Lerab Lingpa." See https://www.lotsawahouse.org/bo/tibetan-masters/fourteenth-dalai -lama/song-devotion-khenpo-jigme-phuntsok, accessed 24 May 2021. Jigmé Phuntsok also traveled in 1993 to many Western countries, including France, England, Germany, and the United States, offering initiations and instructions on many topics to Buddhist and Tibetan Buddhist communities in those countries.

5. The seven major types that Döndrup Gyal specifies are *mgur* that (1) remember the guru's kindness, (2) indicate the source of one's realizations, (3) inspire the practice of dharma, (4) give instructions on how to practice, (5) answer disciples' questions, (6) advise the uprooting of evil, and (7) serve as missives to gurus or disciples. Don grub rgyal, *Bod kyi mgur glu byung 'phel gyi lo rgyus dang khyad chos bsdus par ston pa rig pa'i khye'u rnam par rtsen pa'i skyed tshal,* 194–95.

6. As Döndrup Gyal notes, the words *mgur* and *glu* were used as a single noun, *mgur glu,* in many classical Tibetan literary texts before they evolved into fairly different categories of literary works. He also explores different

types, or sub categories, of *mgur glu*, such as ancient songs of warrior kings (*btsan po'i mgur*), love songs (*la gzhas*), and so on .

7. Don grub rgyal, *Bod kyi mgur glu byung 'phel gyi lo rgyus dang khyad chos bsdus par ston pa rig pa'i khye'u rnam par rtsen pa'i skyed tshal,* 350.

8. Lama Jabb, *Oral and Literary Continuities in Modern Tibetan Literature* .

9. The song was composed spontaneously when Khenpo Jigmé Phuntsok was about to leave for China, and he sang it with tears in his eyes (*ma hwa tsi na'i yul du 'gro grabs byed skabs a bhya'i ming can gyis mig mtha' mas gang bzhin smras pa'o*). See 'Jigs med phun tshogs 'byung gnas, "Skyo glu rgan po'i gdung yus."

10. When Khenpo Jigmé Phuntsok visited the sacred site of Guru Rinpoché in Relwasar in Mandi (India), he composed and sang "The Spontaneous Sound of Uncontrived Song: A Lament Recalling the Great Guru of Oḍḍi-yāna" (*Bla ma o rgyan chen po rjes su dran pa'i gdungs dbyangs ma bcos glu yi rang sgra*). Similarly, when he arrived at Yangleshö in Nepal, he composed and sang "Upon Arriving at Yangleshö." For the originals and translations of these *mgur*, see Lotsawa House: https://www.lotsawahouse.org/tibetan -masters/khenpo-Jigmé-phuntsok/spontaneous-lament-recalling-great -guru and https://www.lotsawahouse.org/tibetan-masters-khenpo-jigme -phuntsok/arriving-at-yanglesho, accessed 27 May 2021.

11. Lama Jabb, *Oral and Literary Continuities in Modern Tibetan Literature,* 233.

12. I have translated the word *skyo shas* as "melancholy" for lack of a better word to indicate a specific kind of sorrow, a deep sorrow born of disillusionment with the world.

13. The expression *thal skya'i zor sna phog* seems to be either an archaic phrase or a local proverb. It is difficult to understand its precise meaning. I have translated it contextually as "to criticize," "to throw ashes at," or quite liter-ally, as "to strike someone's nose with a knife or sickle of ashes."

14. I interpret this verse to be a demonstration of the quality of a mother's love and affection toward her children. Although it is not entirely clear from the text since there isn't a conditional clause or particle, this scene appears to be a hypothetical example, not a literal description of an event.

15. The Four Kāyas (Skt: *catvāraḥ kāyāḥ,* Tib: *sku bzhi*) are the body of reality (*dharmakāya; chos kyi sku*), the body of perfect rapture (*saṃbhogakāya; longs spyod rdzogs pa'i sku*), the emanational body (*nirmāṇakāya; sprul pa'i sku*), and the body of their essentiality (*svabhāvikakāya; ngo bo nyid kyi sku*).

Tibetan Source

'Jigs med phun tshogs 'byung gnas. "Skyo glu rgan po'i gdung yus" [Melancholic song of an old man]. In *Gsung 'bum:* ' *Jigs med phun tshogs 'byung gnas* (1933–

2004) [The collected works of Khenpo Jigmé Phuntsok], 3:127–28. Xiang gang: Xiang gang xin zhi chu ban she, 2002. TBRC W00KG03976.

ADDITIONAL SOURCES

Don grub rgyal. *Bod kyi mgur glu byung 'phel gyi lo rgyus dang khyad chos bsdus par ston pa rig pa'i khye'u rnam par rtsen pa'i skyed tshal: Mgur glu'i lo rgyus dang khyad chos* [The history and characteristics of songs: An analysis of the evolution of Tibetan gur and song]. Lhasa: Mi rigs dpe khrun khang, 1985.

Gayley, Holly, ed. *Voices from Larung Gar: Shaping Tibetan Buddhism for the Twenty-First Century.* Boulder, CO: Snow Lion, 2021.

Jackson, Roger R. "'Poetry' in Tibet: Glu, mGur, sNyan ngag and 'Songs of Experience.'" In *Tibetan Literature: Studies in Genre*, edited by José Ignacio Cabezón and Roger R. Jackson, 368–92. Ithaca, NY: Snow Lion, 1996.

Lama Jabb. *Oral and Literary Continuities in Modern Tibetan Literature: The Inescapable Nation.* London: Lexington Books, 2015.

Terrone, Antonio. "Khenpo Jigmé Phuntsok." The Treasury of Lives. Accessed 24 May 2021. https://treasuryoflives.org/biographies/view/Khenpo-Jigmé -Puntsok/10457.

Tshul khrims blo gros, Bsod dar rgyas, and Bstan 'dzin rgya mtsho. "Snyigs dus bstan pa'i gsal byed gcig pu chos rje dam pa yid bzhin nor bu 'jigs med phun tshogs 'byung gnas dpal bzang po'i rnam thar bsdus pa dad pa'i gsos sman" [Radiant wisdom in troubled times: A brief biography of Khenpo Jigmé Phuntsok]. In *Chos rje dam pa yid bzhin nor bu 'jigs med phun tshogs 'byung gnas dpal bzang po'i gsung 'bum bzhugs so* [The collected works of Khenpo Jigmé Puntsok], 3:364–418. Xiang gang: Xiang gang xin zhi chu ban she, 2002. TBRC W00KG03976.

22

Mourning the Passing of Khenpo Jigmé Phuntsok

INTRODUCED AND TRANSLATED BY HOLLY GAYLEY

I N POPULAR Tibetan music videos, expressions of grief and mourn-
ing proliferated in the years after the passing of the renowned
Khenpo Jigmé Phuntsok (1933–2004).[1] Lyrics and video footage
depict the despondent disciples he left behind and recall his remark-
able contributions to revitalizing Buddhism on the Tibetan plateau in
the post-Mao era. Referred to honorifically by Tibetans with the epithets
"Wish-Fulfilling Jewel" (*Yid bzhin nor bu*) and "His Eminence" (*Skyabs
rje*), Khenpo Jigmé Phuntsok was instrumental in reinvigorating monas-
tic scholasticism among the Nyingma and Kagyu traditions in Eastern
Tibet. He is famous internationally as the founder of Larung Buddhist
Academy, also known as Larung Gar, the largest Buddhist institution on
the Tibetan plateau, located in remote Serta, Sichuan Province.[2] In pop
songs that bemoan his passing, lyrics hail his role in "rekindling the lamp
of dharma" and "healing the damage to the teachings and beings" after the
ravages of the Maoist period.[3]

Reminiscent of the traditional genre "calling the lama from afar" (*bla
ma rgyang 'bod*), devotional laments to Buddhist lamas (teachers) in Ti-
betan pop music invoke sorrow resulting from separation. This may be
due to the lama's passing into *parinirvāṇa*, as with Khenpo Jigmé Phun-
tsok, or living far away in exile, as with the Fourteenth Dalai Lama. In
these cases, devotion is expressed as a longing to encounter the lama and
the stark reality of its impossibility—at least at present. Yet, as the songs
translated in this chapter illustrate, devotion to the lama encompasses
more than faith in an individual teacher; it also signifies a loyalty to Bud-
dhist values and Tibetan culture more broadly.

Eulogies to the Lama

Devotional tributes and laments are part of a wider phenomenon that I have elsewhere termed "eulogies to the lama."[4] These are popular songs performed in music videos, dedicated to one or more Buddhist lamas, that accord with the sentiments expressed in Tibetan ritual and folk genres such as songs of praise (*bstod glu*), supplications (*gsol 'debs*), songs of remembrance (*dran glu*), laments (*gdung dbyangs*), and songs of sorrow (*skyo glu*). Generally, these are found on commercial and monastery-produced VCDs (video compact discs) that feature an image of the lama(s) on the cover with performers grouped in a photo montage below, although they can also be found on the solo albums of individual artists. Eulogies to the lama are generally performed in one of three styles: *dunglen*, a distinctive vocal style accompanied by mandolin; pop songs featuring vocals and musical-instrument digital interface; or a hybrid of the two.

In such eulogies, Tibetan lyrics are routinely composed by Buddhist monks, cleric-scholars, and reincarnate lamas, while the performers are popular singers who model devotion, such as singing with palms folded in reverence or prostrating before a photo of the lama. Video shots of the singers are interspersed with or overlaid onto footage of the lama presiding over large-scale ritual gatherings. The lama is typically surrounded by Tibetan and Han Chinese followers, who display devotion by bowing in greeting, listening with rapt attention, or offering khatas (white ceremonial scarves). Given the ubiquity of music videos in private homes and public spaces in Tibetan areas of China, since the popularization of VCDs in the late 1990s and DVDs more recently, eulogies to the lama have played a noteworthy role in encouraging an affective orientation of devotion toward specific lamas as representatives of Buddhism more broadly, especially among younger Tibetans.

Pop music and *dunglen* videos evoke devotional forms of Buddhist practice while also overlaying new meanings. In the songs in these videos, the lama represents a range of functions, both old and new—as a moral exemplar, an object of veneration for Tibetan and Han Chinese followers, a luminary who dispels the darkness of ignorance, a wish-fulfilling jewel and bearer of good fortune, a transmitter of Buddhist wisdom, and a compassionate guide to benefit beings. Since the 1980s, Buddhist leaders have become a unifying force, guiding Tibetans in preserving their culture and values during the massive social changes resulting from state-driven modernization efforts.[5] Their words of advice, originally composed in poetry and song, have been adapted in pop music videos and included in monastery-produced VCDs. Tibetans are encouraged to practice virtue, send their children to school, preserve Tibetan culture and language, and engage in a unified "path forward" (*mdun lam*) grounded in Buddhist values. In this way, Buddhist devotion has become intertwined with the ethno-nationalist vocabularies of loyalty (*la rgya*) and unity (*mthun sgril*) as Tibetans seek out an alternative modernity in Buddhist terms.[6]

TEARS OF SORROW FOR THE LATE KHENPO

In this chapter, I offer translations of three devotional laments released in the years following Khenpo Jigmé Phuntsok's passing, as well as three songs of advice, two composed by Khenpo Jigmé Phuntsok himself and another by a Larung Gar monk about the path forward for Tibetans. The latter is resonant with the Khenpo's advice in an influential work he composed in 1995, *Heart Advice to Tibetans for the Twenty-First Century*, and filmed onsite at Larung Buddhist Academy.[7] These songs provide an opportunity not only to recall his greatness but also to make Khenpo Jigmé Phuntsok present visually through photographs and videos and to evoke and transmit his advice.

The first song, "Tears of Sorrow" (*Skyo gdung gi mig chu*), written by Ngawang Lozang and performed in *dunglen* style by Dubhé, came out the year after Khenpo Jigmé Phuntsok's passing on a commercial VCD titled *Meeting the Turquoise Dragon*. The VCD title and the lyrics and visuals of this song play with the paradox of the lama's physical absence in the mundane world and his ongoing presence in audio-visual materials, in the collective memory of his followers, and as an enduring enlightened presence in the dharmakāya.[8] In "Tears of Sorrow," even as his loss is mourned in emotionally charged language, Khenpo Jigmé Phuntsok is memorialized through photographs documenting his travels in China, India and Nepal; his encounters with eminent Buddhist leaders such as the Tenth Panchen Lama; the treasure objects that he revealed; and iconic moments in the transformation of Larung Gar from an encampment to an official Buddhist academy in 1987. As the "blue cuckoo" (*khu byug sngon mo*) of Tibet, Dubhé gives voice to the grief of Tibetans at large: the Khenpo's "multitudes of followers reduced to anguish" as the song puts it. Its verses persistently ask what hope is left without him, and my translation attempts to capture the intensity of emotion and mirror its affective terms.

Amid expressions of loss is the promise of the Khenpo's continuity in more ethereal realms and a request to return via reincarnation.

Since the Khenpo's advice is highlighted in devotional laments such as "Tears of Sorrow," referencing his "wise sayings," "nectar of oral instructions," and "melodies of dharma," it seems appropriate to include several songs of advice in this chapter. "Potent, Timely Advice" (*Dbang gi dus gtam*) is a song by Khenpo Jigmé Phuntsok performed on a 2004 VCD, *The Conch That Heralds the Fortunate Era*, in *dunglen* style by Dubhé.[9] This song of advice asks Tibetans to follow an ethics of non-harming and benefiting others; to observe the Buddhist values of love and compassion for all, both Tibetans and other nationalities; to practice accumulating merit and purifying obscurations as a collective; and to observe an ecumenical spirit for the sake of unity among Tibetans. Because of the density of advice, in longer lines of eleven syllables, the translation loses some of its poetic value in order to maintain the message. For Khenpo Jigmé Phuntsok and other contemporary Buddhist leaders, Tibetan unity—as grounded in Buddhist values—is paramount for cultural survival as well as for progress. In this way, "Potent, Timely Advice" contains more than generic dharma instructions; it includes advice geared for contemporary Tibetans facing distinctive challenges under Chinese rule, hence its potency and timeliness.

Another song by the Khenpo on the same VCD has a more visionary tone. "The Distant Call of Ne'u Chung" (*Ne'u chung rgyang glu*) evokes the prophetic voice of Ne'u Chung, one of the maidens of Ling in Tibet's Gesar epic. Similarly to "Potent, Timely Advice," this song highlights the collective agency of Tibetans as a people, connected to benevolent forces from the distant past: the great lamas of yore and Gesar of Ling, the mythic hero of the world's longest epic, whose kingdom of Ling is understood locally to have been centered in northern Kham and Golok, the areas surrounding Serta. Using the notion of *tendrel*, which can refer to "auspicious coincidence" or, more technically, the Buddhist concept of "dependent origination" (*rten 'brel*), the song suggests that the present-day signs of fortune in the Golden Valley of Serta (Gser rta, alt. Gser ljongs) are portents of an auspicious future. This future entails the prosperity of Tibetans, flourishing of the Buddhist teachings, and victory over demonic forces, a coded reference to the devastation of the Maoist period. "The Distant Call of Ne'u Chung" features penetrating vocals by Kyicham performed *a capella*, with flute interspersed between and images from a Tibetan festival and performance of the Gesar epic. The haunting vocals and flute are, of course, impossible to capture in translation, but the lyrics are evocative nonetheless. My translation maintains the parallel structure of successive signs of fortune, while attempting to convey the stark images, simplicity of language, and cadence of epic verse.

THE POP STAR AND THE MONK

The sorrow of separation is poignantly taken up in "A Broken Heart" (*Yid re skyo*), the best-known of several collaborations between the leading pop star Kunga and the monk lyricist Lo Jamyang.[10] Despite the title of this widely circulated music video, it is not a song about love gone awry but instead a devotional lament. Referencing the contemporary "sun, moon, and star" (*nyi zla skar gsum*) of Tibet in its first stanza, the song bemoans the loss of the *sun* crossing peaks, likely referring to the Dalai Lama's going into exile in 1959; the *moon* hidden by the clouds, gesturing to the unofficial Eleventh Paṇchen, whose whereabouts remain unknown; and the *star* that slipped through the clouds, namely, the Seventeenth Karmapa Ogyen Trinley Dorje, who escaped into exile at the turn of the millennium. In the music video, only the Karmapa's image appears. Photographs of the Dalai Lama are not allowed to be publicly displayed in China, so the bodhisattva of compassion Avalokiteśvara stands in his place, while the Tenth Paṇchen is shown instead of his reincarnation because of political sensitivity.

As Kunga sings amid a cluster of stūpas, these three are cast as relatives who can no longer be met in person, a source of heartbreak. The second stanza is dedicated to Khenpo Jigmé Phuntsok. Kunga provides a role model of devotion for urban youth by prostrating before a picture of him while dressed in army fatigues with an MP3 player around his neck. In an eight-syllable meter common among Tibetan songs in Eastern Tibet, the lyrics recount: "Now, all alone, I can no longer hear his advice. / Unable to meet the lama—the heartbreak!" Here again the loss of the Khenpo and his ongoing advice are mourned, and the refrain extends that sense of loss and longing, captured in its repetition in the original and the translation. The song concludes with a stanza dedicated to parents, who will inevitably depart in old age, severing one of the crucial ties that urban Tibetan youth have to their heritage, another heartbreak. Each stanza represents a loss not only of esteemed figures but of the cultural knowledge they hold.

Another song composed by Lo Jamyang and performed by Kunga contains advice on the path forward for Tibetans, anchored in Khenpo Jigmé Phuntsok's legacy. "The Path Forward for Tibetan Youth" (*Gangs phrug gi mdun lam*) traces a young Tibetan's quest for advice from a mountain range, a Buddhist cleric, and a village elder. The advice for the path forward that he receives has to do, first of all, with loyalty to the snow mountains. It is not surprising, then, that the Snow Land (*gangs ljong*) of Tibet, and not a more specific Tibetan region, serves as homeland (*pha yul*) in this song. The second stanza features advice from a cleric, who states that the path forward is to study the traditional domains of knowledge, which include Tibetan medicine, visual arts, grammar, logic, and "inner knowledge" involving Buddhist topics. Here Kunga is filmed on location in Serta and other sites in Golok: in front of the Gesar Palace, a site identified in a vision by Khenpo Jigmé Phuntsok; in front of the large stūpa at the county seat in Serta; and on the hill overlooking the massive and rustic "city of dharma" (*chos kyi grong khyer*), that is, Larung Gar. Each stanza is followed by a refrain that Kunga performs as a rap sequence reiterating the advice. This gives the didactic call and response a youthful flare, while the parallelism is signaled by *E ma*, a calling sound maintained as a foreignizing feature in the translation. The third and final stanza, featuring advice from an elder, suggests that Tibetans have a united path forward. Thus, according to this song, the path forward includes loyalty to homeland, continued engagement with cultural forms of knowledge, and unity across generations, all tied to the Khenpo and Larung Gar through the setting of the music video and contents of the lyrics. A devotional impulse is thereby linked to the land of Tibet, its culture, and its people.

Awaiting His Return

The final song translated in this chapter, "Elegy" (*Dran gdung*), was recorded three years after the Khenpo's passing by Sherten, a native of Golok, the nomadic region just north of Serta. Similar to "Tears of Sorrow," "Elegy" conveys intense sorrow and longing for reunion. Khenpo Jigmé Phuntsok's advice is recollected, and its loss as an ongoing inspiration mourned. His well-known slogan "Don't lose self-determination; don't disturb the minds of others" is quoted in the lyrics, hearkening to the Khenpo's call for Tibetans to uphold their moral character and preserve their cultural heritage while remaining on good terms with other nationalities or ethnic groups.[11] This is his reworking of the Chinese term promoting "ethnic unity" (Ch: *minzu tuanjie*). Rather than unity among nationalities within the Chinese motherland, however, the Khenpo calls for unity among Tibetans and harmony in terms of interethnic relations. This song ends with a poetic request for his swift return via reincarnation: "Though the youthful sun of your presence / set over the western peaks some time ago, / once more, as guide for those to be trained, / I pray for you to swiftly return." In translation, it is always challenging to try to capture the density of language—this song has six-syllable lines— and distinctiveness of poetic metaphors in Tibetan. Unfortunately, the somber melody and rich timbre of Sherten's voice cannot be reproduced on the written page.

Nonetheless, through this selection of songs, I hope the reader gains some sense of the profound loss that Tibetans have experienced with the passing of each Buddhist teacher who provided a vital link to their cultural and religious heritage prior to the 1950s. Those lamas who like Khenpo Jigmé Phuntsok survived the socialist transformation of Tibetan areas and the attendant destruction of Buddhist institutions during the Cultural Revolution were instrumental in revitalizing Tibetan culture from the 1980s forward. The reality on the ground remains precarious, given repeated shifts in Chinese Communist policies toward minority groups. It is therefore all the more remarkable that Larung Buddhist Academy continues to flourish, despite tight strictures, as an epicenter for Tibetan erudition, with a new generation of Buddhist leaders continuing to balance innovation and cultural preservation.

Tears of Sorrow
Ngawang Lozang, performed by Dubhé

Emanation who coalesces the wisdom of all buddhas,
with golden sword of insight, love, and strength,
on hundred-petaled lotus seat, you always remain
at the crown of my head, bestowing supreme knowledge.

In the Snow Land, medicinal valley of dharma,
you heal the damage to the teachings and beings.
From the tree of your physical form with noble lineage,
your wise sayings unfurl leaves of discernment.

For beings with feeble merit in degenerate times,
the ragged and untamed who keep bad company,
you were a wish-fulfilling gem, crowned by sun and moon,
that dissolved into the space of dharmakāya—what sorrow!

Accomplished paṇḍita, learned in the five domains,[12]
master of realization, only friend to living creatures,
supreme refuge, glorious, precious lama,
gone to the pure realm of bliss—can it be true?

When you left for the domain of mother ḍākinīs,
as a teaching on impermanence and illusory body,
I, a naïve youth of the same flesh and bone,
wept uncontrollably in a stream of tears.

When you, lama, a great leader and protector,
left for the palace of ḍākinīs in Dhumathala,
you left behind a constellation of disciples,
multitudes of followers reduced to anguish.

For folks like me obscured by the five poisons,[13]
to whom shall we look for hope? Who will bestow
the supreme medicine, the nectar of oral instructions?
Thinking this way, my sorrow grows ever more.

The wish-fulfilling gem, granting needs, has been crushed,
the lamp of complete dharma without bias extinguished,
the only ancestral lama, ultimate refuge, departed,
Kyé ma, alas, now what hope is there left?

Your smiling face like the presence of the moon,
your sweet voice resonant with melodies of dharma,
your great compassion sustained us—what kindness!
Recalling this, I feel helpless, my lifeline broken.

Considering all this, from the expanse of dharmakāya,
like a magical display or the moon reflected on water,
emanate once again within the maṇḍala of the senses.
Please return swiftly for the good of all—without delay!

Potent, Timely Advice
Khenpo Jigmé Phuntsok, performed by Dubhé

The wisdom of primordial truth, aware and empty,
Mañjuśrī resides as an indelible dot at the heart center.
At the festival of benefit, blessed nectar falls as rain;
may it bring what's needed for prosperity everywhere.

Atop the wish-granting tree is the vine of Three Trainings.[14]
Fortunate dharma siblings gather as lotus petals of faith.
Listen to this heart advice of a kind old father,
arising from the pure milk lake of best intentions.

Through this faraway song of our fine karma and wishes,
let's gather in cool medicinal valleys of the snow mountains
to engage in bodhisattva activity as master-disciples conjoined,
to gather merit and purify obscurations. This is my heart advice.

Don't draw divisions between the views of various sects.
This rejects a unified dharma and leads to ruin for both sides.
Hold fast to your heritage, where your karmic flower fell,
while respecting all other traditions. This is my heart advice.

All beings of the three realms have been our kind parents,[15]
so protect them impartially with great love and compassion.
Don't hold one's own people as friend and others as enemies;
be an unbiased guide for the downtrodden. This is my heart advice.

While a good heart is the essence of sublime dharma,
beneficial conduct is the foundation for human mores.
Avoid harmful behavior, shameless and deceitful;
uphold our noble, pure traditions. This is my heart advice.

From now onwards, as our teachers and crowds of followers
assemble as one massive body, it's wondrous to engage in virtue.
Teaching the skills to master appearances and experiences,
deliver all beings to a blissful state. This is my heart advice.

In this way, accumulate the roots of virtue at all times;
the fruition, combined together, will ripen for all beings.

May qualities of renunciation and realization spread without limit
and effortlessly accomplish the great benefit of infinite beings.

The Distant Call of Ne'u Chung
Khenpo Jigmé Phuntsok, performed by Kyicham

To the west, a rainbow arises amid light mist,
illuminated by sunrays shining from the east.
This is a sign that the field crops will mature.
Not arranged by *tendrel*, it's a natural occurrence.

When understanding arises in faithful minds,
based on compassion from the lamas of yore,
this is a sign that dharma practice will flourish.
Not arranged by *tendrel*, it's a natural occurrence.

When happiness arises in this Golden Valley,
based on compassion of the warriors of Ling,
this is a sign that demonic forces will be overcome.
Not arranged by *tendrel*, it's a natural occurrence.

Understand these signs, heartfelt friends across lifetimes.
Have a joyful mind, all you gathered in the crowd.

A Broken Heart
Lo Jamyang, performed by Kunga

Southward, the sun crossed the peaks.
Westward, the white moon is hidden by clouds.
Winter's falling star slipped through the mist.
You, three relatives, I can no longer meet—the heartbreak!

Ah . . . sun, moon, and star

Winter's falling star slipped through the mist.
You, three relatives, I can no longer meet—the heartbreak!

In the seminal point of the earth, lower Do Kham,[16]
advice from the revered lama vividly resounds.

Now, all alone, I no longer hear his advice.
Unable to meet the lama—the heartbreak!

Ah . . . my lama

Now, all alone, I no longer hear his advice.
Unable to meet the lama—the heartbreak!

You, mother and father, showed me great kindness.
As your braids grow and your time to depart draws near,
now I can no longer receive your kindness.
Myself still young and naïve—the heartbreak!

Ah . . . mother and father

Now I can no longer receive your kindness.
Myself still young and naïve—the heartbreak!

The Path Forward for Tibetan Youth
Lo Jamyang, performed by Kunga

I, a Tibetan youth, was born at the foot of snow mountains
and never forget the kindness of the pure snowy ranges.
E ma, what is the path forward for friends of snow mountains?
Protect our loyalty from the depths of the heart.

Our homeland is the Snow Land of Tibet:
never forget loyalty as the relatives of snow mountains!

I, a Tibetan youth, went to the land, Golden Valley,
and engaged in discussion with a cleric.
E ma, relatives of snow mountains, what is our path forward?
The path forward is to study the traditional domains of knowledge.

A request to Tibetan youth who remain loyal to snow mountains:
study the domains of knowledge allied with the snowy ranges.

I, a Tibetan youth, went to a big town
and asked the advice of an elder there.

E ma, what is our path forward as Tibetan youth?
The path forward is in accord with your relatives.

> Our homeland is the Snow Land of Tibet:
> uphold a single path forward in accord with our relatives!

Elegy

Lungtok Tenzin, performed by Sherten

Sole refuge, world guardian,
dharma lord, gem fulfilling wishes,
As of today, three years have passed,
since your bodily presence dispersed.

Wretched, without a protector,
we students recall your kindness.
Bearing sorrow, these months and years,
we remain, seeking to bring you back.

> Ohhh . . .
> Bearing sorrow, these months and years,
> we remain, seeking to bring you back.

Each time I recall your form,
A stream of tears bursts forth.
Each time I recall your speech,
Grief wears me down.

With great courage and strength,
you revived Buddha's teachings.
For rekindling the lamp of dharma,
we'll never forget your kindness.

> Ohhh . . .
> For rekindling the lamp of dharma,
> we'll never forget your kindness.

"Don't lose self-determination;
don't disturb the minds of others."

Your advice on the two systems,[17]
we can never, ever forget.

Though the youthful sun of your presence
set over the western peaks a while ago,
Once more, as guide for those to be trained,
I pray for you to swiftly return.

Ohhh . . .
Once more, as guide for those to be trained,
I pray for you to swiftly return.

NOTES

1. For studies on this important figure, see Gayley, "Ethics of Cultural Survival"; Germano, "Re-membering the Dismembered Body of Tibet"; and Terrone, "'Anything Can Be an Appropriate Treasure Teaching!'"

2. For the voices and innovative approaches of Khenpo Jigmé Phuntsok and his successors at Larung Gar, see the recent anthology edited by Gayley, *Voices from Larung Gar*.

3. The phrases "rekindling the lamp of dharma" (*bstan pa'i sgron me sbar ba*) and "healing the damage to the teachings and beings" (*bstan 'gro'i rgud pa sel ba*) can be found in songs translated in this chapter, "Elegy" and "Tears of Sorrow," respectively.

4. See Gayley, "T-Pop and the Lama." There I trace devotional tributes to Buddhist teachers or lamas in Tibetan pop music in the years 2004 to 2007 on the basis of several dozen monastery-produced video compact discs. My overview in this section is largely distilled from that previous publication.

5. There are certainly dissenting voices about the influence of lamas among urban Tibetan secular intellectuals, who regard Buddhism more broadly as an anathema and counterproductive to modernization efforts, state-sponsored or otherwise. See Wu Qi, "Tradition and Modernity."

6. See Anna Morcom, *Unity and Discord* (2004) and Lama Jabb, "Singing the Nation: Modern Tibetan Music and National Identity" (2011) on how Tibetan pop music promotes unity and loyalty among Tibetans within a secular framework. For examples of music videos of this type, see "Two Songs about Tibetan Unity" on *High Peaks Pure Earth*, posted on August 31, 2010: highpeakspureearth.com/two-songs-about-tibetan-unity-mentally-return -and-the-sound-of-unity.

7. *Dus rabs nyer gcig pa'i gangs can pa rnams la phul ba'i snying gtam.* See Gayley, "Ethics of Cultural Survival," for a study of this work; and Gayley, *Voices from Larung Gar,* for a translation of its preamble.

8. The song employs various euphemisms to reference Khenpo Jigmé Phuntsok's passing, including dissolving into the space of dharmakāya (the abstract "truth body"), departing for blissful pure realms, leaving for the domain of mother ḍākinīs (female tantric deities), and residing in a ḍākinī palace in Dhumathala, the epicenter of Padmasambhava's mythic homeland of Oḍḍiyāna.

9. Dubhé first met the Khenpo around 2000 in Chengdu, visited Larung Gar twice, and was invited by monks to perform on this VCD as well as on *Meeting the Turquoise Dragon,* both dedicated to Khenpo Jigmé Phuntsok and featuring multiple singers. Interview with Dubhé in Chengdu in May 2007. This and others interviews with dunglen and pop artists, including Kunga and Sherten, were conducted with Khonthar Gyal and Anne-Laure Cromphout during the summer of 2007.

10. "A Broken Heart" and "The Path Forward for Tibetan Youth" appear on several of Kunga's albums. The first, titled *Re sgug gi mdun lam,* was a CD dedicated to Khenpo Jigmé Phunsok with his photo on the cover and below that photos of the pop star and monk duo, Kunga and Lo Jamyang. Kunga met the Khenpo once in Chengdu, and Lo Jamyang studied at Larung Gar. The title was condensed to *Re sgug* (Waiting) on the VCD version cited in the bibliography, and a follow-up compilation *Re sgug 2* was subtitled "Lhasa Girl" (*Lha bu mo*), after one of Kunga's better-known love songs. See Warner, "Hope and Sorrow," for a discussion of the YouTube reception of *Yid re skyo.*

11. My gloss of *rang tshugs ma shor / gzhan sems ma dkrugs* is based on a commentary on the slogan by Khenpo Rigzin Dargye titled *The Lantern That Illuminates Discernment according to the Two Systems* (*Lugs gnyis blang dor gsal ba'i sgron me*). Composed in 2004, this work was published and distributed by Larung Gar without any publication information.

12. Given the context, I take this *gnas lnga* to mean the *rig gnas lnga,* or five domains of traditional knowledge: logic, medicine, visual arts, grammar, and "inner knowledge" involving Buddhist topics.

13. The five poisons are the five negative emotions (Skt: *kleśa*) of classic Buddhism: passion, aggression, pride, jealousy, and delusion.

14. The Three Trainings (*bslab gsum*) are the core aspects of the Buddhist path—ethics, meditation, and knowledge.

15. On the basis of the schema of reincarnation, Buddhist texts routinely suggest that across innumerable lifetimes all sentient beings have been our parents at one point or another. This becomes one argument for universal love and compassion.

16. Do Kham (*mdo khams*) refers to Eastern Tibet.
17. "Two systems" (*lugs gnyis*) refers to secular and religious perspectives.

Tibetan Sources

Dubhé. *Dbang gi dus gtam* [Potent, timely advice]. Composed by Mkhan po 'Jigs med phun tshogs. *Bkra shis rdzogs ldan bsu'i ba'i dung sgra* [The conch that heralds the fortunate era]. Chengdu: Chengdu Yinxiang Chubanshe, 2000.

———. *Skyo gdung gi mig chus* [Tears of sorrow]. Composed by Ngag dbang blo bzang. *G.yu 'brug kha sprod* [Meeting the turquoise dragon]. ISRC CN-H09-05-301-00/V.J6. Xining: Qinghai Kunlun Yinxiang Chubanshe, 2005.

Kunga. *Gangs phrug gi mdun lam* [The path forward for Tibetan youth]. Composed by Blo 'jam dbyangs. *Re sgug* [Waiting]. China Record Chengdu Company, 2004.

———. *Yid re skyo* [A broken heart]. Composed by Blo 'jam dbyangs. *Re sgug* [Waiting, wishing]. Chengdu: China Record Chengdu Company, 2004.

Kyicham. *Ne'u chung rgyang glu* [The distant call of Ne'u Chung]. Composed by Mkhan po 'Jigs med phun tshogs. *Bkra shis rdzogs ldan bsu'i ba'i dung sgra* [The conch that heralds the fortunate era]. Chengdu: Chengdu Yinxiang Chubanshe, 2000.

Sherten. *Dran gdung* [Elegy]. Composed by Lung rtogs bstan 'dzin. *Rigs zhen gyi 'bod pa* [New spring melody]. Xining: Qinghai Kunlun Yinxiang Chubanshe, 2007.

Additional Sources

Gayley, Holly. "The Ethics of Cultural Survival: A Buddhist Vision of Progress in Mkhan po 'Jigs phun's *Heart Advice to Tibetans for the 21st Century*." In *Mapping the Modern in Tibet*, edited by Gray Tuttle, 435–502. Sankt Augustin, Germany: International Institute for Tibetan and Buddhist Studies, 2011.

———. "T-Pop and the Lama: Buddhist 'Rites out of Place' in Tibetan Monastery-Produced VCDs." In *Religion and Modernity in the Himalaya*, edited by Megan Sijapati and Jessica Birkenholtz, 43–62. New York: Routledge, 2016.

———, ed. *Voices from Larung Gar: Shaping Tibetan Buddhism for the Twenty-First Century*. Boulder, CO: Snow Lion, 2021.

Germano, David. "Re-membering the Dismembered Body of Tibet: Contemporary Tibetan Visionary Movements in the People's Republic of China." In *Buddhism in Contemporary Tibet: Religious Revival and Cultural Identity*, edited by Melvyn Goldstein and Matthew Kapstein, 53–94. Berkeley: University of California Press, 1998.

Lama Jabb. "Singing the Nation: Modern Tibetan Music and National Identity." *Revue d'Etudes Tibétaines* 21 (2011): 1–29. https://himalaya.socanth.cam.ac.uk/collections/journals/ret/pdf/ret_21_01.pdf.

Morcom, Anna. *Unity and Discord: Music and Politics in Contemporary Tibet.* London: Tibet Information Network, 2004.

Terrone, Antonio. "'Anything Can Be an Appropriate Treasure Teaching!': Authentic Treasure Revealers and the Moral Implications of Noncelibate Tantric Practice." In *Tibetan Studies: An Anthology,* edited by P. Schwieger and Saadet Arslan, 397–426. Sankt Augustin, Germany: International Institute for Tibetan and Buddhist Studies, 2010.

Warner, Cameron. "Hope and Sorrow: Uncivil Religion, Tibetan Music Videos, and YouTube." *Ethnos* 78.4 (2013): 543–68, https://doi.org/10.1080/00141844.2012.724433.

Wu Qi. "Tradition and Modernity: Cultural Continuum and Transition among Tibetans in Amdo." PhD diss., University of Helsinki, 2013.

23

In Praise of Jetsünma Mumtso

INTRODUCED AND TRANSLATED BY
PADMA 'TSHO (BAIMACUO)

Jetsünma Mumé Yeshé Tsomo (abbreviated Mumtso)[1] has achieved iconic status among the Tibetan nuns at Larung Gar,[2] the most significant and influential Buddhist institution in Tibetan areas of China. She is both the director of Larung Gar and niece of its founder, the great Khenpo Jigmé Phuntsok (1933–2004).[3] For this reason, Jetsünma Mumtso has become one of the outstanding women and female lamas in Tibetan Buddhism today, respected and praised by nuns and monks alike. The poem translated in this chapter, titled "In Praise of Jetsünma Mumé Yeshé Tsomo: A Sonorous Melody of Threefold Devotion," is an example of one such praise. It was authored by Khenmo Norzin, one of the numerous *khenmos* (female cleric-scholars) trained at Larung Gar through its promotion of nuns' education, and published in the Tibetan women's journal *Gangkar Lhamo* in 2012.[4]

Jetsünma Mumtso was born in 1966 in Khyushar in Serta County, Sichuan Province (Gser lung phyug mo zhes pa'i ru lag khyug shar). She grew up with her uncle, Khenpo Jigmé Phuntsok, and became a *śrāmaṇerī* (novice nun) at the age of 17. As the first nun to earn the title of *khenmo* at Larung Gar, she received teachings and pure transmissions of esoteric and exoteric Buddhism directedly from Khenpo Jigmé Phuntsok.[5] According to numerous prophecies by Lerab Lingpa among others,[6] she was recognized as the emanation of Yeshé Tsogyal, Machik Labdrön, Yumchen Dakmé, Nangsa Öbum, and Mingyur Peldrön (1699–1769),[7] all significant female figures in Tibetan Buddhism. In 1989 Jetsünma Mumtso was enthroned and become the main female lama of Gyabzi (Rgya bzi) Monastery.[8] Later, in 2000, she was recognized and enthroned as the reincarnation of Mingyur Peldrön at Mindrolling Monastery and accepted the inheritance of the lineage teaching of Mindrolling.[9] In addition, Khenpo Jigmé Phuntsok recognized Jetsünma as a vajra master authorized to give various Dzogchen empowerments to all monastics, including *tulkus, khenpos,* and *khenmos,* as well as all dharma students from all over the world. After Khenpo Jigmé Phuntsok passed away in 2004, Jetsünma Mumtso assumed his responsibilities as the director of Larung Gar. In that role, she gives teachings and annual empowerments, such as Vajrasattva, to disciples at Larung Gar.

The poem "In Praise of Jetsünma Mumé Yeshé Tsomo: A Sonorous Melody of Threefold Devotion" expresses respect for and veneration of Jetsünma Mumtso on behalf of the nuns at Larung Gar. It was first published in *Gangkar Lhamo* under the simple title "Jetsünma" in 2012. Its author, Khenmo Norzin (b. 1973), lived in the pastoral area of Drango (Brag mgo) until arriving at Larung Gar in 1990 and became a nun when she was 17.[10] She learned Tibetan grammar and reading from her father and then studied Tibetan poetry after she became a nun. In 2005, Khenmo Norzin started her *khenmo* exam, with its rigorous series of oral explanations (*'chad rgyugs*), recitations (*blo rgyugs*), and written exams (*yig rgyugs*) about the five major subjects of exoteric Buddhist study.[11] After she passed her Prajñāpāramitā exam, she was allowed to teach a grammar course beginning in 2007. She earned the *khenmo* certification in 2013, after passing all the exams, and then started to teach the major subjects of exoteric Buddhist study. She enjoys reading and writing Tibetan literature and has produced two literary works: the first is devotional, expressing her respect and gratitude for Buddhist lamas and tantric deities, as well as the joys and sorrows of her own life, while the second is an edited collection of nuns' poetry.[12]

I was able to interview Khenmo Norzin several times about her poetry, her life, and her views on women's issues. When I asked what she thought about the status (*thob thang*) of Tibetan women, she traced gender inequities to traditional cultural patterns, since women have not had the same opportunities as men until recently. Yet she noted that even with improved opportunities, women still lag behind men. For example, the Buddhist teachers who are able to excel in public projects, such as building schools and supporting monasteries, remain predominantly male. Women's equality (*bud med kyi 'dra mnyam*) is a prevalent theme in essays published in *Gangkar Lhamo*. In essays I have translated and analyzed elsewhere, Larung Gar nuns and *khenmos* emphasize the importance of education in bolstering the confidence and courage of Tibetan women to pursue advanced Buddhist studies and also become teachers and writers themselves, thereby contributing to Tibetan literary and cultural production.[13]

Thanks to the extraordinary efforts to educate nuns at Larung Gar, there are now more capable women teachers. Jetsünma Mumtso has led the way as one of the rare *khandromas* (realized women)[14] in contemporary Tibet who is also a monastic. For nuns, she provides a role model and an example. In this devotional praise, rendered in ornate *kāvya* poetic style, the virtuous qualities of Jetsünma Mumtso are extolled in elevated terms. Thus, the formal literary style matches the august character of its subject. Jetsünma Mumtso is characterized as an influential teacher whose "unmistaken speech" inspires "goosebumps from unshakable faith" and "invigorate[s] fortunate students" to attain realization by following in her footsteps. Moreover, her elevated stature is attributed to her virtue and monastic discipline as much as to her realization. In explaining why she wrote this poem, Khenmo Norzin stated simply, "I wrote this poem to show devotion and respect to Lama Mumtso, from the depths of my heart and mind." The translation that follows attempts to capture this respect by using refined and precise yet effusive language. Because of the elaborate meter and technical dharma terminology, each line is divided into two parts for readability in English.

In Praise of Jetsünma Mumé Yeshé Tsomo:
A Sonorous Melody of Threefold Devotion
Norzin of Drango

To Samantabhadrī, mother of buddhas, in the vast space
    encompassing the unsurpassable great emptiness,
to Sarasvatī, lady of speech, in the sambhogakāya pure land
    resplendent with rainbow-colored lights,
to the great learned Yeshé Tsogyal, exhibiting the play of manifest form,
    taming whatever needs to be tamed,
and to the fusion of these three into one, the *ḍākinī* noble lady
    Mumé Yeshé Tsomo, I bow down.

You are an emanation of the great mother Dagmema,
    Nangsa Öbum, and Mingyur Peldrön,[15]

and the symphony of your unmistaken speech,
    is the vajra command of buddhas and bodhisattvas.
When heard in its distilled essence
    by the assembly of fortunate students endowed with devotion,
it gives rise to goosebumps from unshakable faith
    in the depths of our hearts.

Your sublime form, with the signs and marks, unquenchable to behold,
    is elegantly adorned by the saffron robes.
Your divine melodious voice with sixty qualities,
    inaugurates a celebration of the definitive secret dharma.
With your mind of great affection beyond reference points,
    please take us poor, miserable wretches as your disciples,
while you grace the crown of the hundred thousand ḍākinīs
    at Pema Khandro Ling in Do Kham.[16]

In the fertile soil of this field of pure discipline,
    you plant the seeds of bodhicitta
and harvest the fruition of the indivisible buddha bodies,
    the apex of vehicles: Ati view, meditation, and conduct.
Through the power of ripening, you invigorate fortunate students
    toward the stage of vidyādharas.[17]
I bow down to the chief of ḍākinīs, Mumé,
    victory banner of the Buddhist teachings and practice of sūtra and tantra.

In the palace of Dhumathala, ornamented with an array
    of limitless enjoyments,
at the zenith, on a lofty golden throne,
    expressing the level of your merit,
you are the supreme dharma queen of the definitive meaning,
    our karmically destined lama.[18]
Like the moon amid constellations of stars,
    you are the dazzling ornament of sacred ḍākinī lands.

The three secrets of your liberation story, noble lady,
    are beyond the sphere of my feeble mind.
By the power of your virtuous deeds
    in the pearl necklace of the succession of your lives,
    only a fraction of which are mentioned here,

May I not be separated from your body, speech, and mind,
  and thus enjoy the profound and vast dharma.
May your enlightened activities be exceptional
  as you engage in benefitting the teachings and beings.

NOTES

1. Rje btsun ma mu med ye shes mtsho mo, alternatively Jetsünma Mumtso (Rje btsun ma Mu mtsho), Khandro Mumtso (Mkha''gro Mu mtsho), or Lama Mumtso (Bla ma Mu mtsho).

2. Larung Gar, also known as Larung Buddhist Academy of the Five Sciences (Bla rung lnga rig nang bstan slob gling), is located in Serta, Ganze Prefecture, Sichuan. For an overview of the second generation of leaders at Larung Gar, see Gayley, *Voices from Larung Gar.*

3. Khenpo Jigmé Phuntsok (Mkhan po 'Jigs med phun tshogs) was an incarnation of Tertön Sogyal (1856–1926), also known as Lerab Lingpa. He was one of the most important Buddhist lamas for Tibetans in contemporary China after the Cultural Revolution.

4. On the development of the *khenmo* (*mkhan mo*) degree at Larung Gar, see Padma'tsho, "How Tibetan Nuns Become Khenmos"; and Liang and Taylor, "Tilling the Fields of Merit."

5. Padma'tsho (Baimacuo), "How Tibetan Nuns Become Khenmos," 12.

6. Don skyid, *Rje btsun ma mu med ye she mtsho mo'i rnam thar ma bcos dad pa'i rang mdangs.*

7. These are (1) one of the central Nyingma progenitors from the eighth century, (2) the eleventh-century founder of the ritual Chöd, (3) the wife of Marpa the Translator, (4) the legendary revenant of Tibetan opera, and (5) the daughter of Terdak Lingpa and an important female teacher in the Nyingma tradition at Mindrolling Monastery in Central Tibet.

8. Don skyid, *Rje btsun ma mu med ye she mtsho mo'i rnam tar ma bcos dad pa'i rang mdangs.* See also Liaorong Azha Kanbu and Mu cuo Kong xing mu, *Se da la rong wu ming fo xue yuan yuan zhang Men cuo shang shi de zhuan ji.*

9. Don skyid, *Rje btsun ma mu med ye she mtsho mo'i rnam tar ma bcos dad pa'i rang mdangs.*

10. Khenmo Norzin (Mkhan mo Nor'dzin), interview by author, 2018.

11. The five major subjects (*gzhung bka' pod snga*) include Prajñāpāramitā (*phar phyin*), Madhyamaka (*dbu ma*), epistemology (*tshad ma*), Abhidharma (*chos mngon pa*), and Vinaya ('*dul ba*).

12. Nor'dzin, "Sgra dbyangs dkar mo'i'gyur khugs" and "Btsun ma'i smyug tshogs."

13. Padma'tsho, "Tibetan Nuns Writing on Equality and Education."

14. The Tibetan term *khandroma* (*mkha' 'gro ma*) translates the Sanskrit *ḍākinī*.

It refers to a class of female tantric deities and is also used as an epithet for realized Buddhist women.

15. As mentioned above, these are (1) the wife of Marpa the Translator, (2) the legendary revenant of Tibetan opera, and (3) the daughter of Terdak Lingpa, who played a crucial role in the reconstruction of Mindrolling Monastery in Central Tibet.

16. The nunnery at Larung Gar in the region of Do Kham in Eastern Tibet.

17. *Vidyādhara* means "wisdom holder" and represents an advanced stage of realization.

18. The term *lha skal* usually refers to one's karmically destined *yidam*, or tutelary deity, indicated by where the flower falls when the disciple tosses it into a maṇḍala during a tantric initiation. In this case, the author clarified that it refers to Jetsünma Mumé Yeshé Tsomo as the "karmically destined lama."

TIBETAN SOURCE

Nor 'dzin, Mkhan mo. "Rje btsun ma mu med ye shes mtsho mo la bsngags pa dad gsum ngag gi sgra dbyangs" [In praise of Jetsünma Mumé Yeshé Tsomo: A sonorous melody of threefold devotion]. *Gangs dkar lha mo* [Goddess of the snowy range] 2 (2012): 1–2.

ADDITIONAL SOURCES

Don skyid. *Rje btsun ma mu med ye she mtsho mo'i rnam tar ma bcos dad pa'i rang mdangs* [The natural expression of genuine faith: The life of Jetsünma Mumé Yeshé Tsomo]. In *Mkha' 'gro'i chos mdzod chen mo* [Ḍākinīs' great dharma treasury], 13:302–38. Lhasa: Gu ji chu ban she, 2017.

Gayley, Holly, ed. *Voices from Larung Gar: Shaping Tibetan Buddhism for the Twenty-First Century.* Boulder CO: Shambhala, 2021.

Liang, Jue, and Andrew Taylor. "Tilling the Fields of Merit: The Institutionalization of Feminine Enlightenment in Tibet's First *Khenmo* Program." *Journal of Buddhist Ethics* 27 (2020): 231–62.

Liaorong Azha Kanbu and Mu cuo Kong xing mu. *Se da la rong wu ming fo xue yuan yuan zhang Men cuo shang shi de zhuan ji* [A biography of Master Mencuo, abbot of Larong Wuming Buddhist Academy]. Accessed 10 June 2022. https://read.goodweb.net.cn/news/news_view.asp?newsid=37533.

Nor 'dzin. "Btsun ma'i smyug tshogs" [A collection of writings by nuns]. Kha ba rig gnas sgrig sbyor khang. Unpublished manuscript. 2022.

———. "Sgra dbyangs dkar mo'i 'gyur khugs" [The reverberations of the goddess's song]. Me tog dkar po'i sgrig sbyor khang. 2014.

Padma'tsho (Baimacuo). "How Tibetan Nuns Become Khenmos: The History and Evolution of the Khenmo Degree for Tibetan Nuns." *Religions* 12 (2021): 1–18.

———. "Tibetan Nuns Writing on Equality and Education." In *Living Treasure: Buddhist and Tibetan Studies in Honor of Janet Gyatso,* edited by Holly Gayley and Andrew Quintman. Boston: Wisdom, 2023.

24

Tracing the Footsteps of
Tibetan Mothers

INTRODUCED AND TRANSLATED BY
MIRANDA AROCHA SMITH

IN AN INTERVIEW in Xining in 2015,[1] Wo Jik Jil (*Bod gzhug skyid*) expressed concern over the state of the educational system in Tibet and highlighted the key role of mothers as educators, maintaining the connection between children and their native Tibetan language. When she was young, Wo Jik Jil's parents encouraged her devotion to her studies at the local primary, middle, and high school and nurtured an enthusiasm for reading Tibetan literature, especially classic works, in her spare time. Wo Jik Jil expressed concern about the fate of her native language and her hope that Tibetan mothers can serve as a vital link between children and Tibetan linguistic and cultural traditions. Also important to Wo Jik Jil is a woman's ability to express her emotions and her life experiences through verse.

Born in the pastoral village of Kargya in Guide County, Qinghai Province, in 1983, Wo Jik Jil received a bachelor's and a master's degree in Tibetan medicine from Qinghai University and a certificate in international health from Johns Hopkins University. An author of both poetry and prose, she lives in Xining where she balances work and motherhood and is also affiliated with the Qinghai Tibetan Medical Study Institute. In 2011 she received first prize in the First National Tibetan Women's Writing Competition for her poem "Who Is That Strong One Who Can Lift Half the Sky?" (*Gnam gyi phyed ka 'degs pa'i gyad mi de su yin*). In her spare time, she coordinates a writing circle for women poets in Qinghai and participates in virtual communities of writers through WeChat. She is a contributor to *The Milk Pail Hook* (*Bzho lung*), the first anthology of Tibetan women's poetry, published in 2005 through the Demoness Welfare Association for Women, founded by Tibetan writer and women's advocate Palmo. Her first book, *Daybreak* (*Skya rengs*), is part of a five-volume collection of texts exclusively by women writers called *Collection of Modern Tibetan Women Writers* (*Bod kyi deng rabs bud med rtsom pa po'i dpe tshogs*), published in 2015 by Sichuan Nationalities Publishing House.

Drawing from Tibetan literary traditions and steeped in orality, Wo Jik Jil's poetry collection *Daybreak* utilizes a variety of verse forms, retaining and adapting traditions as well as engaging in experiments with form and content. In *Daybreak*, she primarily utilizes free verse, in combination with elements of *gur* (*mgur*, songs), *layi* (*la gzhas*, love songs), *kāvya* (*snyan ngag*, ornate poetry), and her own stylistic innovations, to express themes such as women's roles, the importance of home and childhood, concern for the fate of language, and the challenges of inter-ethnic cultural encounters. Particularly resonant in her work is the theme of the importance of women, especially their voices and self-reflection through writing poetry, and their everyday interactions in work and family life. Whether writing about her own feelings, describing women's everyday lives, or critiquing historiography, Wo Jik Jil resituates women as central actors and comments on their lives with both praise and criticism.

Wo Jik Jil's poetry often dives into memories of hometown and childhood (her own and her daughter's). In the poems, she imaginatively traverses the path back to her hometown and renders scenes of the pastoral village and her own childhood from memory. Concern for the loss of these times and past places weighs heavily on the work. However, writing verse allows Wo Jik Jil to revisit and regard experiences from the past at a close distance in language and preserve them for future generations. Her memories, recorded in verse, serve as a resource for others; throughout *Daybreak*, she invites readers to return to these scenes from the past as they build toward the future.

In *Daybreak*, Wo Jik Jil visits historic locations such as Lhasa's Barkhor neighborhood, around the Jokhang Temple with its Tibetan architecture, shops, and restaurants. The temple, considered a main spiritual center of Tibet, attracts pilgrims from across the plateau and serves as a vital symbol of Tibetan identity, culture, and politics. Historically, the temple's construction is associated with the introduction of Buddhism to Tibet, and it houses the Jowo statue of Śākyamuni, one of Tibet's most sacred statues. Encircling the temple is the Barkhor circuit (*bar skor*), one of Tibet's most well known traditional circumambulation paths, or *korlam* (*skor lam*). The sight of women traversing the *korlam* is a source of consolation for the poet as she visits a changed Lhasa and its sacred sites, which she compares to a dream.

In the poem translated below, "Mothers in the Barkhor Circuit" (*Bar skor gling gi a ma lags*), the poet finds solace and strength in the sight of women circumambulating and attending to the presence of the revered Jowo Śākyamuni, among other buddha images. The women perform *korra* (*skor ra*), the practice of circumambulating a sacred site, often while chanting mantras, counting beads on a mālā, repeatedly prostrating, and/or spinning prayer wheels. Through these everyday religious practices, laywomen emerge as heroic figures with the power to maintain traditions that link past and future generations.

In the poem, Wo Jik Jil expresses admiration for the compassion and dependability of mothers who gather at the Barkhor. Emotions in the poem are difficult to classify as neatly secular or religious, as these qualities weave across various stanzas. As she watches the older generation of women, Wo Jik Jil notes their empathy for the Jowo, in addition to the devotion one might expect; watching the mothers "trying to relieve the grief and loneliness / of the gold-faced Jowo and his assembly" triggers the poet's own emotional response in the first person: "In Lhasa I suddenly feel like crying." Later on in the poem, Wo Jik Jil notes the "fixated attachment" of the mothers, which suggests that their empathetic response to the Jowo could be more maternal than devotional. At the same time, the Jowo's import as an object of religious devotion is affirmed and augmented by the mothers' cyclic act of *korra*. Yet in the last stanza, the goosebumps indicative of devotion are worn away by sun and rain and prove less enduring than the steadfastness of the Barkhor mothers in their maintenance of tradition.

To Wo Jik Jil, the activities of the mothers fill a gap left by the Sixth Dalai Lama Tsangyang Gyatso, who has left no trace behind, not even a footprint. Tsangyang Gyatso is known in popular imagination for his unconventional lifestyle: he rejected the life of a monk and is said to have left the Potala Palace at night to roam the streets of Lhasa, galivanting around the Barkhor neighborhood and visiting taverns and outlying villages. He composed love songs and poems regarding his many romantic exploits, writings that remain popular to this day. In the wake of his absence, the poet commands the reader to instead contemplate the steadfast mothers who remain as a significant source of cultural continuity: "In case that is another path, / We need to think more." The vision of mothers circling the Barkhor generates emotion in the speaker that endures and extends into the present: "their relaxed but swift walking style circling the Barkhor— / I'm still feeling it." Her statement reverberates with nostalgia and longing to return to Lhasa, the remembered scene, and the traditions the scene renders. At the same time, the poem's ambiguity and open-endedness in this description invite the reader to reflect on the mothers' footsteps and to contemplate her own emotional response to them.

The scene of women circumambulating the temple also reminds Wo Jik Jil of "learning to draw *Ka Kha*," the Tibetan alphabet, and she goes on to compare the pacing to "golden radiance from the bones of our ancestors." Here, the women's pious walking is a metaphor for the preservation of Tibetan language and culture, and the physical movement has the capacity to link past and present generations. Their gait is relaxed and swift, and their attitude determined as they circle the Jowo, a symbol of Tibetan culture and history. Since the 1960s, Chinese has been the language of instruction in almost all middle and high schools in the Tibet Autonomous Region; in recent years, the government has reportedly taken steps to extend this teaching into primary schools and kindergartens as well. In the final stanzas, the poet lingers in quiet contemplation and invites the reader to turn to the mothers as a source of consolation. Although devotion is ephemeral, easily dispelled by changes in the weather, the mothers are a stable presence, giving the poet hope that "ancient things will endure," as their footsteps conjure the image of drawing the Tibetan alphabet.

Daybreak includes a large number of free verse poems, which utilize irregular stanzas and line lengths and reflect Wo Jik Jil's inheritance of *gur*. *Gur* stands out from other Tibetan poetic forms for its metrical variety, which ranges from rhythmically simpler patterns of four syllables per line to complex, highly ornamented verses of up to twenty-one syllables that rival the complexity of ornate *kāvya* poetry.[2] Wo Jik Jil's poems generally reflect a loose structure, with line lengths ranging from short (3 or 4 syllables) to long (16 syllables) in a single poem. "Mothers in the Barkhor Circuit" is typical of Wo Jik Jil's *gur*-influenced free verse. Reflecting her inheritance of both free verse and *gur*, Wo Jik Jil employs asymmetrical and flexible metrics, a simplicity of language and style, contemporary content, and a focus on subjective experience and inner feelings. In this translation, I render Wo Jik Jil's flexible metrics through English-language free verse and maintain a connection to Tibetan language in the poem by leaving key terminology and cultural concepts untranslated. As much as possible, I adhere to Wo Jik Jil's decisions regarding line breaks and stanza lengths.

Mothers in the Barkhor Circuit
Wo Jik Jil

Lhasa is a deep dream still dreaming.
Why not, sometimes it looks like an ancient old man with his old stories.
How much time has passed
since we labeled it and now recognize it as Lhasa?
Which of Lhasa's various-colored murals should we carve in our minds?

It looks just like a movie of the secret forms of material things.
In Lhasa, sometimes I lose myself again and again,
and sometimes I find myself again and again.

Only the mothers circling the Barkhor
are trying to relieve the grief and loneliness
of the gold-faced Jowo and his assembly.
In Lhasa I suddenly feel like crying.

In the Barkhor circuit
no footprint of Tsangyang Gyatso,
nor the unborn face of the mother.
Decorated with book cloth and apron,
pairs of hands holding a maṇi wheel and mālā,[3]
group of mothers encircling the *korlam*—
in case that is another path,
we need to think more.

With weather extremes of hot and cool
people might get angry and faces might turn reddish-black.
Still I see the face hidden in the cool shade of the moon,
the pair of eyes that are clear and clean like water.
Even now I am still seeing
their relaxed but swift walking style circling the Barkhor—
I'm still feeling it.

The mothers at Barkhor circuit
are like mothers of Lhasa's Jowo

unable to loosen the knot of fixated attachment.
They're stable there, calves not carrying them anywhere but that place.
If I contemplate the situation quietly, what does it mean?
The order of their pacing back and forth is
something like learning to draw *Ka Kha*.
Why not—could this be golden radiance from the bones of our ancestors?

In the Barkhor circuit,
though you have goosebumps when you feel great devotion,
the sun's red heat will melt them away.
The arm hair rising out of pure devotion
inevitably disappears in clouds and rain.
Only the mothers around the Barkhor
bring me the warm sense that ancient things endure.
They walk away, leaving me a last testament.

Notes

1. Wo Jik Jil, interview by author, 15 June 2017.
2. Jackson, "'Poetry' in Tibet."
3. A maṇi wheel, or more commonly, prayer wheel, is a hollow cylindrical device that assists in the repetition of mantras; it is filled with a long paper scroll on which many thousands or millions of mantras are printed. It is commonly carried in the left hand and spun while counting a rosary, or mālā, in the right hand and reciting mantras. See Buswell and Lopez, *Princeton Dictionary of Buddhism*, 526.

Tibetan Source

Bod gzhug skyid. "*Bar skor gling gi a ma lags*" [Mothers in the Barkhor Circuit]. In *Skya rengs* [Daybreak], 5–7. Sichuan: Si khron mi rigs dpe skrun khang, 2015.

Additional Sources

Buswell, Robert E., and Donald S. Lopez. *The Princeton Dictionary of Buddhism*. Princeton, NJ: Princeton University Press, 2013.
Jackson, Roger R. "'Poetry' in Tibet: Glu, mGur, sNyan ngag and 'Songs of Experience.'" In *Tibetan Literature: Studies in Genre*, edited by José Ignacio Cabezón and Roger R. Jackson, 368–92. Ithaca, NY: Snow Lion, 1996.

25

Praise to the Nubri Valley

INTRODUCED AND TRANSLATED BY MASON BROWN

NUBRI IS an ethnically Tibetan valley in Nepal's Ghorka district that has been a part of Nepal since the 1850s. It has had some Tibetan settlement since at least the thirteenth century, when it belonged to the Tibetan kingdom of Mangyul Gungthang, or lower Ngari. Like Tibetan songs from other areas, Nubri songs often employ spatialized language that evokes the hierarchies of the maṇḍala.[1] On the Tibetan plateau, this "mandalization process" has been used to recenter Tibetan (masculine) agency and decenter the hegemonic narratives of the PRC by placing Buddhist lamas in morally higher, or central, positions.[2] I argue that through such spatialization, Nubri songs recenter Nubri in relation to Nepal and exile Tibet as a valorized highland culture in a similar mandalization process.[3]

Folk songs in Nubri are considered traditional in the sense that they are generally orally transmitted, are of anonymous authorship, and conform to longstanding genres. New songs are always being composed, however, and these days the composers are often known and sometimes are lamas. *Töshay* (*bstod gzhas*), which literally means "song from Tö (Upper Tibet)," can also be translated as "praise song." The *töshay* translated below was recorded by the Nubri singer Pema Dhondrup, and the lyrics were written by the contemporary lama Tulku Karma Rinpoché, of Serang Gompa, who was born in Bhutan.[4] Lineage connections between Nubri and the Himalayan kingdom have historical precedents that may date from the late seventeenth century.[5] The genre *töshay* is considered to be semiclassical—akin to "chamber music"—and is historically associated with the Muslim community of Lhasa, who were often hereditary musicians there in the nineteenth and twentieth centuries.[6] This history serves to mark the song as Tibetan even as it proclaims itself a Nubri song.

When talking about devotion in the context of Tibetan Buddhism, one would ordinarily be referring to the one-on-one relationship between guru and disciple. Here, however, Tulku Karma is expressing a collective devotion to land, tradition, and community. Ultimately, he posits the suitability of Nubri as an object of veneration for the whole world. Spatially, Tulku Karma's text delineates the upper limit of the valley as Pungyen (*Spungs rgyan*, Mount Manāslu), literally "Ornamented Heap," which lies above the villages of Sama (Rö) and Samdo, with Larkye Pass on its shoulder; and the lower limit as Sertrang (*Gser sbrang*, Serang Himal),[7] literally "Golden-Bee Mountain," which towers above the villages of Trok and Bi in lower Nubri (Kuthang). The song calls the mountain deity Pungyen, or Manaslu in Nepali, "the palace of the Lords of the Three Families," referring to the bodhisattvas Avalokiteśvara, Mañjuśrī, and Vajrapāṇi. In Buddhism, the meaning of teachings and practices is often said to have three levels — outer, inner, and secret. On the outer level, Pungyen is a snow mountain, and on the inner level it is the palace of either the Lords of the Three Families or Cakrasaṃvara, depending on the pure perception of individual lamas; what it is on the secret level is, apparently, a secret. Pungyen can also refer to the worldly protector deity of the mountain.[8] Sertrang, or "Golden-Bee Mountain," is cited as the "practice place of Orgyen Pema," or Padmasambhava (also known as Guru Rinpoché), and it is a site of pilgrimage.

The song defines Nubri as comprising four villages, Rö (Sama) and Lö in upper Nubri and Bi and Trok (Prok) in lower Nubri. The villages are compared to the Four Harmonious Friends, characters from a jātaka tale in which an elephant, a monkey, a hare, and a crow mutually agree on their respective ages and live amicably together.[9] This cheery language reads somewhat like a tourism add (an impression strengthened by the last verse, calling visitors from around the world "siblings of previous lives" who will be welcomed "with gladness, faith, and joy") and belies real tensions that have existed between upper and lower Nubri. However, it can also be seen as a call for alliance between the peoples of the two ends of the Nubri Valley as well as between them and outsiders who might be able to help them in their relative poverty and putative isolation. Indeed, the rest of the text highlights the strong Buddhist faith of the people of Nubri and the importance of their Milarepa- and Guru Rinpoché–related pilgrimage sites, which they all value highly and in which many Western dharma seekers also have an interest. Accordingly, this song is at once a "traditional" Nubri song and also intended for a contemporary and cosmopolitan audience.

In terms of mandalization, this song places Nubri at the high point and in the center. Tulku Karma Rinpoché employs the common Tibetan trope "roof of the world" to place Nubri and its primary sacred mountain, Pungyen, in the upper position, with Sertrang peak defining the lower boundary of the maṇḍala and Lake Kel in the middle. Once this environment is delineated, it is populated with deities (the Lords of the Three Buddha Families), lamas (Guru Rinpoché, Milarepa, and "the rest"), and villages (Rö, Lo, Bi, and Trok). Finally, it invites foreigners to enter this mandalic framework. In this song's mandalization, Nubri is complete in itself, without reference to other places, and thereby recentered in a geographic cosmology of its own. In praising Nubri, Tulku Karma Rinpoché highlights it as a sacred site for pilgrimage, a beautiful and blessed place, arousing devotion and a desire to visit it in Buddhists and tourists alike. The music video posted to YouTube in May 2016 and seen by more than ten thousand viewers contains footage of local sites and culture to add to the appeal.

Nubri Praise Song: Auspicious Melody
Tulku Karma Rinpoché

At the top of the world
there is a happy country,
the pleasant land of Nubri,
the homeland of us youth.

Above is Pungyen Snow Peak
the palace of the Lords of the Three Families.
Below is Sertrang Snow Peak
the practice place of Orgyen Pema.

In the middle is blue Lake Kel
our spirit-lake surrounded by local deities.
Mountains, lakes, and forests are assembled
like the jewelry of the world.

When the Lords of the three Buddha Families
Padmasambhava, Milarepa, and the rest,
came to this place
they blessed the very land.

Above are both Rö and Lö;
below are both Bi and Trok.
These four beautiful districts
are like the Four Harmonious Siblings.

The Three Jewels are the protectors
of the lineage of our ancestors
who know the workings of karma, and what to adopt or abandon.
These are the distinguishing features of our land.

Visitors from around the world
are our relatives of previous lives.
We will welcome them
with gladness, faith, and joy.

NOTES

1. Maṇḍalas are two- or three-dimensional representations of the cosmos in Buddhism and Hinduism.
2. See Makley, *Violence of Liberation*, 61–72; and Gayley, *Love Letters from Golok*, 21–24.
3. See Brown, "From Pungyen to Palyul."
4. A version of this translation and parts of the accompanying text appear in Brown, "Meaning, Melody, and YouTube in Irish and Tibetan Traditional Musics"; and Brown, "From Pungyen to Palyul."
5. Childs, "Brief History of Nub-ri," 18.
6. Samuel, "Songs of Lhasa." As in many cultures, musicians of low caste (often Muslims) provided musical entertainment for the Lhasa aristocracy. Over the course of the twentieth century these musical practices (of actually playing the music) spread to the middle and upper classes.
7. This can also be spelled *Gser thang*, or "golden plain."
8. Khenpo Gyaltsen, personal communication, 9 September 2017.
9. Jātaka tales are stories of the Buddha's previous lives, drawn from the sūtras.

Tibetan Source

Pema Dondrup. *Nub ri bstod bzhas bkra shis sgra dbangs* [Nubri praise song: Auspicious melody]. Composed by Tulku Karma Rinpoché. Available at https://www.youtube.com/watch?v=RRAmiBv5g5Q, posted 26 May 2016.

Additional Sources

Brown, Mason. "From Pungyen to Palyul: Recentering Identities through Alliance and Music in Trans-Himalayan Nepal." PhD diss., University of Colorado Boulder, 2018.

———. "Meaning, Melody, and YouTube in Irish and Tibetan Traditional Musics." *American Music Research Center Journal* 27 (2017): 7–24.

Childs, Geoff. "A Brief History of Nub-ri: Ethnic Interface, Sacred Geography, and Historical Migrations in a Himalayan Locality." *Zentralasiatische Studien* 31 (2001): 7–29.

Gayley, Holly. *Love Letters from Golok: A Tantric Couple in Modern Tibet.* New York: Columbia University Press, 2016.

Makley, Charlene. *The Violence of Liberation: Gender and Tibetan Buddhist Revival in Post-Mao China.* Berkeley: University of California Press, 2007.

Samuel, Geoffrey. "Songs of Lhasa." *Ethnomusicology* 20.3 (1976): 407–49.

CONTRIBUTORS

WILLA BLYTHE BAKER is an independent scholar, teacher, and translator in the Tibetan Buddhist tradition. She is the founder of Natural Dharma Fellowship and its retreat center, Wonderwell Mountain Refuge in New Hampshire, where she guides meditation retreats. She received her doctorate from Harvard University, and was a visiting lecturer in Buddhist ministry at the Harvard Divinity School from 2013 to 2017. She is the author of several books, including *The Wakeful Body* (Shambhala, 2021), *The Arts of Contemplative Care* (Wisdom, 2012), and *Everyday Dharma* (Quest Books, 2009). She is the translator of Tāranātha's lamrim text, *Essence of Ambrosia: A Guide to Buddhist Contemplations* (Library of Tibetan Works and Archives, 2005), and *Appearances Unleashed: A Memoir of Jigme Lingpa* (forthcoming from Shambhala in 2024). Her articles and translations have appeared in the *Journal of the International Association of Buddhist Studies, Tibet Journal, the Journal of Buddhist-Christian Studies, Buddhadharma,* and *Lion's Roar*. In 2005 she was formally certified as a teacher (tripon lama) in the Kagyu lineage of Tibetan Buddhism after twelve years of monastic training and two consecutive three-year retreats.

LARA BRAITSTEIN is associate professor of Indo-Tibetan Buddhism at McGill University. She has also taught at the Karmapa International Buddhist Institute (KIBI) in New Delhi and the Rangjung Yeshe Institute in Kathmandu. She teaches Mahāyāna and Vajrayāna Buddhist philosophy, Buddhist hagiography, and Tibetan/Himalayan Buddhist literature and historiography. She translated the fourteenth Shamarpa's *Path to Awakening* and is the author of *The Adamantine Songs: Study, Translation, and Tibetan Critical Edition,* a study of Saraha's Mahāmudrā poems. Her recent research is dedicated to untangling the history and representation of the tenth Shamarpa, Chodrup Gyatso.

JOSHUA BRALLIER (FORMERLY SHELTON) is a scholar of Tibetan Buddhist studies with interests in Tibetan hagiography (*rnam thar*) and narrative literature, Buddhist cosmology, gender and sexuality in tantric Buddhism, and the critical study of men and masculinities. His dissertation research attends to the life and writings of the nineteenth-century tantric adept Do Khyentsé Yeshé Dorjé, querying the role of masculinity in Do Khyentsé's subject formation, religious life, ritual career, and enduring lineages. He received his MDiv in Indo-

Tibetan Buddhism from Naropa University in 2016 and his MA in Buddhist studies from the University of Colorado Boulder in 2018, and he is currently completing his PhD in Buddhist studies at Northwestern University under the guidance of Sarah Jacoby.

MASON BROWN is a musician, ethnomusicologist, and producer with expertise in the musical traditions of the United States, Ireland, Nepal, Japan, and Tibet. He holds a PhD in Ethnomusicology from the University of Colorado Boulder. Based in Michigan, he is currently a visiting faculty member at Kathmandu University and project codirector, with Anna Stirr, of the National Endowment for the Humanities Scholarly Editions and Translations grant, "Nepali Folk Performance: The Works of Subi Shah."

LOWELL COOK is an independent scholar and translator of Tibetan literature. He completed his MA in translation, textual interpretation, and philology at the Rangjung Yeshe Institute in 2017. He is the author of *Tibetan Pure Land Buddhism: Mipham Rinpoche on Self-Power and Other-Power* and the translator of Sangngak Tenzin Rinpoche's *White Conch Spiraling toward Happiness: Poems of a Tibetan Master.* His translations and writings have appeared on the websites *84000: Translating the Words of the Buddha, Journal of Tibetan Literature, Los Angeles Review of Books, Lotsawa House, TibShelf,* and *Yeshe.* He is the recipient of a National Endowment for the Arts grant to translate *A Frostbitten Flower and Other Stories: The Complete Fiction of Dondrup Jyel.* His aspiration is to share the richness of Tibetan literature with the world. He lives with his wife and two sons, spending his time pretending to practice and translate.

JETSUN DELEPLANQUE is a postdoctoral fellow in Buddhist studies at George Mason University. He recently completed his PhD at the University of Chicago's Divinity School in the Department of the History of Religions. His dissertation, titled *"Visions of Theocracy: The Rise of Ecclesiastical Power in Tibet and the Founding of the Bhutanese State,"* explores the dynamics that led to the founding of the Bhutanese theocracy of Shabdrung Ngawang Namgyel (1594–1651) in the seventeenth century. He received a BA in the study of Religions and Tibetan from the School of Oriental and African Studies in London and a master's degree in theological studies from the Harvard Divinity School.

RENÉE L. FORD is a postdoctoral fellow at Aarhus University in Aarhus, Denmark, where her project is titled "Heart Openings: Love in Religious Traditions," and a catalog researcher and translation coordinator with the Khyentse Vision Project. Renée researches faith and devotion in Nyingma tantric and Great Completeness (*rdzogs pa chen po*) practices. She completed her PhD under the auspices of Dr. Anne C. Klein at Rice University.

HOLLY GAYLEY, associate professor of religious studies at the University of Colorado Boulder, is a scholar and translator of contemporary Buddhist literature in Tibet. Her research areas include gender and sexuality in Buddhist tantra, ethical reform in contemporary Tibet, and theorizing translation, both literary and cultural, in the transmission of Buddhist teachings to North America. She is the author of *Love Letters from Golok: A Tantric Couple in Modern Tibet* (2016), coeditor of *A Gathering of Brilliant Moons: Practice Advice from the Rimé Masters of Tibet* (2017), translator of *Inseparable across Lifetimes: The Lives and Love Letters of Namtrul Rinpoche and Khandro Tāre Lhamo* (2019), and editor of *Voices from Larung Gar: Shaping Tibetan Buddhism for the Twenty-First Century* (2021). Her articles on an ethical reform movement spearheaded by cleric-scholars at the Larung Buddhist Academy in Serta have appeared in the *Journal of Buddhist Ethics, Contemporary Buddhism, the Journal of Religious Ethics,* and the *Himalaya Journal.*

PALDEN GYAL is a PhD candidate in modern Tibetan and late imperial Chinese history at Columbia University. He holds a BA in philosophy and an MA in philosophy of religion. His dissertation project, tentatively entitled "Shifting Terrains of Authority: Buddhist Government in the Sino-Tibetan Borderlands, 1720–1950," focuses on the practices of governance and the political and institutional history of Tibetan communities in the Sino-Tibetan borderlands in the context of Qing imperial expansion into Inner Asia.

SARAH HARDING completed a three-year retreat in 1979 under her teacher, Khyabjé Kalu Rinpoché. She was associate professor of religious studies at Naropa University for twenty-five years, now retired, and has been a translation fellow of the Tsadra Foundation since 2000. Her published translations include *Creation and Completion; Machik's Complete Explanation; Niguma: Lady of Illusion; The Life and Revelations of Pema Lingpa; The Treasury of Knowledge: Esoteric Instructions; Four Tibetan Lineages;* and *The Treasury of Precious Instructions,* volumes 11: *Shangpa Kagyu,* 13: *Zhijé,* and 14: *Chöd.* She is currently working on a translation of the second book of volume 12, on Shangpa Kagyu. She has contributed chapters to various anthologies, written published and unpublished articles, and translated many practice manuals for private use.

LAMA JABB was born and brought up in the Dhatsen tribe, a nomadic community in northeastern Tibet. He studied in Tibet, India, and the United Kingdom, where he received his DPhil at the University of Oxford. He is currently a Supernumerary Fellow in Tibetan and Himalayan Studies and the head of the Tibetan and Himalayan Studies Centre at Wolfson College. He teaches Tibetan language and literature in the Faculty of Asian and Middle Eastern Studies, University of Oxford. Lama Jabb's research and writing centers on the interplay between the Tibetan literary text and oral traditions, literary criticism, translation theory and practice, and contemporary Tibet. He is the author of the book *Oral and Literary Continuities in Modern Tibetan Literature: The Inescapable Nation* (2015) and many scholarly articles, including "The Mingled Melody: Remembering the Tibetan March 10th Uprising" (2019), "The Wandering Voice of Tibet: Life and Songs of Dubhe" (2020), and "Currents of the Tibetan National Epic in Contemporary Writing" (2022).

SARAH H. JACOBY is an associate professor in the Religious Studies Department at Northwestern University. She specializes in Tibetan Buddhist studies, with research interests in Buddhist revelation (*gter ma*), religious autobiography and biography, Tibetan literature, gender and sexuality, the history of emotions, and the history of Eastern Tibet. She is the author of *Love and Liberation: Autobiographical Writings of the Tibetan Buddhist Visionary Sera Khandro* (Columbia University Press, 2014), coauthor of *Buddhism: Introducing the Buddhist Experience* (Oxford University Press, 2014), and coeditor of *Buddhism beyond the Monastery: Tantric Practices and Their Performers in Tibet and the Himalayas* (Brill, 2009).

CHIME LAMA is a Tibetan American writer, translator, and multi-genre artist based in New York. She holds an MA in divinity from the University of Chicago and an MFA in creative writing from Brooklyn College. She teaches creative writing at the Rochester Institute of Technology (RIT) and serves as poetry editor of *Yeshe: A Journal of Tibetan Literature, Arts and Humanities*. Her work has been featured in the *Exposition Review, The Margins, Street Cake, Volume Poetry,* and *Cadernos de Literatura em Tradução* (Notebooks of literature in translation), among others. Her poetry collection, *Sphinxlike,* is forthcoming from Finishing Line Press.

ORIANE LAVOLÉ is a PhD candidate in religious studies at Stanford University, focusing on Tibetan Buddhism. She obtained an MA in translation, textual interpretation, and philology from Rangjung Yeshe Institute in Boudhanath, Kathmandu. Prior to starting her PhD program in 2020, she lived in Kathmandu and worked as Kyabgön Phakchok Rinpoché's oral interpreter and director of his translation group, Samye Translations (formerly Lhasey Lotsawa Translations and Publications), which translates a variety of textual genres drawn primarily from the Chokling Tersar, or New Treasures of Chokgyur Lingpa, and produces books based on the teachings of its lineage masters. Lavolé occasionally translates sutras as part of the 84000 project.

JUE LIANG is an assistant professor in the Department of Religious Studies at Case Western Reserve University. She is currently completing her first book, entitled *Conceiving the Mother of Tibet: The Early Literary Lives of the Buddhist Saint Yeshé Tsogyal.* She is also working on a second project, tentatively titled *Thus Has She Heard: Theorizing Gender in Contemporary Tibetan Buddhism.* As a scholar of Buddhist literature, history, and culture in South and East Asia, she reflects in her research and teaching continuities as well as innovations in the gender discourses of Tibetan Buddhist communities. She is also interested in the theory and practice of translation in general and translating Tibetan literature in particular.

ALISON MELNICK DYER is an associate professor of religious studies at Bates College. Her scholarship considers the intersection of gender, authority, and privilege among Tibetan Buddhist monastic communities. Her book *The Tibetan Nun Mingyur Peldrön: A Woman of Power and Privilege* offers a historical and literary analysis of Mingyur Peldrön's life and considers how women negotiate authority in religious institutional contexts. She is currently studying the role of gender and the impact of education in Drikung Kagyu monastic institutions. She holds a PhD and an MA in religious studies from the University of Virginia and a BA in Asian languages and cultures from the University of Michigan.

NATASHA L. MIKLES is an assistant professor in the religious studies program at Texas State University in San Marcos. Having completed her doctoral work at the University of Virginia, Natasha's current research focuses on the role of popular literature like the Gesar epic in developing Buddhist doctrine and lived Buddhist practice. She also is an aficionado of stories about hell in any religious tradition and has done comparative work on the intersection of hell, narrative, and religious ritual. Natasha's research has been published in several academic journals, including the *Revue d'Etudes Tibétaines, Material Religion,* and *Culture and Religion,* and she edited the volume *Religion, Culture, and the Monstrous: Of Gods and Monsters* (Lexington Press, 2021). Natasha is the founder and lead editor of the *Journal of Gods and Monsters.*

CHRISTINA LEE MONSON was a Buddhist teacher and Tibetan language translator and interpreter with more than thirty years of study, translation, and practice experience in Buddhism. Her initial interest in Asian philosophy led her to immerse herself in the study of religion as an undergraduate student at Brown University. Later, she focused her studies on Tibetan Buddhism while completing graduate work at the University of Wisconsin–Madison. Since her first trip to Nepal in 1989, she studied and practiced the treasure revelations of Sera Khandro under the close supervision of her principal teacher, Chatral Sangyé Dorjé, himself a direct disciple of Sera Khandro. With his guidance, Christina worked with a team of Tibetan scholars to compile and edit a comprehensive version of Sera Khandro's collected works (*gsungs 'bum*) in Tibetan language, which was printed in a first edition in Nepal in 2020. She spent time translating portions of Sera Khandro's works into English as a Tsadra Foundation translator and scholar. Her upcoming publications include translations of a volume of Sera Khandro's *shaldam*, or spiritual advice, entitled *A Dakini's Counsel: The Spiritual Instructions, Letters and Advice of Sera Khandro Dewé Dorje, the Dakini from Central Tibet*, and of Sera Khandro's biography of her lama and consort, Drimé Özer, entitled *An Utpala Garland of Blooming Flowers to Ornament the Ears, A Chariot of Devotion to Enlighten the Heart*.

PADMA 'TSHO (BAIMACUO) is a professor in the Philosophy Department of Southwest University for Nationalities in Chengdu, China. She holds a PhD from Sichuan University in Chengdu and an MA from Central Nationalities University in Beijing. She was an instructor at Front Range Community College in 2016–17. Her areas of research and teaching include Tibetan Buddhism, ritual, and culture, as well as the education of Buddhist nuns in Tibetan areas. She has published numerous articles in several languages and two books. Her articles have appeared in anthologies, such as *Eminent Buddhist Women* (edited by Karma Lekshe Tsomo) and *Voices from Larung Gar* (edited by Holly Gayley), as well as numerous journals, including *Religions, Contemporary Buddhism, China Tibetology*, the *Journal of Ethnology, Sichuan Tibetan Studies*, and *Asian Highlands Perspective*. In the last decade, Professor Padma'tsho has been a visiting research scholar at several North American universities, including Harvard, Columbia, the University of Virginia, and the University of Colorado Boulder.

RACHEL H. PANG is an associate professor of religious studies at Davidson College. She received her MA and PhD degrees in Tibetan and Chinese religions from the University of Virginia, and her Honors BA in English and religion from the University of Toronto. Her research focuses on Buddhist life writing, Tibetan poetry, nonsectarianism in nineteenth-century Tibet, and the collected works of Shabkar Tsokdruk Rangdröl. Her research articles have appeared in *a/b: Auto/biography Studies, Himalaya, Numen*, the *Journal of Buddhist Ethics*, and the *Revue d'Etudes Tibétaines*, as well as in several edited volumes. Her translations of some of Shabkar's songs on vegetarianism can be found in *The Faults of Meat* (Barstow, 2019).

ANDREW QUINTMAN is an associate professor of religious studies at Wesleyan University, specializing in the Buddhist traditions of Tibet and the Himalayas. He has written extensively on the literary corpus of the Tibetan poet Milarepa. His English translation of *The Life of Milarepa* was published by Penguin Classics in 2010. His book *The Yogin and the Madman: Reading the Biographical*

Corpus of Tibet's Great Saint Milarepa (Columbia University Press, 2014), received the American Academy of Religion's 2014 Award for Excellence in the Study of Religion, the 2015 Heyman Prize for outstanding scholarship from Yale University, and an honorable mention for the 2016 Association of Asian Studies' E. Gene Smith Book Prize.

GEDUN RABSAL is a senior lecturer at Indiana University Bloomington, where he teaches Tibetan language and culture in the Department of Central Eurasian Studies. His publications include an autobiographical account, *Go Into Exile!* (*'Gro skyabs bcol la 'gro*); research on Tibetan literary history, *A Comprehensive History of Tibetan Literature* (*Bod kyi rtsom rig gi byung ba brjod pa rab gsal me long*); and Tibetan-language translations of works such as Ernest Hemmingway's *The Old Man and the Sea* and Jack Kerouac's *On the Road*.

MIGUEL SAWAYA holds a BA in jazz performance from UCLA and an MA in Indo-Tibetan Buddhism from Naropa University. After completing the year-long Translator Training Program at Rangjung Yeshe Institute, Kathmandu University's Centre for Buddhist Studies, he worked there for six years as a Tibetan language instructor and interpreter for Buddhist philosophy courses taught by monastic instructors. He has translated for the 84000 Project and interprets for several Tibetan Buddhist teachers in a variety of contexts. He is currently a doctoral candidate in the Department of Religious Studies at the University of Virginia.

RIGA SHAKYA has a PhD in Tibetan history in the Department of East Asian Languages and Cultures (EALAC) at Columbia University. He is broadly interested in the connected histories of state and empire building across China, Tibet, and the Himalayas, as well as in the convergence between early modern knowledge systems and colonial modernity. His dissertation project examines issues of multi-ethnic rule, translation, and historiographical practice through a study of the role of Tibetan aristocratic elites and their visions of the Qing imperial project in Tibet and greater Inner Asia during the eighteenth century. He is the founding editor of *Waxing Moon: Journal for Tibetan and Himalayan Studies*, supported by the Center for Digital Research and Scholarship, Columbia Libraries.

MIRANDA AROCHA SMITH is a doctoral student in Buddhism at Northwestern University. She holds an MTS in Buddhism from the Harvard Divinity School (2015), an MFA in creative writing from the University of Texas at El Paso (2012), and a BA from Mount Holyoke College (2006). She was awarded a research fellowship by the China-US Scholars Program for 2021–22.

Dominique Townsend is an associate professor of Buddhist studies at Bard College. She is the author of *A Buddhist Sensibility: Aesthetic Education at Tibet's Mindröling Monastery* (Columbia University Press, 2021); *Shantideva: How to Wake Up a Hero*, an adaptation of the classic text for young readers (Wisdom, 2015); and a collection of poems, *The Weather & Our Tempers* (Brooklyn Arts Press, 2014). Her research interests include the interplay between the religious and the secular, Tibetan Buddhist dreams and dreaming, aesthetics, poetics, and translation theory.

Trungram Gyaltrul Rinpoché (a.k.a. Trungram Gyalwa Rinpoché) is an independent scholar who holds a PhD in Indo-Tibetan Buddhist studies from Harvard University. Recognized as a young child by the sixteenth Karmapa as a Kagyu *tulku*, Gyalwa Rinpoché studied at Rumtek Monastery and the Nalanda Institute for Higher Buddhist Studies in Sikkim. The fourth head of the Trungram lineage, he holds the Nyengyu (*snyan rgyud*) lineage, has received extensive transmissions in the Kagyu and Nyingma schools, and teaches in the spirit of the Rimé (nonsectarian) movement. He is the founder of the Dharmakaya Center for Wellbeing, the Trungram International Academy, and Buddhist Relief Services. His activities are worldwide but largely based in Nepal and the United States.

Nicole Willock is an associate professor of Asian religions at Old Dominion University in Norfolk, Virginia. Translating from Tibetan and Chinese languages, her research examines Tibetan literature and intellectual history. She is the recipient of Foreign Language and Area Studies (FLAS) fellowships, the Fulbright-Hays Doctoral Dissertation Research Abroad (DDRA) fellowship, and the American Council of Learned Societies' (ACLS) Robert H. N. Ho Family Foundation Research Fellowship in Buddhist Studies. Her articles include "Thu'u bkwan's Literary Adaptations of the Life of Dgongs pa rab gsal" (2014), "Maps and Territory in the 1950s: The Writing of the *Dan tig dkar chag—A Guide to Dan tig Monastery*" (2016), and "'*Avadāna* of Silver Flowers': A Discussion on Decolonization and Anti-Colonial Translation Practices for Tibetan Poetry," co-written with Gedun Rabsal, in the *Journal of Tibetan Literature* (2022). Her first book is *Lineage of the Literary: Tibetan Buddhist Polymaths of Socialist China* (Columbia University Press, 2021).

INDEX

abuse of power: and the need to address it, 2, 5–6, 27–28; "proxemic desire" fostered by devotion to an external teacher, 5, 18n10

Amdo Province: *dunglen* ("to strum and sing") as a popular musical form in, 44, 49; *ngakpa* community of Zhopong village in, 180

Aris, Michael, 38

avadāna (*rtogs brjod*, "testament of realization"): Tsongkhapa's biographical *avadāna* of Chennga Drakpa, 56–57. See also Jigmé Lingpa (1729/30–1798): *Turning the Wheel*

bardo (*bar do*): defined, 13, 18n23, 48n1; translation as a liminal *bardo*-like zone between two languages, 13, 32–33, 35, 47–48

Bays, Gwendolyn Bays, 116

Benjamin, Walter, 32, 40, 48

Bhum, Pema, 65n20

Bhutan: edition of *The Great Perfection of Hell*, 203, 210n2; founding by Shabdrung Ngawang Namgyel (1594–1651), 143, 145; Paro Taktsang, 248; recitation by wandering bards, 38; Sertang Pangri transformed by the bird Turquoise, 218, 220; Tsang Khenchen's exile to, 143–45; Tulku Karma Rinpoché's birth in, 286

"calling the lama from afar" (*bla ma rgyang 'bod*) song form: elements of spiritual songs of devotion, 136; invoked in contemporary Tibetan pop music, 8, 257; Khyentsé Wangpo's "Emissary of Renunciation" related to, 188; Kunga Drolchok's use of, 135

Catford, J. C., 42

Chokgyur Dechen Lingpa (1829–1870), 189, 197

Chökyi Wangchuk: "The Dream on Which I Dare Not Think," 205–10; *The Great Perfection of Hell*, 11, 202–4

Christianity: Jigmé Phuntsok compared with St. Francis of Assisi, 248; Milarepa's preaching to the animals compared with St. Francis of Assisi, 69; theistic associations related to devotion, 4; Tower of Babel story, 34

"Cloud Banks of Nectar." See Longchen Rabjam Drimé Özer (alt. Longchenpa, 1308–1364): "Cloud Banks of Nectar"

Coleridge, Samuel Taylor, 9, 34

conviction. See *mögü* (*mos gus*); *yiché* (*yid ches*, confidence)

ḍākinī (tantric female deities, Tib: *khandroma*): *ḍākki* and *ḍākkima* in Sera Khandro's "A Teardrop of Devotion," 227–29, 232n6; imagined by students in *guruyoga* practice, 101; Jetsünma Mumtso identified as, 275–76; Khenpo Gangshar on the meritorious scent that delights mother beings and *ḍākinī*, 239; palace in Dhumathala, 264, 270, 276; as a term, 277–78n14; Üza Khandro as Sera Khandro's nickname, 225–26. See also Niguma

dak nang (*dag snang*): Khandro Rinpoché on, 7, 28–29; transmissions by Dudjom Lingpa, 220n2; transmissions by *tertons* in the Nyingma tradition, 212

Traditions and Transformations in Tibetan Buddhism

This series investigates the stability of Tibetan religious culture from its historical beginnings in the sixth century through the modern era as well as how the religious tradition has changed in reaction to historical realities, technological transformation, and social unrest. To facilitate an interdisciplinary approach, the series publishes projects on four interconnected themes: ritual traditions and textual transformations, Tibet in its historical milieu, Tibet and the modern world, and Tibetan Buddhism in diaspora.

Printed in the USA
CPSIA information can be obtained
at www.ICGtesting.com
CBHW020404011124
16730CB00005B/553

9 780813 950693